Gated Communities in China

Moving beyond conventional accounts of gated communities and housing segregation, this book interrogates the moral politics of urban place-making in China's commodity housing enclaves. Drawing on fieldwork and survey conducted in Shanghai, Pow critically demonstrates how gated communities are bound up in the cultural reproduction of middle-class landscape that is entrenched in the politics of the good life – defined in terms of a highly segregated landscape secured and maintained through the territorialization of privilege, lifestyle and private property.

The study challenges the concept of gated communities as simply 'spatial containers' of social classes and argues that Shanghai's gated enclaves may be more fruitfully analysed as critical sites of and for the production and consumption of an exclusive lifestyle where nascent middle-class sensibilities and identities are being (re)presented, cultivated and lived. In the final analysis, the book addresses an overarching normative concern by examining how social–spatial differentiation and exclusion in Shanghai's gated communities potentially disrupt, challenge and unsettle the modern ideals of urban life. By adopting a geographical–moral perspective, this book illuminates the moral complexities and ambiguities of place-making in Shanghai's increasingly polarized urban landscape.

As the first book-length academic study on gated communities in China, this book will appeal broadly to those with interests in urban studies and urban social development in China.

Pow Choon-Piew is Assistant Professor in the Department of Geography at the National University of Singapore.

Routledge Pacific Rim Geographies

Series Editors: John Connell, Lily Kong and John Lea

Gated Communities in China

Class, privilege and the moral
politics of the good life

Pow Choon-Piew

 Routledge
Taylor & Francis Group

LONDON AND NEW YORK

For my family

First published 2009
by Routledge
2 Park Square, Milton Park, Abingdon, Oxon OX14 4RN

Simultaneously published in the USA and Canada
by Routledge
270 Madison Ave, New York, NY 10016

*Routledge is an imprint of the Taylor & Francis Group, an informa
business*

© 2009 Pow Choon-Piew

Typeset in Times New Roman by Prepress Projects Ltd, Perth, UK
Printed and bound in Great Britain by the MPG Books Group

British Library Cataloguing in Publication Data
A catalogue record for this book is available from the British Library

ISBN10: 0-415-47810-3 (hbk)
ISBN10: 0-203-87620-2 (ebk)

ISBN13: 978-0-415-47810-6 (hbk)
ISBN13: 978-0-203-87620-6 (ebk)

Contents

Illustrations

Figures

Tables

Acknowledgements

This book began as part of doctoral dissertation research that spans several different places. I would like to express my appreciation to my dissertation advisor at the University of California Los Angeles (UCLA), J. Nicholas Entrikin, who has been a great source of moral support and intellectual inspiration. From the start of my graduate programme, Nick has been immensely encouraging and provided invaluable guidance along the way while allowing me the freedom to independently pursue my own research interests. I must also express my gratitude to my doctoral committee members, Cindy Fan, John Agnew and Yunxiang Yan, as well as Denis Cosgrove at UCLA, for their mentorship and advice. The financial assistance of UCLA Geography Department and Graduate Division (summer research grant in 2003 and the Henry Bruman Fellowship Award 2005–06) are also gratefully acknowledged here.

Over in Shanghai, Li Yihai and the staff at the Foreign Affairs Office in the Shanghai Academy of Social Sciences (SASS) were most helpful during my stay in Shanghai. At the East China Normal University, Huang Li and her colleagues greatly facilitated my research and gave me the opportunity to present some of my findings at a graduate seminar. In addition, I also want to acknowledge the cooperation and inputs of numerous respondents in Shanghai who made this research possible.

Back home in Singapore, I am very grateful to the National University of Singapore (NUS) for the financial support and research grants which made this book possible. My gratitude also goes to the faculty and staff at the Department of Geography at NUS, in particular Victor R. Savage, Lily Kong, Shirlena Huang, Henry Yeung, Peggy Teo, Brenda Yeoh, Tim Bunnell, T. C. Chang, Godfrey Yeung and Tracey Skelton. I am equally grateful to Harvey Neo, who has been my tireless friend and comrade-in-arms for over a decade (and still counting), as well as Justin Lee for his friendship and generosity in LA.

Last but not least, I am most thankful to my family in Singapore, who remain steadfast in their support for all my academic and personal endeavours – my parents, in particular my mother, my sisters and their families all deserve special mention. Bryan, Freda and Xiang shared my journey in their own ways. My wife Tracie and daughter Gilda continue to provide the much needed emotional moorings that anchor my work and family life. This book is dedicated to them all.

I should also mention that this book extends significantly from arguments first outlined in the following journals: an earlier version of Chapter 4 appeared in *Urban Geography*, Volume 28:2 (co-written with Lily Kong); Chapter 5 draws from a paper published in *Social and Cultural Geography*, Volume 8:2; and Chapters 6 and 7 are built upon arguments that were presented in *Urban Studies*, Volume 44:8 and *Geografiska Annaler* Volume 91:2 respectively. Finally, I would like to acknowledge the helpful and patient editorial staff at Routledge as well as two anonymous reviewers for their insightful comments on my draft manuscript.

1　Introduction

Gated communities and the lure of the good life

Before I built a wall I'd ask to know
What I was walling in or walling out,
And to whom I was like to give offence.
Something there is that doesn't love a wall,
That wants it down . . .

Robert Frost, 'Mending Walls', 1915, in Latham (1979: 39)

A man of substantial means might have a shoulder-high wall around his property,
over which it was easy to peep and see the good points of the house. But a really
high official might have a wall many times a man's height so that no one not let in
by the gate could realize the beauty and wealth of the palace.

Confucius, *Analects* (XIX, 23), quoted in Moore (1984: 223)

Introduction

Barely a mile away from the runway of Shanghai's Hongqiao Airport in the
Minhang District, a huge tract of suburban housing estate dominates what was
formerly an 800 mu (over 50 hectares) plot of paddy-field. Comprising a mix of
high-rise apartments, townhouses and villas, the privately developed and owned
housing estate known locally as 'Vanke Garden City' is arguably Shanghai's first
large-scale 'middle-class' housing enclave built by Vanke Property Development,
one of China's most prestigious housing developers.[1] Notwithstanding its location near a noisy airport, Vanke Garden City has, over the years, proven to be
immensely popular with 'new middle-class' home-buyers and is widely regarded
as an icon representing the dawn of Shanghai's modern commercial housing
development in the 1990s. Surrounded by 2-metre-high wrought-iron gates and
concrete walls around its perimeter, the suburban private housing enclave comes
equipped with high-tech surveillance technologies and is guarded round-the-
clock and patrolled by more than 280 privately employed security guards on site.
A prominent sign erected outside the main entrance announces in bold Chinese
characters that the premises belong to a private community and non-residents
are not allowed to enter. Another sign at the front gate further proclaims that the

gated commodity housing enclave belongs to a select group of 'Model Civilized Residential Quarters' (*shifan wenming xiaoqu*) that have been hand-picked by local district officials as exemplary of a 'civilized' modern living environment. Within the enclave, all housing clusters have electronic gated access and residents pay a monthly maintenance fee to enjoy condominium facilities such as swimming pool, club house, tennis courts, spas, landscape gardens and, all in all, a 'new lifestyle' (*xinshenghuo fangshi*) for those who can afford the escalating prices of commercial housing in Shanghai. In Vanke Garden City, commercial house prices have more than doubled over the past years, with prices now ranging from 800,000 yuan to over 3 million yuan.[2]

As one enters the gated neighbourhood, security personnel wearing crisp military uniforms can be seen prominently standing guard at street corners and road intersections, directing traffic while eagerly keeping on eye out for trespassers. The interior of the estate is further adorned with well-manicured garden landscaping, brightly lit pavements and meticulously clean pavements that are a far cry from the congested and dirty streets outside. Trash bins and manhole covers within the gated estate are all emblazoned with the conspicuous corporate logo of Vanke's developer. Along the pavements, sounds of birds chirping and children laughing are emitted from tape recorders hidden under shrubs and tress. Overall, every minute detail and sensory pleasure in the neighbourhood has been meticulously planned and orchestrated to create a picturesque and pristine living environment – the hallmarks of what Vanke Corporation calls a 'new concept housing' (*xinzhuzai linian*) and 'new housing movement' (*xinzhuzai yundong*) that are aimed at promoting a new elegant and modern lifestyle (*youya xiandai shenghuo fangshi*) tailored to the desires and aspirations of the 16,000 'new middle-class' residents and some expatriates residing within.

On first impression, these newly constructed residential estates (*xinjian zhuzai xiaoqu*) in Shanghai seem to resemble the California-style 'gated communities' found throughout North American cities and elsewhere (see Blakely and Snyder, 1997; Webster *et al.* 2002; Low, 2003; Glasze *et al.*, 2006). Like many of the middle-class gated enclaves in Asia and Southeast Asian cities (see Connell, 1999; Leisch, 2002; Dick and Rimmer, 2003; Waibel, 2006), these affluent residential enclaves in Shanghai are planned as self-contained 'mini-cities' that display a distinct form of class territoriality with clearly marked out spatial boundaries and zones that are zealously guarded and fortified by high walls, fences, surveillance technologies and private guards. The houses in these gated communities are further designed in a bewildering and eclectic mix of styles combining European classical traditions, baroque, Spanish revival and a pastiche of modernist and post-modernist architectural motifs that are often out of synch with the surrounding environment.

Intrigued by the development of these private housing estates, I approached several local scholars and friends to find out more about these *fengbi xiaoqu* (literally meaning enclosed or sealed residential estate). Then, a well-meaning colleague with extensive fieldwork experiences in Shanghai cautioned that the 'gated community phenomenon' is more a 'Western academic preoccupation' that may not resonate well with the pressing housing concerns of local residents and even academic researchers in China. Although I too was wary of uncritically importing 'Western' urban theories and debates without paying adequate attention to the particular conditions and local realities in China, a quick internet search on the term *fengbi xiaoqu* revealed hundreds of entries related to the topic posted by Chinese netizens and the media. For example, one posting detailed an ongoing legal feud in an up-market residential community (*gaodang xiaoqu*) in the Pudong area, where residents were unhappy that the property developer had reneged on a promise to fully enclose the private neighbourhood and had rented out office spaces within the premises.[3] Reportedly, the residents were concerned that the presence of offices would compromise the safety and exclusive character of their neighbourhood even though gates and fences had been erected around the premises. In scores of other postings, some urban residents complained that they had found themselves being 'locked out' of their own neighbourhood when up-market gated enclaves began to appear in the surrounding areas from the mid-1990s. More significantly, a news posting by the state-run Xinhua news agency announced that from 2003 it would be mandatory for all newly built residential estates in Shanghai to be secured with surveillance cameras, infra-red detection systems and police warning devices at the neighbourhood boundaries. Although it is not required for walls and fences to be put up in all new residential estates, the guideline implicitly endorsed the building of gated residences in an attempt to promote neighbourhood safety and 'modern' housing management practices throughout the municipality. (Some of the local people I spoke to, however, criticized this policy as an attempt by the local government to 'subcontract' security to citizen groups and private companies in order to relieve itself of the financial burden of having to employ more police personnel on the ground.[4]

In my subsequent interviews and interactions with residents in Shanghai, I noticed that most people seem to take the presence of walls and gates in their neighbourhoods for granted. When I asked my respondents to draw what they would consider to be an ideal neighbourhood layout, many of their sketches depicted enclosed housing compounds with onsite facilities, parks and green spaces (Figure 1.1). Further discussion with the local residents on the different motivations for 'gating up' invariably led to the issue of culture and tradition in China. When it was suggested that gated residences are popular in Shanghai because of the public perception of a rising crime rate, a respondent[5] who lives in an up-market suburban gated neighbourhood promptly corrected me:

> It is interesting that you get the impression Shanghai is 'unsafe' because people are moving into gated residential areas. This is obviously a misunderstanding. The cultural difference between the East and the West is the reason. In China, people have the tradition of building [en]closed houses with very high walls and a strong defence system. It does not mean Shanghai is unsafe . . . It is the style in the country. Just take for example, all the universities in China have high walls that separate the campus from the outside . . . so [Chinese]

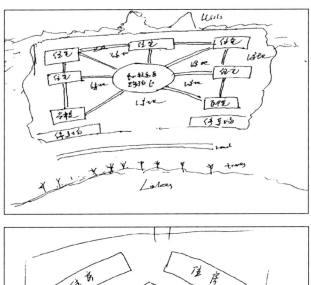

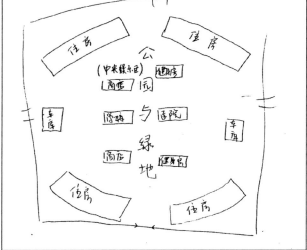

Figure 1.1 Sketches by respondents of their ideal neighbourhood layout.

people visiting America will be very surprised to see there are no walls in their universities.

If the above view is correct, then it would be reasonable to assume that the development of gated communities in China has been shaped by the 'inner workings' of culture and tradition more than by the 'discourse of fear' or any other factors commonly alluded to in the gated communities literature. In other related discussions, some scholars have suggested that the cultural and socialist legacies of China's 'collectivist-oriented culture' and strong political control may be some of the underlying reasons contributing to the present phenomenon of gating in Chinese cities (Y. Huang, 2006), although the meaning and constitution of the 'collectivist culture' have been dramatically altered from one based on lineage, clans and work-unit affiliations to contemporary social divisions marked by emerging class distinction, consumption and lifestyle patterns (D. Davis, 2000). Webster *et al.* (2006: 168) further observe: 'Gates are unremarkable in China. As one developer put it, "walls are the tradition here"'.

To be sure, Chinese architectural canons and urban history are replete with examples of enclosed housing forms ranging from the ancient walled cities in the Shang and Chou dynasties, through the residential wards (*fangli*) found in the Tang dynasty, to the enclosed courtyard houses (*siheyuan*) of the gentries and walled villages in the countryside, and later the walled 'work-unit compounds' constructed in the post-1949 socialist era (see Wheatley, 1971, Heng, 1999; Knapp 2000). As John Friedmann (2007) further points out, walls and gates have always been important symbolic markers of place in China. Quoting the work of Xu (2000), Friedmann notes that walls in China are used to define human relationships and serve as a symbol of the spatial ordering of life. Similarly, William Jenner in his book *The Tyranny of History* (1992: 83–102) devotes an entire chapter to consider the pervasiveness of walls (both literal and symbolic), boundaries and enclosed spaces throughout Chinese history. In Shanghai during the Republican era in the 1920s and 1930s, as the historian Lu Han Chao (2000: 20) describes, 'a typical residential neighbourhood in the city was a walled and gated compound consisting of several rows of identical attached houses'.

Given the long historical trajectory of walled housing traditions in China, it is perhaps not surprising that 'culture' and 'tradition' have so frequently been invoked as justifications for gating up in modern Chinese cities. Such 'culturalist' explanations are, however, problematic when one begins to probe deeper into the meanings of 'culture' and what kinds of 'work' culture performs. More pointedly, whose culture and tradition do present-day gated communities represent? Both walls and gates may reflect historical Chinese legacies and cultural practices of maintaining hierarchical human relationships, separating the sacred from the profane, the civilized from the barbaric, but, as Laura Ruggeri (2007: 103) points out, whereas the residents of traditional walled villages belonged to a clan and shared common ancestors, the inhabitants of the new gated communities share only the dream of living in a safe and socially homogeneous environment. To explain away the modern gating phenomenon in contemporary Chinese cities as the product of an immutable cultural tradition or social norm is clearly to ignore the complexities of urban change and its underlying social–cultural processes.

Indeed, what is further incongruous about these strong culturalist claims and explanations for gating is that in modern China, where historical buildings and architecture including old city walls and gates have been wantonly destroyed, first in the socialist period (especially during the Cultural Revolution in the 1960s and 1970s) and later to make way for modern skyscrapers in the 1990s, it seems odd to suggest that the age-old cultural practice of building walled residential compounds is preserved intact and perpetuated 'for the sake of cultural continuity'. By focusing only on the apparent cultural and physical *form* of gatedness in Chinese architectural styles, culturalist explanations fail to recognize how the underlying *functions, meanings* and *symbolism* of gates and walls have changed dramatically over time. Indeed, the ancient city gates (*lao chengmen*) and city walls (*lao chengqiang*) of old Shanghai that were first erected during the feudal times for protection against external threats (such as the marauding Japanese pirates off the coast) later marked the physical and symbolic boundaries between the 'Chinese part' of the city and the encroaching foreign concessions following the Opium War in the mid-nineteenth century. Interestingly, at the dawn of the Republican era in 1911, most of the city walls and gates in Shanghai were torn down by the new Nationalist government, who considered the ancient city walls an archaic sign of feudal backwardness that was incompatible with the modernizing visions of post-dynastic China.[6] Gamble (2003: 118–124) further observes that, although schools, offices, factories and housing projects in Shanghai are often gated and organized according to work-unit or *danwei* system, since economic reform many schools and local government offices have begun 'tearing down walls and setting up shops' (*poqiang kaidian*) by incorporating commercial functions within their compounds in order to raise revenue. Evidently, urban forms such as gates and walled compounds as well as their underlying meanings and symbolism do not fall into a fixed form of cultural stasis that is bounded in time and space.

Furthermore, such culturalist arguments seem to posit urban forms as the product of an ineluctable cultural logic and the dictates of a static cultural tradition. In many ways, such overtly culturalist explanations echo Duncan's (1980) earlier objections on the 'superorganic' cultural explanation that seems to reify the notion of culture by assigning it independent ontological status and causative power. In his widely debated paper, Duncan makes a trenchant critique on the so-called 'traditional' American cultural geography during the 1960s and 1970s that he claimed had sought primarily to understand and explain human spatial variations by recourse to the notion of culture as a process *sui generis* – that is, as a thing irreducible to the actions of individuals (Duncan, 1980: 185). Explanations of geographical phenomena using the superorganic argument are framed wholly at the abstract cultural level, giving short shrift to the role of individuals as active and meaningful social actors. Whereas Duncan's critiques are levelled at what he sees as the methodological flaws of traditional cultural geography, the concern of this study here, without revisiting the debates (see D. Mitchell, 1995; Duncan, 1998; Mathewson, 1998; Shurmer-Smith, 1998), is to take his critique as a starting point to examine the cultural politics of gated communities in contemporary Shanghai.

In this book, I argue that gated communities in Shanghai cannot be adequately understood as a taken-for-granted urban cultural form as alluded to in the above discussions or the *inevitable* diffusion of an 'American-style' urbanism throughout the world. Although both of these views do find some resonance in this study, it is important to provide a more nuanced account that pays close attention to the local complexities and contested moral geographies of the city as well as the politics of middle-class place-making in Shanghai's gated communities.[7] Specifically, I ask what the role is of (middle-)class cultural practices and place-making strategies in the territorial production/consumption of privileged landscapes in Shanghai's gated communities. To what extent is this cultural process interpenetrated by existing political–economic structures in China and linked more broadly to the pursuit of urban modernity as evinced by the emergence of new modern housing enclaves such as Vanke Garden City? More pertinently, in China, where economic class and status distinctions are becoming more pronounced after three decades of economic reform and 'open-door' policies, how does urban landscape, more specifically, new middle-class housing landscape, help to (re)produce nascent class identities, privileged lifestyles and neoliberal forms of urbanism that are entrenched in the ethos of private property and individualism?

Gated communities – a contested 'global' urban form?

The proliferation of what are commonly known as 'gated communities'[8] and 'fortified enclaves' in cities throughout the world has generated great concern and debates among urban scholars and city planners. Typically, these debates have been polarized between those who view gated communities as symptomatic of the imminent breakdown of the society at large, culminating in the 'revolt of the elites' (Lasch, 1995) – the retreat of upper middle-class citizens from the meaningful public sphere – and those who consider gated communities as innovative and efficient ways of organizing and (re)distributing public goods. That gated communities have generated such widespread concern and contention is understandable, especially in view of the rapid diffusion of such urban forms across cities throughout the world. In the United States alone, it has been estimated that there are easily in excess of 20,000 gated communities with more than 3 million housing units that are bounded by walls and entrance gates (Blakely and Snyder, 1997; Low, 2003: 15; Sanchez *et al.* 2005). Similarly, gated communities can also be found in virtually every major city in Europe, South America, the Middle East, South Africa, Asia and Southeast Asia (see, for example, Graham and Marvin, 2001; Coy and Pohler, 2002; Hook and Vrdoljak, 2002; Dick and Rimmer, 2003; Miao, 2003; Grant, 2005; F. L. Wu, 2005; Genis, 2007; Rosen and Razin, 2008).

Contemporary discussions on gated communities are, however, often marked to a large degree by polemics, with supporters and detractors on each side roundly condemning or celebrating the spread of gated community developments. Such polarized debates fail to take account of the local subtleties and complexities of meanings attached to these housing projects as well as the varied ways that gated communities take shape in particular urban contexts. Typically, the emergence of gated communities is seen as the physical manifestation of global urban trends emanating from the United States (see, for example, Dick and Rimmer, 2003). It is, however, ironic to note how much 'critical' urban scholarship tends to view gated communities as a universally dominating urban form originating from the United States (in particular Los Angeles), without adequately considering how such an urban phenomenon is locally received, contextualized and 'reworked' in a myriad of different settings.

Recent housing reform in China has led to the 'rolling back' of the state in public housing provision and the (re)commodification of the housing market.

Accompanying the housing reform is the emergence of new commercially developed housing estates, known locally as *xinjian xiaoqu*, with many of them being built along the lines of upper- and middle-class gated enclaves. For many Chinese residents who are moving into these privately managed gated communities, what is the attraction or the appeal of gated living? What exactly are they trying to safeguard and defend behind these walls and what are they attempting to 'wall out'? Furthermore, what is the role of the state in promoting the development of gated residential enclaves and how can gated communities be understood in the specific context of Shanghai and, more broadly, in terms of the 'privatization' and 'neoliberalization' of urban China? As Ong and Zhang (2008: 2) carefully point out, there are multiple meanings, localizations and entanglements of the term 'privatization' in contemporary China. Even as privatization in the form of profit-making business and entrepreneurialism is raging in some areas, privatization as an official state policy is still widely eschewed or denied. By focusing on housing consumption and, in particular, gated communities in Shanghai, this book critically examines housing privatization in China as a variegated process with widespread ramifications beyond just the economic sphere, which, in some instances, throws open (semi-)autonomous spaces where individuals are relatively free to pursue and realize their own desires, self-interests and new lifestyles, albeit within the parameters set by the state. Housing consumption, in particular the ability to buy into the exclusive gated lifestyle of China's newly minted commodity housing enclaves, has become the basis for lifestyle differentiation and the formation of new modern urban(e) identity and status distinction. In these terms, this book makes the case for considering gated communities in Shanghai as *key sites of and for middle-class spatial formation*, where class cultural practices and place-making strategies are enacted and where nascent class identities are being cultivated, staged and contested.

Although the term 'gated communities' has gained much currency (and notoriety) in recent debates, especially in 'critical' planning literature, the definition of what constitutes a gated community remains surprisingly ambiguous and problematic. Analytically, the concept of gated community conjoins two distinct terms: 'gated' – the nature of being enclosed (or 'gatedness'); and 'community' – commonly referring to the association of individuals bound together in a shared locale by common interests. Yet there are no necessary relations between gates and communities, or for that matter exclusion. One could, for example, think of the presence of gates without necessarily engendering a sense of community, in much the same way as the mere presence of gates does not always signal exclusion (think of the ornamental gates of public gardens). Conversely communities can and do exist independent of the presence of gates. In fact, some of the predominantly white middle-class suburbs in North America are arguably prime examples of residential communities that can be highly exclusionary yet exist without the physical presence of gates (Baumgartner, 1988; Jacobs, 1996; Duncan and Duncan, 2003). What then makes the conjoining of the two terms as 'gated community' analytically useful and significant in describing enclosed/fortified neighbourhoods?

Urban scholars have defined gated communities as simply 'residential developments surrounded by walls, fences, or earth banks covered with bushes and shrubs with secured entrances' (Low, 2003: 12). Others have emphasized that gated communities are 'residential areas with restricted access in which normally public spaces are [now] privatized' (Blakely and Snyder, 1997: 2). Specifically, Blakely and Snyder (1997) have identified three main categories of gated communities in the United States. In 'lifestyle communities' such as retirement villages, golf/leisure community clubs and suburban 'new towns', shared public spaces and local amenities have become privatized and controlled more as a social statement than as a security feature. These developments reflect the 'notion of shared territory and exclusive rather than inclusive sharing values' (Blakely and Snyder, 1997: 55). By contrast, 'prestige communities' may lack the shared recreational facilities in lifestyle communities. The purpose of gating here is to symbolize residential distinction as well as to enhance and protect the image and property value in the neighbourhood. In the third category, 'security zone community' is created predominantly out of fear of crime and outsiders. In security zones, residents rather than developers are the ones who initiate the erection of gates and barricades in an attempt to defend the neighbourhood from both 'real' and/or 'perceived' threats.

Although these three categories of gated communities are essentially ideal types, in reality their distinctions and characteristics often overlap. In a conference on gated communities, Atkinson and Blandy further define a gated community as a 'walled or fenced housing development to which public access is restricted, characterized by legal agreements which tie the residents to a common code of conduct and (usually) collective responsibility for management' (2005: 178). Yet, despite several attempts at defining gated communities and documenting the litany of problems associated with such attempts, researchers have mostly focused on more formal (political–economic) and legalistic aspects of 'gatedness' while paying little attention to the cultural politics that underpin the territorial organization of urban spaces and social life.

Middle-class place-making and the good life

To the extent that gated enclaves symbolize *living up* the urban good life, a major objective of this book is to examine how the 'cultural reproduction' of privileged groups in Shanghai's gated communities is implicated in territorial politics of exclusion and the formation of a highly exclusionary landscape. As I will argue in the book, the territorial production and consumption of gated communities are invariably bound up in the politics of place-making, more specifically, the cultural reproduction of middle-class landscape that is underpinned by a politics of 'the good life' – defined in terms of a secession from society through the territorial defence of privileged lifestyle, privacy, private property and, ultimately, securing the 'civilized' moral enclaves to keep out the disenfranchised masses of urban poor and migrant workers.

By cultural reproduction, I am not referring to the passive passing down and enculturation of cultural traditions or the transmission of a fixed set of values and cultural practices. Rather, cultural reproduction in this study refers to the myriad of ways in which the lifestyles, attitudes, beliefs, values, identities and dispositions of particular social groups such as the middle class are actively being *worked out* politically and economically *in space*, thereby reinforcing the visibility and distinctiveness of group structures and its membership. However, class here is not seen as a static and monolithic category of analysis but as a practical category[9] and cultural process that needs to be worked out (or in Bourdieu's terms a 'return to practice' by paying attention to the 'modus operandi' of culture). As E. P. Thompson (1966 [1963]) further pointed out in his seminal work, middle-class formation, far from being fixed and stable, is an ongoing (and often fragmented) process of being constructed. For him, class is viewed not so much as a 'structure' or even as a 'category', but as 'something which in fact happens' (and can be shown to have happened) in human relationships. 'No actual class formation in history is any truer or more real than any other, and class defines itself as, in fact, it eventuates' (Thompson, 1978: 150). More recently, L. Zhang (2008) argues that this processual approach opens up a new space for rethinking class beyond strictly economic terms and rigid structural divides and is particularly useful to understand class-making in post-Mao China, where a distinct middle-class culture is amorphous. By conceptualizing middle-class culture reproduction in processual terms, I also emphasize that class-cultural practices *take place* in actual localities/ sites 'by transforming specific spaces in arenas, or stages, for the performance of its own class logics and narratives' (Leichty, 2003: 257). This is what I will refer to in the book as the place-making strategies of the middle class in Shanghai. In these terms, landscape and other elements of culture are used to define membership in a social group through reaffirmation of members' values and the exclusion of non-members. This process involves not only conscious sociopolitical action but also collective action based on unarticulated, taken-for-granted values and ways of thinking (Duncan, 1992).

As Jenks (2005: 114) further notes, the idea of cultural reproduction 'makes reference to the emergent quality of the experience of everyday life' and 'serves to articulate the dynamic process that makes sensible the utter contingency of, on the one hand, the stasis and determinacy of social structures and, on the other, the innovation and agency inherent in the practice of social action'. The residential landscape, in this case Shanghai's gated communities, serves as an important repository of group symbols and social practices and is the vehicle through which the identity and cultural practices of a class or status group are maintained and spatially reproduced (see Jacobs, 1996; Duncan and Duncan, 2003). Privileged groups such as the nouveau riche middle class in Shanghai, who possess the power and resources to build and shape urban spaces, further seek to protect themselves behind fortified enclaves in search of 'the good life', which revolves around the private consumption of a 'wholesome' and 'civilized' residential landscape while turning their back on the 'disorderly' and 'insalubrious' public life.

Central to the book are themes related to the concept of middle-class territoriality, power and space. Whereas there are copious amounts of work that examines the territoriality of states and regions, relatively few studies have focused on the effects and functions of 'micro-scale' territoriality on urban social life. Specifically, how do privileged groups in the city shape and organize space for their own use while keeping out 'less deserving others' and what kinds of cultural resources or tools do they draw upon in the process? How do middle-class residents in Shanghai's gated communities inscribe their own cultural/moral logic onto the urban landscape, thereby transforming the nature of public/private spaces and civic life in the city? More significantly, what can the proliferation of privately developed and managed gated communities in Shanghai tell us about the changing state–society relations in China and how can we reconceptualize the role of the reform-era Chinese state in urban provision and social control?

It is important to state at the outset that this study rejects the simplistic notion that gated community residents are dictated to and manipulated by their material-ist class interests, which drive them relentlessly towards territorial behaviours. Moving beyond standard commentaries on gated communities typically devoted to issues of class segregation and urban fear (M. Davis, 1990; Caldeira, 2000), this book explores the social and cultural meanings given to these increasingly common forms of urban housing in Shanghai and challenges the commonly held assumption that gated communities are simply the 'containers' of social class. Beyond such narrow and static depictions of class antagonism, it is analytically more fruitful to examine the development of Shanghai's gated communities as being bound up in the cultural (re)production of a 'geography of otherness' (Sibley, 1988, 1995; Till, 1993) that pits the 'civilized' (*wenming*) and 'cultured' (*you wenhua*) lifestyles and values of the privileged urban(e) residents against the swelling numbers of urban poor – the 'uncivilized' peasant and migrant workers (*minggong*), who are often marginalized and treated as inferior 'outsiders' (*waid-iren*) in the city (Ma and Xiang, 1998; Solinger, 1999a; L. Zhang, 2001). Although material/class interests remain important determinants of lifestyle and residential choices, economic distinctions are at the same time reinforced and constituted by particular 'ways of thinking' that render specific individuals or groups as 'irre-deemably different' and inferior to the dominant group.

To this extent, gated communities yield a highly exclusionary spatial politics that not only valorizes and affirms the desirable place qualities and identities of Shanghai's middle-class dwellings and their inhabitants but at the same time excludes and denigrates those 'outsiders' who do not fit into the purported land-scape ideals and values. Yet when focusing on the contested cultural geographies of gated communities, we must be careful not to lose sight of broader structural forces that shape social–cultural processes (and vice versa). As Duncan and Duncan (2003: 4) note:

> Structural and institutional bases . . . have too often been studied without more than a cursory reference to the sentiments and emotions behind place-making practices. Similarly studies of sense of place, place attachment and belonging are often studied in isolation from the political economic flows and processes that are central to place production.

By combining the political economy and cultural politics approaches, this study aims to bring together both macro and micro perspectives; structure and agency; culture and economy. Culture, in this sense, is not considered as simply an afterthought or the 'residual category' of political economic process; neither is culture treated as a superorganic entity that exists independently in and of itself. Rather, culture is conceived as the 'very medium through which social change is experienced, contested and constituted' (Cosgrove and Jackson, 1987: 9). In other words, culture provides the 'tool-kits' (materials and resources) from which individuals and groups construct strategies of actions to suit particular circumstances. As this study will later demonstrate, landscape and other elements of culture are actively being mobilized by middle-class residents of gated communities to define membership in a social group through affirmation of the members' values, preferences and desires – to the exclusion of non-members.[10] Fundamentally, the book argues that Shanghai's gated enclaves may be more fruitfully viewed as critical sites of production and consumption where nascent middle-class interests, aesthetic sensibilities and identities are being territorially defined, (re)presented and contested.

Contextualizing the study and research

The study was carried out over a period of 12 months from May 2004 to May 2005 with a subsequent revisit to the field in June 2007 (see Appendix for a detailed discussion on research methodologies and fieldwork). Shanghai was chosen as a case study for its dynamic real estate market, which allows us to readily examine the growth of gated communities and its impact on urban life (a trend that may otherwise take several more years to be apparent in other Chinese cities). For example, in 1997, 70 per cent of total completed houses in Shanghai were commercial houses (X. Q. Zhang, 1999: 602). By 2002, 87.45 per cent of the total floor space sold was for commercial houses, constituting 69 billion yuan sales revenue or 6 million residential buildings (see *China Statistical Yearbook 2002*).

Although Shanghai may not be wholly representative of housing conditions in other Chinese cities, this project uses Shanghai as a 'base model' from which comparative studies with other Chinese cities can be established (see, for example, F. L. Wu and Webber, 2004; Y. Huang, 2006; Zhang, 2008). Another justification for choosing Shanghai as a case study is to offer what Caldeira (1999) calls a 'caricature view of reality'. In her study on gated communities in São Paulo, where urban inequality and spatial segregation are particularly visible, choosing a case study with an exaggerated form of a phenomenon is 'a way of throwing light onto some of its characteristics that might otherwise go unnoticed' (Caldeira, 1999: 115). In Shanghai, private gated communities are often designed as exclusive 'lifestyle enclaves' but at the same time they also incorporate the 'prestige factor' and security as part of the overall appeal of the housing development. Gating is a necessary though not sufficient condition for defining gated communities. In this study, I identify gated communities in Shanghai as commercially developed private residential enclaves where lifestyle, prestige and security rank paramount in the overall design and 'packaging' of the residential landscape.[11] In addition, gated communities manifest a distinct form of territoriality in which the omnipresence of gates, fences, surveillance technologies and privately employed security personnel seeks to secure the 'real' and 'symbolic' boundaries of the commodity housing enclave, with the explicit goals of 'keeping out' non-residents and spatially sorting out 'unwanted social elements'. Many of these gated communities in Shanghai are also designed as self-contained enclaves and are managed by 'professional' property management companies overseeing the operation of neighbourhood amenities and services (club houses, tennis courts, fitness centres, schools, supermarkets, restaurants, medical centres, laundry shops, etc.) that are intended to create a self-functioning community, thereby minimizing physical and social contact with the 'outside world' (*yi waijie geli*).

In order to gain a deeper insight into the management of gated communities and the everyday life of its residents, I stayed in Vanke Garden City (known locally as *Wanke Chengshi Huayuan*) and conducted community ethnographic fieldwork[12] over a period of 12 months (see Figure 1.2). Vanke Garden City – a

Figure 1.2 Main entrance of Vanke Garden City (top); cluster layout of houses in the estate (bottom). Source: author's photograph, 2005.

52-hectare commodity housing enclave referred to earlier in the introduction – is located in Qibao town in the Minhang district,[13] not far from Hongqiao Airport, and is bordered by Qixing Road and Zhongchun Road to the east and west and Xingzhan Road and Xinlong Road to the north and south (see Figure 1.3). The gated community, built on former paddy-fields in the suburbs, was occupied in 1994. It was one of Shanghai's earliest large-scale gated communities and remains, arguably, the most comprehensive and 'mature' (*chengshu*) middle-class gated neighbourhood in Shanghai. Because of the scale of its development, Vanke Garden City has been divided into 'old' and 'new' zones, which are further sub-divided into three phases and several subdevelopments containing a wide array of social amenities, retail shops, medical facilities and restaurants (see Tables 1.1 and 1.2). As a successful prototypical middle-class gated community, the Vanke Garden City residential model has also been replicated in many other Vanke housing development projects in various parts of Shanghai and other Chinese cities such as Beijing, Wuhan, Tianjing, Shenyang and Shenzhen (see *Vanke Corporate Report 2000*: 68–69).

This research is not confined to a single case study. In addition to ethnographic fieldwork in Vanke Garden City, I also surveyed a number of gated communities in different districts in Shanghai. Drawing on real estate data from a variety of sources, including newspapers, magazines and journals, I visited and sampled over 80 commercial gated communities in 11 districts in Shanghai, including those in outlying municipal districts of Jiading and Songjiang. During these visits, I took photographs, recorded my observations and spoke to housing agents as well as residents. Although this study is primarily interested in 'middle-class' private gated communities, gated housing complexes in Shanghai, to be sure, do not all belong to a uniform category. As Webster *et al.* (2006) point out, China's modern gated cities may range from private high-end gated communities, through master-planned private suburbs and enclosed former work-unit residential

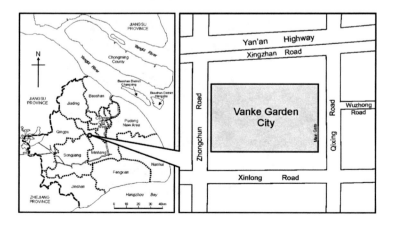

Figure 1.3 Location of Vanke Garden City in Shanghai's Minhang District.

Table 1.1 Vanke Garden City housing statistics

		'Old' zone	'New' zone			
	Vanke Garden City	First and second phases	Vanke 'Land of Dreams'	Vanke 'Lily Garden'	South zone second phase	South zone third phase
Total occupied area (m²)	520,000	200,000	114,000	38,000	91,000	78,000
Total building area (m²)	683,000	392,000	130,000	18,000	54,000	88,000
Plot ratio	1.31	1.96	1.14	0.48	0.6	1.13
Housing types		Mid- to low-rise condominium apartments	Four-to-five storey condominium apartments	Villas and townhouses	Villas, townhouses, garden houses	Mid- to low-rise condominium apartments
Year of occupancy		1994	2001	2002	2003	2004
Number of households	6,194	3,979	1,075	99	320	721
Number of residents	16,207	9,948	2,688	297	1,120	2,154

Source: Vanke (2004).

Table 1.2 Amenities and business in Vanke Garden City

Type of amenity or business	Number of premises
Financial institutions/banking	2
Retail based	30
Food and beverage/restaurants	42
Service-based (e.g. laundry, housekeeping, home repair and remodelling)	59
Educational services	6
Medical	3
Total	142

Source: author's survey.

neighbourhoods, to the enclosure of former rural collective territories ('village condominiums' or 'green ghettoes'), etc. In addition, some gated communities may cater to expatriates, local residents or both (see Appendix on methodology for further discussion on the distinctions between middle-class gated communities and high-end gated communities or what Giroir (2002) describes as 'golden ghettoes'.

Organization of the book

This book is organized into eight main chapters. Following this introductory first chapter, which outlines the research agenda and methodologies employed, the second chapter reviews some of the relevant concepts and theories framing the study. Chapter 3 then examines how macrostructural processes such as urban reform and the housing commodification policies implemented by the central and local governments since the late 1980s and 1990s have laid the groundwork for the emergence of commodity housing enclaves or gated communities and a new privileged group of middle-class private property owners. What is noteworthy here is how the Chinese state through its 'post-welfare' housing policies has played a crucial role in shaping the development of gated communities in contemporary Shanghai.

After setting out the broad contextual overview, Chapter 4 proceeds to look at how gated communities and their residential landscapes are being manipulated and packaged to appeal to the tastes and aspirations of middle- and upper-class housing consumers in Shanghai. Specifically, the chapter examines how representations of 'the good life' (*xingfu shenghuo*; *meihao shenghuo*) are being shrewdly packaged, and sold to and consumed by residents of gated communities. As will be apparent, such neoliberal representations of the good life draw explicitly on various idealized notions of domestic life and the foreign 'suburban' landscape that not only reflect the prestige and wealth of its inhabitants but also embody the exclusivist housing aspirations of the middle-class residents. Besides the enhancement of prestige and social distinction, gated communities are also private havens for urban elites who desire greater privacy away from the prying eyes and interference of the 'nosy' public. Chapter 5 in turn focuses on the relationship between the 'public' and 'private' in Shanghai and pays particular attention to how gated communities have transformed public and private spaces and relate to changing notions of civic life as well as experiences of individual/household autonomy and urban citizenship. In particular, this chapter provides a fine-grain analysis of the meanings and functions of privacy in the Chinese context and how privacy is tied in to the proprietary attitudes of the residents, which mirror neoliberal claims on individualized rights of seclusion and the prevailing ethos of privatism and individualism.

In so far as class distinctions are experienced primarily through processes of cultural differentiation and spatial demarcation, Chapter 6 extends the analysis further to unravel the 'moral geographies' of gated communities by demonstrating how territoriality and social–spatial exclusion in gated enclaves are undergirded by a strong moral order that defines and frames spaces according to the purported 'civilized' moral values of middle-class urban residents. Through mobilizing a cultural repertoire of morally charged stories told by residents about 'others' and themselves, the normative framing of space is, however, not politically neutral or innocent as it excludes those who do not fit into the 'civilized' landscape visions of gated community residents. By inscribing and mapping their own moral–cultural logic onto urban spaces, residents of gated communities thus attempt to 'soften' and 'naturalize' the exclusionary landscape by reconstituting it as pristine 'cultured' spaces befitting Shanghai's 'cultivated' managerial class.

At another level, these moral–spatial hegemonic discourses of gated communities are also inflected by historically contingent ideas in China regarding the 'city' (*cheng*) and the 'countryside' (*xiang*) – between the civilized lifestyles of cultivated urban(e) folks as opposed to the rustic and 'uncultured' ways of the peasants and migrant workers (the 'outsiders' in the city) who lead an uneasy co-existence with the privileged urban class in Shanghai's increasingly segregated spaces. To the extent that Shanghai's gated communities signify privileged status and codes of distinction, these codes are sometimes subverted and even resisted by different social groups who engage them on a daily basis. Chapter 6 further interrogates the paradoxical spatial logic of exclusion in Shanghai's gated communities and highlights some of the resistance to gated living in the city. Specifically, the chapter argues that outsiders are not *simply* excluded from the privileged spaces of gated communities but are fundamentally constituted as an immanent group within its contested moral geographies. Although tendencies towards neighbourhood privatization and gating are prevalent in Shanghai, gated communities also generate various ambiguities and resistances amongst competing social groups in the city and are hence fraught with internal contradictions and tensions.

Chapter 7 brings together all the themes and issues that have been discussed in the preceding chapters to address a central concern in the book: how human endeavours to shape places according to certain desired ideas and images are implicated in the territorial conflicts and struggles to include (and exclude) certain groups of people; and how these practices potentially undermine the normative ideals of openness and diversity in modern urban life. The book will conclude by examining some of the broader significance and implication of this study for understanding the cultural politics of urban space and middle-class spatial practices as well as comparative analysis of gated communities developing elsewhere. Beyond the unique particularities of individual case studies, as the last chapter suggests, cross-cultural comparative research that explores regional and national variations in residential gating may yet point the way towards developing an integrated critical theory on urban enclosure and fragmentation (see Low, 2007).

2 Making middle-class spaces

Privilege, territoriality and the moral geographies of exclusion

Walling in/out privilege

The city and its residential landscapes are not mere 'bricks and mortar' but spaces encoded with multiple social–political meanings and cultural significations. As Delores Hayden (2002) notes, housing form carries many aesthetic, social and economic meanings that have profound influences on the well-being of urban life and the community. Indeed, housing form not only carries with it the utilitarian function of providing the proverbial 'roof over one's head' but also is complex social text laden with symbolic material culture. As Alfred Marshall (2001 [1907]: 58) remarked:

> House-room satisfies the imperative need for shelter from the weather: but the need plays very little part for the effect demand for house-room . . . relatively large and well appointed house-room is, even in the lowest social ranks, at once a 'necessary for efficiency', and the most convenient and obvious way of advancing a material claim to social distinction. And even in those grades in which everyone has house-room sufficient for the higher activities of himself [*sic*] and his family, a yet further and almost unlimited increase is desired as a requisite for the exercise of many of the higher social activities.

Although a number of scholarly works have demonstrated how the house is a physical manifestation of the complex social relationships, symbolizing status and social differentiation as well as reflecting psychological and ideological processes of the builders and its inhabitants, few urban forms or housing developments have received so much public attention and academic scrutiny since the late 1990s as privately organized, and often secured, housing developments or what are often called gated communities (Glasze *et al.*, 2006: 1). In particular, Blakely and Snyder (1997) consider gated communities as manifesting a number of social tensions 'between *exclusionary aspirations rooted in fear and protection of privilege and the values of civic responsibility*; between the trend toward privatization of public services and the ideals of the public good and general welfare; and between the *need for personal and community control of the environment and the dangers of making outsiders of fellow citizens*' (Blakely and Snyder, 1997: 3, emphasis added). In an edited volume on the global rise of private urban neighbourhoods, Webster and Glasze (2006: 222) further elaborate that gated communities signify a distinct shift in the way cities are organized, providing a new model for financial civic/public goods. They represent an extreme decentralization of decision-making and create new socio-spatial divides and micro-societies by breaking down traditional social geographies and altering patterns of urban insecurities. Their popularity has also spawned a commodified neighbourhood industry, creating micro-territories with their own local constitution and enhancing the conspicuousness of home-based consumption.

For their harshest critics, gated communities have often been diagnosed as an 'urban pathology' (M. Davis, 1990) that is associated with destructive forms of 'splintering urbanism' (Graham and Marvin, 2001) and other detrimental social impacts such as the excessive encroachment of private property on public spaces; the undermining of traditional forms of citizenship bonding and civic trust; the exacerbation of social–spatial polarization and urban inequality; and, ultimately, the disintegration and eventual destruction of society at large and meaningful public life (see Sennett, 1992; Caldeira, 2000; Webster *et al.*, 2002; Low, 2003; Glasze *et al.*, 2006).

In the United States alone, it has been estimated that the number of people living in gated communities increased from 4 million in 1995 to 8 million in 1997 and 16 million in 1998 (Low, 2003: 15). However, the rise of gated enclaves is by no means a distinctly 'American' phenomenon that diffuses throughout the world, as this new urban housing form can also be found in nearly every major city in the world[1] and may be the result of somewhat different local contexts and historical factors. As Webster *et al.* (2002: 316) point out, a 'development plucked from an international repertoire of concepts and designs may serve a subtly different purpose in Beijing than it does in Baltimore'. Researchers thus need to be wary of the danger of exporting the gated communities debate without adequately considering the institutional, social, economic and cultural contexts in which such gated housing developments are emerging elsewhere in the world. For example, in South Africa, fortified 'secure communities' are seen as a consequence of institutionalized racism in the apartheid era and high crime rates in the post-apartheid era. Gated enclaves in South Africa are inhabited not only by the rich but also by people from varied income groups and ethnic backgrounds. In Lebanon, gated communities first emerged during the civil war; in Saudi Arabia, gated compounds provide families with a sense of privacy and identity but also as a way to contain expatriate ('Western') cultures in the predominantly Muslim country. Fear of crime and police brutality further spurred the sprawl of gated enclaves in Latin America, whereas suburban gated complexes on the Mediterranean coast of Western Europe (Spain, Portugal and France) often serve as holiday homes for wealthy elites (see, for example, Caldeira, 1999, 2000; Coy and Pohler, 2002; Jurgens and Gnad, 2002). More commonly, the rise of contemporary gated communities has been interpreted as a physical manifestation of the 'global city–dual city' hypothesis (Marcuse, 1997a; Webster *et al.*, 2002). Specifically, it has been argued that global economic restructuring has led to the valorization of certain 'command-and-control' functions in key 'global cities' where urban inequality and income/class polarization have also intensified and become increasingly prevalent. In this context, gated communities are seen as exclusive sites where local and global elites organize their consumption and production as well as social and leisure activities (see F. L. Wu and Webber, 2004).

Whereas such broad interpretations focus on the macroeconomic factors, the development of gated communities has also been shaped by (and in turn shapes) the changing tastes and lifestyles of upper- and middle-class residents who see gated living as offering promises of the good life. In this conception, individual/ household preferences, changing lifestyle aspirations and security concerns are seen as important factors that account for the popular appeal of gated communities. For example, in Maxwell's (2004) analysis of online advertisements of gated communities in Canada, several social and lifestyle factors such as security, friendliness, social homogeneity, convenience, active lifestyle, privacy and exclusivity have been emphasized. These marketing discourses idealize and commodify place as buyers are led to believe that their lives might just be a little more like the fantasy promised in the marketing brochures if they purchase a home in a particular gated development.

The global diffusion of American 'popular culture' and images of the 'suburban dream home' have also been linked to changing consumer preferences (see Taylor, 1999; Fraser, 2000; King and Kusno, 2000; Harvey, 1997; F. L. Wu, 2004). Often emphasized in these studies are the roles of 'place imagineers' and 'place entrepreneurs' (property developers, architects and design professionals) in constructing and marketing gated communities as embodying various utopian and edenic visions of a perfect living environment – a highly controlled and manipulated space that is free from the dangers and unpleasantness of the 'outside' world. Within these purported utopian landscapes, the 'New Urbanist' paradigm holds sway as developers and planners opportunistically adopt various 'neo-traditional' neighbourhood designs and 'eco-friendly' environmental rhetoric to appeal to a niche market of 'lifestyle-conscious' housing consumers (see McCann, 1995; Till, 2001). Fraser (2000) further examines luxury housing advertisements in Shanghai and argues that the main mechanism by which these advertisements render private housing desirable and inviting is through the marketing of an imagined 'oasis' (*lüzhou* or *lühua*). As Fraser (2000: 27) notes, '[o]asification commodifies green pleasant aspects of a constructed nature to create a buffer zone between the individual apartment and its larger social and spatial contexts'.

For King and Kusno (2000: 43), the new architectural reference of contemporary Chinese cities such as Shanghai and Beijing further entails 'the crossing over of certain Euro-American urban artefacts such as the skyscraper, luxury apartment building and the suburban villa to the urban space of China'. In particular, the design of luxury apartments and 'high-class' villas is managed by a team of international property consultants who select from a broad cultural repertoire of 'European and US style houses' with private gardens, golf courses, advanced security features and 'quality Western fixtures' as well as design inspirations ranging from 'the American' to 'the Nordic', 'the Baroque', 'the Mediterranean', 'the Classic European' and 'the Georgian' (King and Kusno, 2000: 57).

Similarly, Grant's (2005) study on real estate advertisements for Ghana's gated communities reveals how themes such as safety and security, privacy and seclusion, community prestige and sense of community are frequently invoked in the marketing rhetoric. Many of the gated communities also rely extensively on 'transnational' housing designs to appeal to potential Ghanaian home buyers, many of whom have lived and worked abroad. F. L. Wu (2004) further argues that developers in Beijing exploit globalization by transplanting foreign cityscapes in the form of Western-style townhouses as a means of niche marketing. Wu demonstrates how the global imagineering of a purportedly 'Western' suburban lifestyle in these gated villa estates, appealing to the upwardly mobile urban rich in the Chinese capital, is however rooted in the contradictions of late socialist housing commodification policies in China. King's (2004) analysis of the 'villa phenomenon' in India and China provides further examples of the global–local nexus in shaping and inflecting real estate developments in various cities. Commenting on the case of India, King observes that many of the real estate advertisements are directed at flattering the cosmopolitan nature of potential investors, in particular the affluent and footloose non-resident Indians.

Though superficially similar to some North American (sub)urban landscapes, many of these new residential urban forms (the enclosed villa estates) in places as varied as Beijing, Shanghai, Delhi, Hyderabad and Bangalore all display quite different transnational, post-colonial flows of capital and culture as well as the particularistic dynamics of locality that underpin their production and consumption. Through the selective appropriation of these transnational spaces, foreign 'exotic' housing designs thus serve as the 'symbolic capital' that bestows upon their owners 'a reputation for competence and an image of respectability and honorability' (Bourdieu, 1984: 185). In this way, aspiring upper- and middle-class home-buyers may attempt to establish for themselves their own 'habitus' by which they can be identified and with which they can identify (McCann, 1995: 227).

No matter what strategies of 'enchantment' are being deployed in the advertising and marketing of gated communities, at the core of the production and consumption of gated communities is the notion of territoriality and its control of urban space and social life. The following section will now examine the theoretical relevance of territoriality in the construction of privileged middle-class landscape and the remaining two sections will consider related concepts of public/private spaces and the moral geographies of exclusion.

Marking out middle-class territoriality

Territoriality, as Sack (1986) contends, refers to the 'primary geographical expression of social power, and the means by which space and society are interrelated'. This view of territoriality differs markedly from ethological approaches that see territoriality among animals (including humans) as being genetically determined behaviours, an inherent drive among animals to gain and defend exclusive properties or spaces (see, for example, Adrey, 1997). To put it simply, human territoriality is the securing of social power through the control of space.[2] According to Sack (1986: 21–23), territorial action combines three necessary characteristics or 'tendencies': first, classification by area; second, communication by spatial markers such as boundaries; and, third, enforcement of access. Classification by area entails the categorization of objects by their location in space, rather than by type. The enactment of territorial strategy through classification can be very efficient in certain circumstances as it avoids the problem of enumeration, relying instead on the abstract logic of spatial classification. Communication further marks out territories through certain spatial markers such as sign, boundary or a statement about possession or exclusion. Classification and communication are in turn bolstered by the third tendency of enforcement, which limits the freedom of movement, access and control through various spatial interventions. Sack's work further demonstrates how spatial power in the organization of production and consumption of space evolves from primitive, pre-modern and modern capitalist societies.

To be sure, the theme of power and space is an enduring one in social theory. For example, Weber's definition of modern state power draws specifically on the idea of an administrative state legitimately exercising its coercive force over a territorially demarcated area. Mann (1984) further elaborates how state autonomy flows principally from the state's unique ability to provide a territorially centralized form of organization. Departing from both Weber's and Mann's focus on the state and its bureaucratic regulations, Foucault emphasized what he called the 'capillary functioning of power', which penetrates wide and deep into social life through the spatial disciplining of subjects at the periphery. One of the strengths (albeit also weaknesses) in Foucault's conception is the idea that power is omnipresent but at the same time also diffuse and fluid, hence making it difficult to pin down analytically.

Although social theorists have examined the spatial foundations of modern social power, one of the key limitations in these theories is that they are either overly rigid, in emphasizing formal 'top-down' state power such as in Weberian analysis, or too fluid, as in Foucault's conceptualization of power and space (Herbert, 1996). More fundamentally, studies often pay scant attention to how territoriality actually operates in the 'micro-scale' context, such as in an urban neighbourhood or in a less formalized everyday context (see Peleman, 2003). More fundamentally, the literature on territoriality also often overlooks the role of culture in the territorial organization of spaces and actions. One exception here is Steve Herbert's (1996) study on how territorial strategies and tactics of police officers in the Los Angeles Police Department are underpinned by subcultural norms and values. According to Herbert, central to the operation of police work and organization are normative orders (emphasizing the value of law, bureaucratic regulations, adventure/machismo, safety, competence and morality) that help to structure and explain the territorial behaviours and spatial tactics and practices of police officers in Los Angeles. In a similar vein, like the suburbs documented in North American cities (Baumgartner, 1988; see also Jacobs, 1996; Duncan and

Duncan, 2003), middle-class landscape values and tastes often play subtle roles that underpin and shape the territorial politics of gated communities.

In gated communities, middle-class territoriality is clearly manifested in formal or 'hard' territorial tactics such as the setting up of defensive physical structures (walls, gates, fences, etc.), surveillance and policing of boundaries, and 'turf guarding' actions by homeowners' associations. By setting up territorial boundaries through the explicit zoning of space and further communicating and enforcing territorial exclusivity by constructing spatial markers and restricting access, gated communities are territorial entities par excellence. Blomley (2004a,b), in particular, refers to this as the enactment of property relations that enforces spatial boundaries between owners and non-owners by mobilizing persuasive myths (for example, Locke's powerful 'creation myth' of property whereby *every man has a property in his own person*) and communicative claims that appeal to hegemonic accounts of property rights as individualized, definite, immutable and, almost always, exclusively private.[3] As Blomley (2004a: xvi) argues, real property 'must be enacted upon material spaces and real people including owners and those who are to be excluded' and involves active construction and maintenance of unambiguous spatial boundaries and legible symbols that delineate public and private territories. In this sense, gated communities thus manifest distinct characteristics of modern territoriality through their classification of space and objects into abstract grids that conceptually separate the 'spatial container' from the 'spatially contained'. As Deleuze and Guattarri (1988: 212) observe, 'geometry and arithmetic take on the power of the scalpel. Private property implies a space that has been overcoded and gridded by surveying'. In this abstract view of territoriality, space is perceived as potentially 'emptiable' of its content and may be refilled by overlaying spatial grids and boundaries, hence obscuring any underlying power relations by emphasizing the abstract language of geometric space.

In the zoning of gated communities, the boundaries and perimeters of the enclaves determine the territorial extent of the spatial container. Once these spatial boundaries are fixed, the interior of the enclave is literally emptied out of its content and refilled with new residential communities, thereby obliterating any traces of what had existed before in these spaces. In the suburbs of Shanghai, where private gated communities often occupy spaces where farmlands and agricultural communities once stood, such an observation bears a poignant reminder on the spatial 'violence' wrought through territorial practices and the obliteration of space. Besides such manifest territorial violence, territoriality also operates at a more subtle and ideological level as people actively mobilize different cultural resources and tools (values, symbols, rhetoric of the good life, etc.) to lay claim to their private properties and carve out their own exclusive spaces. As the book will later show, middle-class territoriality operates through a mixture of coercive strategies as well as hegemonic consent through engineering widespread social acceptance of a particular spatial classification (for example, 'my place' versus 'yours') as natural and taken for granted. For example, Taylor (1999) notes that the marking out of the home as women's territory in seventeenth-century Dutch households not only led to the feminization of the home as 'woman's place' but also created a new isolation of women's work. In this sense, territoriality through spatial classification and its visibility provides a means of reifying power and invisible social relations by making explicit and real their potentialities (Sack, 1986: 33).

To the extent that territoriality entails the carving out of 'private' spaces and further controlling and restricting public access to them, it would be necessary for us to be attentive to the various meanings and spatial practices of the 'public' and 'private' and how people actively invoke and construct these (spatial) categories in their everyday life. As the next section will discuss, one critical weakness in gated community research is the underlying assumption that the meanings of 'public' and 'private' are fixed, universal and unproblematic.

Unravelling the public/private

As pointed out by several scholars, the widespread invocations of the 'public' and 'private' amongst scholars in general are not always informed by a careful consideration of the meanings and implications of these concepts in varied contexts (Weintraub, 1995; Drummond, 2000; McDougall and Hansson, 2002). In this regard, one needs to be sensitive to what the concepts of 'public' and 'private' actually mean and, for the purpose of this study, how their meanings and significance have changed and evolved in increasingly neoliberal China. Are there various degrees of 'publicness' and 'privateness' in contemporary Chinese urban society and how are these distinctions and tensions manifested in the everyday lives of people in the society at large as well as within gated communities? More importantly, how do people actively construct and invoke notions of privacy and domesticity in Shanghai's gated communities? Before proceeding further, it is useful to briefly review some of the different ways public–private distinctions are being made.

In contemporary Western literature, public–private distinctions are often discussed in at least four different, albeit related, ways (see Weintraub, 1995). In the liberal economic model, dominant in 'public policy' analysis, the public–private distinction is primarily marked out in terms of the distinction between public state administration and the private market economy. In the classical 'republican virtue' approach, the public realm is conceptualized in terms of the political community and exercise of citizenship rights and obligations, both of which are analytically distinct from the market and the administrative state. Then there is the third, 'dramaturgic', approach of social historical analysis and anthropology, which sees the public realm as a sphere of fluid and polymorphous sociability (see, for example, Aries and Duby, 1991). Last but not least are the feminist and economic history analyses that conceive the distinction between the private and the public in terms of the distinction between family as the private sphere of social reproduction and the public realm of the market economy.

Within gated community research, public–private debates often draw on different strands of the above distinctions. For example, some scholars have argued that gated communities are effective and innovative ways of urban development according to liberal economic principles, as residents are able to decide for themselves whether or not to move into privately developed and managed gated communities that offer a differentiated form of housing product and services. In this way, residents who move into gated communities are expressing a preference for contracting with private developers for the delivery of public goods and services rather than relying on traditional municipal housing provision. Foldvary (1994), for example, arguing from a market realist position, contends that gated communities are efficient because they allow collectively consumed civic goods to be supplied by the market. In a related vein, Webster (2002), adopting an institutional economics approach, argues that gated communities are efficient 'consumption clubs' that avoid the 'free-rider problem' inherent in public goods provision as gated community residents are full-paying proprietors bounded by explicitly assigned property rights over their neighbourhoods. However, little is mentioned by these authors about the problem of social inequity and urban segregation associated with gated communities.

On the other hand, critical scholars have roundly censured gated communities for contributing to the breakdown of the social compact and view the retreat of privileged upper- and middle-class residents into their private enclaves as anti-social decisions to avoid the 'messy' affair of civic engagements with the wider public/political community. Overall, the public–private debates in gated communities research have emphasized one or more of the following tensions: between public provision and private provision of civic goods and services; state planning versus market function; efficiency versus equity in service delivery; private space versus shared public space. In the last, gated communities have often been seen as the encroachment of private property onto public streets and amenities, which, if left unchecked, will lead to the eventual demise of public space (D. Mitchell, 1995).

Drawing on the case of São Paulo in Brazil, Caldeira (2000) forcefully argues that fortified enclaves in the city represent an attack on the modern ideals of public space. For Caldeira (2000: 125), private enclaves and the segregation they generate deny many of the basic elements that constitute the modern experience of public life: primacy of streets and their openness; free circulation of crowds and vehicles; impersonal and anonymous encounters of the pedestrian; unprogrammed public enjoyment and congregation in streets and squares; and the presence of people from different social backgrounds interacting and intermingling freely. Similarly, the insidious spread of gated communities in Los Angeles has led Mike Davis (1990) to warn of a 'post-liberal' city where the defence of private luxury enclaves has given birth to an arsenal of security systems that violate shared public spaces and an obsession with the securing of social boundaries through defensive architectural designs (see also Ellin, 1999). Extending the argument further, recent urban scholarship has also examined how gentrification of urban neighbourhoods and the privatization of urban streetscapes have created 'pseudo-public' spaces such as malls and theme parks that are highly regulated, contrived and 'sanitized' arenas for social interaction and intermingling (Zukin, 1991, 1995; Sorkin, 1992; Goss, 1993; Flusty, 2000; Lees, 2001).

Germane to the discussion on the public–private is also the issue of privacy. According to Rapoport (1980: 31), privacy can be defined as 'the control of unwanted interaction' or the individual's 'right to be left alone' (Warren and Brandeis, 1890). In its contemporary usage, the meaning of privacy also extends to suggest something belonging to the individual interest that is not owned by any government (Rossler, 2005). Liberals may trumpet individuals' right to privacy but communitarian thinkers have warned that privacy is not an unmitigated good. Etzioni (2000: 184), for example, argues that good societies 'carefully balance individual rights and social responsibilities, autonomy and the common good, privacy and . . . public safety'. For critics of gated communities, the desire of affluent residents of gated communities to live apart from the masses is further linked to 'neoliberal' discourses on individualized rights of seclusion, privacy and self-protection (see Hook and Vrdoljak, 2002). To this extent, the debates revolving around gated communities manifest the tensions between acknowledging and respecting personal autonomy and individualism versus addressing wider communitarian concerns on the need to promote social integration and civic life (see, for example, Putnam, 2001).

Yet when addressing issues on the public–private divide, we need to be wary that these concepts arise mainly from 'Western' understanding and experiences that may not be readily grafted onto non-Western context. The point here is not to argue that Western academic terms have no relevance in a non-Western context, in this case, Shanghai/China. Rather it is that these concepts offer important insights when examined according to 'local' specificities of time and place. As Zarrow (2002: 121) readily points out, there is no single word in the Chinese lexicon that is the direct equivalent of the English meaning of 'privacy' (in the sense of personal, closed off from the public, inner life, private individual rights and other related concepts). Nonetheless, Chinese concepts of privacy are often subsumed under the political discourse of *si* (personal, self, selfish, private)[4] and developed in relation to the realm of the *gong* (public, public space, open, communal) that predates the modern period.

To be sure, as Bonnie McDougall (2004) points out, despite the common belief that the Chinese have no concept of privacy, there is a well-established tradition of private property and privacy values in traditional and modern China. For example, during the late imperial era in China, there was already extensive (elite) awareness of privacy and appreciation of its benefits. Confucius in the *Analects* had suggested that cultivated Chinese strongly dislike unwarranted intrusions into what they regarded as their private sphere. In order to ensure this right, wealthy elites might erect high walls around their private residences, implying that the right to privacy was a function of one's place or status in society (Moore, 1984: 223). Conversely, the right to *intrude* into other people's privacy is also dependent on one's social status and rank. Yan (2003), for example, observes that individual privacy in traditional Chinese culture existed in a hierarchical context: social superiors could enjoy privacy in relation to those who were ranked lower socially and economically, but not vice versa.

In McDougall's (2002) book detailing the love-letters and intimate lives of the famous Chinese literary figure Lu Xun and his lover Xu Guangping, she further argues that members of the urban elite such as Lu and Xu maintained a coherent and persistent sense of privacy (McDougall, 2002: 2). Despite the well-established tradition of private property and privacy values in traditional and modern China, political rhetoric of the twentieth century emphasized the paramount importance of public good over individualism, subjectivity and private life of the people. In particular, the emphasis on public service as a personal goal and on the public good as a national objective by Chinese political figures throughout the greater part of the twentieth century is partly responsible for the perception that privacy as a value is foreign to China.[5]

During the Republican period (1911–1949), the institution of the family and its relation to the state came under intense scrutiny by cultural, social and economic reformers as well as political parties and the new Nationalist government. After 1949, the new Communist state introduced a much wider range of measures to control people's individual and family lives, culminating in extreme measures such as the rural communal kitchens in the collectivization movements of the 1960s and urban inspection of women's menstrual cycles under the population control laws of the 1970s. Mao, in particular, 'going far beyond Sun Yat-Sen in idealizing the public realm as a supreme good and stigmatizing attachment to private property and private life as merely selfish, laid down a linguistic practice as well as a policy that lasted virtually unchallenged for the better part of forty years' (McDougall, 2004: 3).

In the post-Mao China, however, Yan (2003: 139) argues that, as rural families in Xiajia village become more privatized, family members have become more aware of their individual rights, and hence demand greater personal space and privacy. At a deeper level, this desire for privacy reflects a growing sense of entitlement to individual rights in private life and individualism more broadly. In Shanghai, owing to the overcrowded housing conditions, the lack of intimate spaces and privacy is a perennial concern of residents in traditional neighbour-hoods (Pellow, 1993). As will be shown later in this book, with the development of new commodity housing enclaves, families are beginning to move into independ-ent housing units which afford them greater privacy, individual freedom and the ability to lead a more autonomous life. Such freedom and autonomy are, however, not equally accessible to everyone in contemporary China but rest fundamentally on one's economic ability to buy into private housing enclaves and consume new 'lifestyle choices'[6] that emphasize exclusivity, privacy and prestige.

While the notion of privacy is fast changing in the post-Mao era, what can be said about the 'state-hegemonic public sphere' in China? Here, Kraus's (2000) observation is instructive. For Kraus (2000: 289), Western discussion of China's public sphere often conflates two separate ideas: public sphere and civil soci-ety. In Europe, where civil society grew as the public sphere was transformed, it makes sense to join the two concepts. In China the depth of civil society is open to considerable doubt and hence it makes less sense to conjoin these concepts so tightly. To the extent that scholars often confuse Habermasian ideals of the public sphere as a closely bounded state–civil society combination, the very existence of a public sphere in China often seems to be in doubt. To be sure, the public sphere does exist in China, as in every other society. What is distinctive here is how the Chinese Communist Party (CCP) has reorganized modern Chinese society to create a 'public sphere' over which it could hold power. For Arendt (1998), the emergence of the nation-state and modern industrial economy has precipitated the dominant 'rise of the social' that blurred the old borderlines between the private (household/family) and the political realm of the public. In socialist China, the totalitarian party-state has effectively hijacked the social and transformed society into a massive bureaucratic structure under the rule of the CCP in which society is organized under a massive nationwide administration of 'collective housekeeping' in which 'private interests assume public significance'. Prominent examples of public/state interference in the private sphere include the Chinese state's control of social reproduction activities through compulsory family planning and the Household Registration System (*hukou*), which determines and restricts the residential location of each and every household (see Chan and Zhang, 1999).

Since the decline of the post-Mao work-unit system, the state has to some extent withdrawn from its dominant role in people's daily lives, thereby creating opportunities for social interaction beyond the state's gaze. In this context, the rise of the private housing market and gated communities could be interpreted as the carving out of new domestic spaces that potentially increase personal autonomy away from state control. For example, Deborah Davis (quoted in Fraser, 2000: 43) argues that interior design in Shanghai homes often serves as a vehicle for self-expression outside or in opposition to the claustrophobic control of the Communist party-state. In these terms, it is possible to offer a more nuanced understanding of gated communities in China not so much as representing the bulldozing of public spaces by the private, but rather as offering potential sites where greater personal and household autonomy may be realized (albeit only for those who can afford to move into private housing enclaves).

Paralleling Yang's (1997: 292) observation on the evolution of mass media in urban China, it may be said that 'the post-Mao period has brought about the pluralization, differentiation, and stratification of (media) publics according to class, educational level, region, locality, gender, occupation, and leisure interests, [in the process] fragmenting the state's mass public'. In the words of White (1993: 217), the spread of market relations in China has effectively 'created the basis of, and context for, new forms of sociopolitical participation and organization, to varying degrees independent of and/or in opposition to the Party/state'. For Ong and Zhang (2008), privatization encompasses more than the dismantling of state enterprises, the spread of private property and the spontaneous growth of entrepreneurialism. In particular, privatization is seen as an ensemble of techniques that free up the powers of the self and a multitude of self-interested practices and self-animation associated with neoliberal logic. For them, the most significant aspects of China's privatizing reforms are in the range of new private spaces that comes with the micro-freedom of property ownership and the proliferation of neoliberal values and practices that are focused on animating enterprising subjects who accumulate individual advantages and self-promotion.

Another important point to note is that public and private spheres/spaces are not passively inhabited by people but are actively constructed and enacted in quotidian life. For example, in Drummond's (2000) study on public and private spaces in post-reform Vietnam, people constantly infringe on mundane areas of public spaces such as the street as they go about conducting their own daily affairs and private businesses, hence blurring the public/private, outside/inside divide. Law (2002) further looks at how foreign domestic workers in Hong Kong actively transgress public spaces in the city's central business district every Sunday and in the process transform (albeit temporarily) the monumental public/global spaces into their own private gathering grounds. What these studies suggest is that the 'public' and 'private', far from being innate and fixed social/spatial categories, are actively engaged, negotiated and choreographed by people on a routine basis. In post-reform China, where public/private conventions are rapidly changing, it will be fruitful to further examine how people make use of different cultural tools (symbols, behavioural codes, social practices and discourses) to actively construct and organize their own private life and living spaces away from the hegemonic control of the state.

In so far as gated communities are highly conscious efforts to create an exclusive private universe for urban elites, a moral social order also permeates the territorial organization of space and social life behind the gates. It is to this contested and exclusionary nature of landscape that I will now turn. As will be pointed out, residential landscapes, besides being the repository of personal memories, place attachments and community values, are also often attempts to construct a 'moral geography of otherness' (Till, 1993) that aims to distinguish 'insiders' from 'outsiders' and preserve the 'purity' and 'pristine' nature of private communities and space.

Purified landscape/community and the moral geographies of exclusion

Humanistic geographers often allude to the emotional bond between people and places or landscape. Place attachment or 'topophilia' (Tuan, 1990) manifests itself most clearly in people's attachment to home places, which is at once affective but also exclusive and reactionary. For example, Duncan and Duncan (2001) have explored the 'negative externalities' associated with the attachment to places arising from a search for landscape distinction and prestige that depends on explicit comparisons with other 'lesser' places. In particular, sense of place and the construction of place-identity are seen as a 'positional good' that is underpinned by a highly exclusionary place politics. To this extent, landscape and landscape values play crucial roles in mediating between the politics of exclusion and the representation of space.

As a polysemic term, 'landscape' refers to the appearance of an area, the assemblages of objects used to produce that appearance, and the area itself. Far from being natural or politically neutral, landscape as a social and ideological construct embodies the unequal power relations among different social groups. As W. J. T. Mitchell (1994: 1–2) puts it:

[L]andscape is an instrument of cultural power, perhaps even an agent of power that is (or frequently represents itself as) independent of human intentions. Landscape thus has a double role with respect to something like ideology . . . It naturalizes a cultural and social construction representing an artificial world as if it were simply given and inevitable, and it also makes that representation operational by interpellating its beholder in some more or less determinate relation to its givenness as sight and site.

As I have pointed out in the earlier chapter, landscape, to be sure, is *not* just a product of some naturally evolving culture or tradition. Rather, it is the product of intense negotiation between those with sufficient political and cultural resources to construct and define places and those subjected to such definitions (Western, 1981). Excavating below the surface of the built environment, geographers and other scholars have long explored class, racial and gender issues in the production of landscape as a means to expose its underlying power relations and exclusionary tendencies (see Harvey, 1979; Cosgrove and Daniels, 1988; Jackson, 1989; Monk, 1992; K. Mitchell, 1997; Pile and Keith, 1997). For example, in her analysis of Vancouver's Chinatown, Anderson (1988, 1991) interrogates the historical records of the city to reveal the political, economic and ideological practices underpinning the construction of Chinatown as an ethnic enclave. Drawing on various notions about the supposed biological and social superiority of Europeans, whites in Vancouver came to understand Chinese people as irredeemably different from themselves and regarded the ethnic landscapes of Chinatown as 'naturally unsanitary' (filled with dirty slaughterhouses, sewage lines, airborne diseases, etc.) and plagued with moral depravity and danger (brothels, gambling dens, crime-ridden alleys). Relying on these selective landscape perceptions, white Vancouverites and their government were constantly worried about the 'bad' influence of Chinatown on the health and morality of the entire city and periodically sought to clean up and bring order to the place. Thus, landscape – in this case Vancouver's Chinatown – serves to 'reaffirm a . . . moral order of "us" and "them"' (Anderson, 1988: 145).

Nowhere are such moral geographies of fear and pollution more salient than within the gates of upper- and middle-class housing enclaves, where the idea of maintaining a pristine, clean and wholesome living environment free from the threat of intrusion and pollution by 'social undesirables' (urban poor, vagrants, beggars, migrant labourers) has generated a defensive and divisive urban landscape. But, beyond just a direct mapping of antagonistic class relations, gated communities are also attempts to actively construct an ontological separation between 'us' (i.e. like-minded residents sharing similar lifestyles and values) and 'them' (the 'other' non-residents outside the community with dubious backgrounds); and in the process they determine who 'we' are and what 'our place' is like, as opposed to 'them' and 'their places'. Such socio-spatial distinctions draw widely on select cultural repertoire as people invoke highly charged moral discourses and stories, as well as various normative landscape ideals (such as the desire for an orderly and aesthetic environment) and beliefs (the supposed inferiority of certain racial or social groups such as vagrants and 'outsiders'), which in turn lay the groundwork for exclusionary spatial practices (see, for example, Tuan, 1986; Jacobs, 1996; Cresswell, 1996, 2001; Duncan and Duncan, 2003).

To the extent that gated communities are attempts to construct a moral geography of 'difference' and 'otherness', they also seek to preserve a 'purified community' – one that is free from the unexpected and chaotic messiness of the outside world, and free from experiences that can be emotionally threatening, dislocating and painful (Tajbakhsh, 2001: 170–171; see also Sennett, 1970). Drawing on the anthropological works of Mary Douglas, Sibley (1995) demonstrates how purification of social space often involves the rejection and annihilation of differences and the securing of boundaries to maintain the social homogeneity and the 'purity' of place. In addition, people often construct morally charged stories that draw on the themes of colour, diseases, animals, sexuality and nature, which in turn rest on 'the [central] idea of dirt as a signifier of imperfection and inferiority – the counter reference-point being the white, often male, physically and mentally able person' (Sibley, 1995: 14; see also Wolch and Dear, 1989; Gleeson, 1999; McDowell, 1999). Similarly, in Ervin Goffman's (1963) classic sociological work, he described how society's perceptions shape and discredit particular individuals:

> While the stranger is present before us, evidence can arise of his possessing an attribute that makes him different from others in the category of persons available for him to be, and of a less desirable kind – in the extreme, a person who is quite thoroughly bad or dangerous or weak. He is thus reduced in our minds from a whole and usual person to a tainted, discounted one. Such an attribute is a stigma...
>
> (Goffman, 1963: 15)

In contemporary urban cultural life, the stigmatization of marginal social groups (urban poor, the disabled, ethnic and sexual minorities, etc.) and purification of urban spaces are pervasive as an everyday occurrence such as in modern residential spaces 'where group antagonisms are manifested in the erection of territorial boundaries which accentuate difference or otherness' (Sibley, 1988: 414). Within gated communities, maintaining and defending the purity of space and the 'community' values have become the defining features of 'respectable' and desirable 'middle-class' neighbourhoods where residents marshal a whole arsenal of cultural tools to construct a private world that is pure, pristine and wholesome.

While territorial exclusion and social marginalization have dominated contemporary debates on gated communities, what has been neglected in these discussions so far is precisely how these gated communities actually 'measure up' to the normative ideals of modern urban life as the bastion of openness, social diversity and democracy. In the case of Shanghai's gated enclaves, how do the 'grounded reality' and intersecting roles of local politics and culture shape and influence the normative judgements of places? More pointedly, do privatized 'landscapes of privilege' in gated communities, built on the consumerist ethos of territorially defined membership, privacy and exclusivity, run counter to normative conceptions of what 'good' places are? Arguably, any normative judgement needs to contend with what David Smith (2000: 202) calls a 'context sensitive moral knowledge' of places (its history, culture, politics, etc.). As this book will examine in greater detail later, a foray into the geographical moral conception of place will thus need to grapple with the local complexities and ambiguities of place-making.

Summary

This chapter has provided the conceptual and theoretical scaffolding that frames the study of gated communities and socio-spatial exclusion. A major theoretical underpinning in this book is the notion of middle-class territoriality and other related concepts regarding public/private spaces: privacy, landscapes of exclusion and their implications for the contested moral geographies of the city. The subsequent chapters will now bring together these themes and concepts to bring out their analytical and theoretical significance and shed light on the housing aspirations and motivations of residents in Shanghai's gated communities. As pointed out earlier in this chapter, when applying ('Western') academic concepts and theories such as public and private, it is important to bear in mind the varying local context and particularities. The point here of course is not to deny the relevance of these concepts in a non-Western context, but to counsel their careful usage and application. The next chapter will now set out the general context of Shanghai's recent urban transformation and its housing reform policies.

3 Urban reform, the new middle class and the emergence of gated communities in Shanghai

Economic reform and urban transformation in Shanghai

This chapter provides an overview of the impacts of economic reform and urban restructuring on Shanghai's contemporary urban and housing development. Specifically, I will examine how post-welfare housing reform policies initiated by the central government have led to the emergence of a private housing market centred on the development of commodity housing enclaves targeting the new middle class and nouveau riche in Shanghai. As has been widely documented, contemporary urban development in Shanghai (see Figure 3.1) is directly related to the demise of Maoism in the late 1970s and the establishment of a new economic order by the Chinese Communist Party at the Third Plenum in December 1978 through the implementation of the New Open Door Policy (Y. M. Yeung and Sung, 1996; W. P. Wu, 1999). Initiated by Deng Xiaoping, the main goals of the post-1978 reform policies are, first, to restructure the Chinese economy away from collective forms of ownership and control of the means of production and

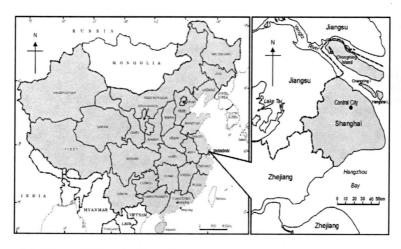

Figure 3.1 China and Shanghai (insert).

towards the growth of individual and private ownership and, second, to increase the allocation of surplus according to market 'efficiency' criteria and towards an increasing role for markets in the circulation of goods, services, capital and wage labour. The larger goal of the reform is to mould capitalism into 'socialism with Chinese characteristics' and to transform China into a modern nation-state (Baum, 1996). In large coastal cities and designated economic growth zones, city officials are encouraged to adopt an 'entrepreneurial' and 'pro-business' outlook to attract investment into their cities and towns (see F. L. Wu, 2003).

In order to link up Chinese cities to the global economy and restructure the city into the global 'space of flows' (Castells, 1996), economic reform began with the creation of four special economic zones (SEZs) in the southwestern provinces of Guangdong and Fujian (Shenzhen, Zhuhai, Shantou, and Xiamen). Subsequently, another 14 coastal cities including Shanghai were established as SEZs in 1984. For Shanghai, however, it was not until 1992, after Deng's stopover in the city during his celebrated southern inspection tour (thus publicly endorsing Shanghai's economic development), that local and central government officials were galvanized into action to push forward various ambitious economic programmes in the municipality. Between 1991 and 1996, US$10 billion was invested in infrastructure, gradually increasing to US$22.1 billion between 1994 and 2000. Specifically, these projects included the construction of inner and outer ring roads, the construction of two subway lines, the construction of tunnels and bridges (Nanpu and Huangpu bridges) across the Huangpu River and major upgrading of Shanghai's port at Waigaoqiao (Y. M. Yeung and Sung, 1996). In addition, the city's telecommunications infrastructure is being upgraded and connected to a new national fibre-optic cable network; and 6 million square metres of new housing is being built per year. In the 1990s, the introduction of housing and land reform measures (more on this later) further encouraged the construction of new housing and propelled many urban redevelopment projects. In the emerging 'consumption-scape', shopping malls, gated communities and skyscrapers have become a ubiquitous sight in the city. The massive make-over of Shanghai in the late twentieth century is particularly significant considering that cities in socialist China were generally considered as consumptive and representing 'decadent bourgeois values'. Whereas the national urban policies in the 1950s and 1960s were geared towards transforming consumer cities into production sites, with emphasis given to industrial development outside the city centre (Y. M. Yeung and Sung, 1996: 274), the new reform urban policies are bent on creating an all-round entrepreneurial and pro-business urban environment that aims to promote comprehensive economic development.

One of the largest-scale transformations in Shanghai undertaken by the Shanghai municipality is the shift to urbanize the peninsula known as Pudong or the area east of the Huangpu River. The development of the New Pudong Area,[1] a 522-km² area, was widely touted as the new model of 'modern' urban development, which is intended to herald the city's new role in the global and regional economy (Olds, 2001). According to the *Summary of the Comprehensive Plan of Shanghai 1999–2020* (2004), city officials further aim to make Shanghai an international economic hub by 2020 and transform it into one of the world's lead-ing economic, financial, trade and shipping centres. As the planning document states, the city's development goals plan to 'give full play to Shanghai's national and international functions as a link and pivot radiating influences outward abroad and inward inland, and further promote joint development of Yangtze River Delta and Yangtze River Economic Zone' (Shanghai Urban Planning Administration Bureau, 2004: 10).

Suburbanization

Alongside these large-scale developmental projects, Shanghai's municipal gov-ernment has also embarked on a massive plan to decentralize the inner-city population into the outlying suburban areas by constructing new cities and town-ships that are connected by extensive highway systems linking these new suburban areas to the city centre as well as to other neighbouring provinces (see Figure 3.2). As part of the 'incipient suburbanization' process in Chinese cities, Shanghai's suburban development, as in other Chinese cities, is the result of a number of fac-tors such as the marketization of urban land, the shift of industrial land to tertiary use, transportation improvement, the availability of foreign and domestic capital and new housing construction in the suburbs (Zhou and Ma, 2000; see also Zhou and Logan, 2005).[2]

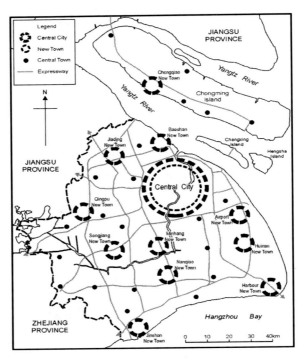

Figure 3.2 New suburban areas and expressways in Shanghai.

According to the *Comprehensive Plan of Shanghai (1999–2020)* ratified by the State Council on 11 May 2001, a 'multi-level' and 'multi-centre' urban system organized along five 'scales' comprising a Central City (*zhongxin cheng*), 11 New Cities (*xincheng*) and 22 Central Towns (*zhongxin zhen*) and scores of other Ordinary Towns (*yiban zhen*) and Central Villages (*zhongxin chun*) has been planned and progressively built. In the new Comprehensive Plan, the Central City surrounded by the Outer Ring Road remains the political, economic and cultural centre of Shanghai whereas the 11 designated New Cities (sometimes referred as 'New Towns') where district or county governments are located are medium-sized cities with important industrial and infrastructural developments (see Table 3.1).

In the next lower hierarchy are the Central Towns, which are small-sized cities, backed by industries and developed from relatively big and systematically organized rural townships. Ordinary Towns in turn are the amalgamation of several existing market towns that are planned according to their locations, transportation and resource endowments. Central Villages are the result of the merging of several rural villages and are new types of modernized rural settlement with distinguishing local features and relatively good infrastructural support and facilities. In addition, 20 large-scale residential districts will also be established between the Inner and Outer Ring Roads in the City Centre accompanied by scores of other small to medium-size residential estates in the suburban areas in the New Cities and Central Towns (Shanghai Urban Planning Administration Bureau, 2004: 44).

Linking up these new cities and new towns is an extensive highway and road system. According to the *Shanghai Metropolitan Transport White Paper* (2002), road mileage in the city had increased exponentially since economic reform began, from 905 kilometres in 1978 through 1631 kilometres in 1990 and 6,641 kilometres in 2000 to 10,451 kilometres in 2003. By 2005, Shanghai's transport planners aimed to increase the length of its principal highway network from 1,188

Table 3.1 Population distribution in Central City area and New Towns

Area	Population (2004)	Projected population (2020)
Central City Area	7,550,000	8,300,000
Minhang New Town	188,000	400,000
Baoshan New Town	241,000	400,000
Jiading New Town	97,000	250,000
Qingpu New Town	58,000	250,000
Songjiang New Town	106,000	300,000
Nanqiao New Town	60,000	200,000
Jinshan New Town	86,000	300,000
Harbour New Town	66,000	200,000
Huinan New Town	44,000	200,000
Airport New Town	33,000	200,000
Chengqiao New Town	51,000	200,000

Source: compiled from Shanghai Urban Planning Administration Bureau (2004).

kilometres in 2000 to 2,340 kilometres. In addition, the city has completed several expressway networks connecting the city to the suburbs including the Huqingping Highway and Xinfengjin Highway. A regional rail transit network has also been planned and built, and is projected to cover up to 540 kilometres by the year 2020. In particular, it is hoped that the construction of the regional rail transit (such as the R4 Line that goes to Songjiang New City and the R1 Line connecting south-wards to the Minhang district) will improve direct accessibility from new cities to the city centre and to speed up suburban development (*Shanghai Metropolitan Transport White Paper*, 2002).

In tandem with the frenzied pace of economic reform and urban restructur-ing, the 'welfare-based' housing provision system has also been jettisoned and commodified, first through sales of 'public housing' and later by encouraging the construction of commercially developed commodity housing. All across Shanghai and the surrounding suburban areas, private commodity housing enclaves have sprung up and are rapidly dominating the urban landscape. As will be discussed in the following, housing commodification is often concerned more with market privatization issues than with social equity and the welfare of urban residents.

Housing reform in Shanghai

Following the Communist Revolution in 1949, urban housing in China was 'de-commodified' and transformed into a form of public welfare under the socialist property regime, whereby the Chinese socialist state and its public agencies and work-units (*danwei*) held the ultimate rights to practically all existing urban properties in the cities. With the exception of a small minority of private home-owners, urban residents all became renters and were allocated housing by their work-units, which were responsible for building and assigning the living quarters of their employees. Thus, urban residents during the pre-reform era were 'suppli-cants' to the state housing mechanism and possessed very limited housing rights (mainly right of occupancy) with virtually no option to own private property (see D. Davis, 2003).

All these were, however, set for change when the Chinese central government, following Deng Xiaoping's economic reform initiatives in 1978, enacted a series of housing reform policies starting with the 'rolling back' of public housing pro-vision accompanied by the 'rolling out' (Peck and Tickell, 2002) of neoliberal policies aimed ultimately at privatizing the housing market and the creation of a full-scale real estate market economy, partly to free the state work-units from the heavy burden of housing provision and partly to promote home ownership and urban consumption (see F. L. Wu, 1996, 2005; D. Davis, 2000, 2003; Li, 2000).[3] Although the Chinese leadership has never espoused neoliberalism (*xinzhiyou zhuyi*) as an official ideology and, as David Harvey (2005) points out, the reforms in China 'just happened to coincide' with the turn to neoliberal solutions in Britain and the United States, the outcome in China nevertheless has been 'the con-struction of a particular kind of market economy that increasingly incorporates neoliberal elements interdigitated with authoritarian centralized control' (Harvey,

2005: 120). It is important to note that urban reform and the liberalization/privatization of the housing market in China does not in any sense signal the complete withdrawal or decline of state power in controlling and managing urban affairs. Rather, the state continues to wield significant influence and important jurisdiction over the housing market. Fundamentally, market reform and privatization in China may be described as the product of the interplay between public and private forces and crisscrossing of both state and market interests. Such 'neoliberalism with Chinese characteristics' or, in the words of Brenner and Theodore (2002), 'actually existing neoliberalism' brings along with it several unintended consequences, precipitating the tremendous upheaval and transformation in urban class relations, public cultures, the rise of private property and institutional changes (see H. Wang, 2003; J. M. He, 2004; Rofel, 2007).

Yet, despite the ideological U-turn of the Communist party-state to embrace neoliberal polices of housing privatization, it was not until the late 1990s that the publicly financed housing system finally gave way to a fully fledged housing market. Even then, as Deborah Davis (2003: 185) contends, housing commodification through the housing monetarization policy (HMP) in China began with a few piecemeal changes in a few selected cities and then stalled or accelerated in response to macro- and micro-level financial and political incentives. I will now briefly trace the different phases of housing reform policies and the HMP that set the stage for the development of commodity housing in gated communities.

Different phases of housing reform policies

Primarily, the HMP entails the restructuring of urban housing market and welfare state accompanied by the transformation of the built environment. Housing commodification initially proceeded on a piecemeal basis as many cities experimented with different housing privatization schemes such as through the selling of state-subsidized housing to employees at a discount and halting the supply of work-unit-supplied housing. Broadly conceived, urban housing reform may be divided into several phases (following Deborah Davis, 2003). In the first phase, from 1980 to 1992, the Chinese government experimented with the selling of housing use rights and the legalization of home ownership. In tandem with housing privatization, urban land reform also led to the commodification and marketization of urban land, replacing the formerly free allocation of land assets[4] (see Zhu, 2002, for a comprehensive review of urban land and property reform). In 1986, the State Land Administration Bureau was established by the State Council to administer the selling and transferring of land-use rights (LURs). This was followed by the revision of the 1986 Land Management Law and the ratification of a 1990 ordinance which allowed cities to sell long-term leaseholds (up to 70 years) by negotiation, tender or auction and to retain 60 per cent of the profit. This new law effectively frees up a vast amount of state land for both local and foreign property investors, propelling massive real estate constructions. Within just seven years (1990–1997), Shanghai built 8.9 million square metres of office space and 3.5 million square metres of retail floor area. In addition, housing reform and privatization have also seen the emergence of full 'commodity' or 'commercial' houses (*shang ping fang*), which are built by property developers and then sold through the housing market and not through the work-unit allocation mechanism.

Concomitantly, during the 1990s, new financial instruments for housing loans and mortgages were introduced to facilitate individual borrowing for home financing, thus laying the groundwork for an emergent housing property market.[5] In the second phase of the housing reform (1993–1997), the State Council started to outline procedures for the selling of public rental flats to sitting tenants throughout the entire country. Heavy discounts, based usually on years of service and occupational ranks, are given to encourage home buying. New owners can purchase the use rights in perpetuity and can bequeath ownership to others and use the property as collateral for loans. After five years of owning the use rights, the owners would obtain full title of the property with the right to sell. At the same time the government raised rents in public-sector housing manifolds in order to 'persuade' the sitting tenants to opt out of the rental mode. The housing reform, however, is not without its problems, as it is seen to encourage home ownership for people who have already benefited from the earlier housing system such as high-ranking cadres, professional and managerial staff of powerful government work agencies and work-units (see Y. Huang, 2003).

Despite the new housing measures aimed at promoting home ownership, only a third of local residents actually held some form of title to their homes by the mid-1990s while the majority of urban residents remained public tenants. The decisive break (or the 'neoliberal moment') came in December 1998 when the State Council announced that no enterprise would be allowed to sell employees housing at below construction costs. It was also decided that, within six months, market rates were to prevail and, except for a small minority of poor families, the government and work-units would stop providing public welfare housing. Essentially, the dual-track property system separating those with full property rights (*quanquan*) and those with only use rights (*shiyong quan*) ended in 1999 when the central government fully legitimized the privatization of housing. In effect, anyone who had purchased a home privately or through subsidized sale of their old public flats (*gong fang*) can now possess most if not the 'full bundle' of property rights, which includes the right of occupancy and use, right to extract income from the property and right of transfer or alienation. Henceforth, after 1999, a new private property regime was established whereby residents who had benefited earlier from below-cost 'fire sales' of formerly public housing can now resell these houses in the property market and put a large portion of the sale price and profit towards a down-payment for a newly built full commercial house. By 2000 most work-unit or *danwei*-based public housing had been privatized in Chinese cities. Newly hired state employees now no longer receive free welfare housing assignments (*fuli fenfang*) from their work-units.

In tandem with the formation of a new property regime, recent amendments to the Chinese Constitution further stipulate that the 'citizens' lawful private property is inviolable' (Article 13 in the Constitution) and that '[t]he State may, in public interest and in accordance with law, expropriate or requisition private property

for its use and make compensation for the private property expropriated or req-
uisitioned' (*Constitution of the People's Republic of China*, 2004).[6] Significantly,
the constitutional amendment now provides legal protection for private property
acquired by Chinese citizens and is widely interpreted as a sign of the state's commitment to boost the housing property market and China's transition to a market
economy. Although the new legal protection has certainly bolstered the claims
of private property owners in China, what has been overlooked in the housing
reform are issues of social equity and the affordability of housing.

As Lee and Zhu (2006: 44–45) argue: 'The linchpin of China's economic
reform policy is the belief that the market, properly regulated and liberated
from all forms of unnecessary interventions, represents the optimal mechanism
for economic development'. The HMP to a great extent follows this neoliberal
logic, in the expectation that ultimately all housing needs could be met optimally
by the market. However, the single-mindedness of the desire to pursue housing
commodification by the Chinese government easily falls prey to a new culture
of 'home' wealth creation, fuelling speculative activities in the private housing
market beyond the affordability ratio set down by the state in the last few years.
The HMP further privileges a certain segment of the population (government
employees and state enterprise workers, especially the cadres) while leaving the
collective enterprise and private-sector workers untouched, not to mention rural
migrant workers in the city, who are not entitled to any forms of social and housing welfare (Lee and Zhu, 2006: 56).

Housing inequality

Although housing and living conditions have generally improved in China in
recent years, urban inequality is still starkly evident, especially in the area of
housing consumption. Y. Huang (2003), for example, notes that residential crowding and housing shortages continue to be a major problem confronting many
Chinese cities such as Beijing and Shanghai. However, current housing reform
policies seem to focus more on the privatization of the housing system and less on
equity issues. For example, people with rural or temporary household registration
status (*hukou*) and those working in the private sector who were disadvantaged
in the former socialist housing system continue to be discriminated against in the
new housing market (Huang, 2003: 611). On the other hand, wealthy families
and those with political connection were able to enjoy a higher absolute value of
housing subsidies during the reform. Deborah Davis (2003), for example, found
out that professionals and managerial staff were often able to make claims on
housing assets beyond their immediate needs and were able to enjoy larger housing subsidies or bargain for larger discounts when purchasing public flats, which
were subsequently resold in the housing market at a substantial profit. In addition, white-collar workers with higher disposable income and the ability to obtain
higher bank loans are also in a far superior position to take advantage of any housing discount and subsidized sale of public flats, compared with their working-class
counterparts. Up until recently, the Chinese government also allowed the entire

amount of the home mortgage (including interest) to be tax deductible in a bid to boost home ownership. Instead of paying taxes, high-income earners began to buy several apartments for speculative purposes.[7] As a result, the privatization of what was formerly a welfare housing benefit laid the foundation for residential segregation by economic class and undermined the relative equality of lifestyle that had prevailed in earlier years (D. Davis, 2003: 195). This has led housing experts to observe critically that, whereas early reforms had the potential to create a more transparent and universal system that could benefit all residents, later reforms to capitalize housing stock as a personal asset generally favoured managerial and professional staff or the 'new middle class' (see next section).

In fact, it was estimated that in 1995 the richest 10 per cent in China owned 60 per cent of private housing assets and a similar estimate has been made for the late 1990s. When market forces penetrate so deeply and widely that capital accumulation becomes possible, former cadres and current managers, professionals or the new middle class tend to gain disproportionately in reaping the rewards of housing privatization. What is even more alarming is that commodity housing, which now dominates most of the new housing supply, is practically beyond the economic means of most low-income and even middle-income households (Y. Huang, 2003; Zhang, 1999). In Shanghai, for example, the average selling price for commodity houses in 2003 was at approximately 5,118 yuan per square metre (compared with the national average of 2,777 yuan). Given that the average worker's income in Shanghai is about US$1,400 (or 11,550 yuan) per annum, it would take more than 20 times the annual wage income of an average two-worker household to finance a 100-m² commercial apartment (*Shanghai Economy Yearbook 2003*; *China Statistical Yearbook 2002*). In fast-growing areas such as the Pudong New Area, housing prices has even gone up to beyond 10,000 yuan per square metre.[8] According to a survey done by the State Development and Reform Commission (SDRC), the average ratio of housing price to disposable income in Shanghai has reached 15.4:1, far surpassing the acceptable range of 4:1 to 6:1 for developing nations (*Xinhua News*, 10 March 2005).

Whereas average-income households can hardly afford the escalating prices of commodity houses, the housing situation of Shanghai's migrant population is even more dire. W. P. Wu's (2002) study on the housing options of migrant workers in Beijing and Shanghai reveals that migrant communities suffer from systematic housing discrimination and are largely excluded from the mainstream housing distribution system. The recent housing reform has mostly overlooked the needs of the migrant population. Acquiring either use right or ownership right of municipal and work-unit housing is out of the question for migrants without local *hukou* because the linkage between household registration and urban amenities is largely intact. Commercial housing, the only real property sector open to them, is beyond the purchasing power of most migrants (Wu, 2002: 114). Left without many options, migrant communities often end up staying in crammed housing quarters that are spread out in suburban areas.

Whereas low-income households and migrant workers have been disenfranchised in the new private housing market, the burgeoning new middle class and nouveau riche in China have been quick to capitalize on the speculative housing market to reap substantial benefits. The next section will now focus on the new middle class and nouveau riche and their role in pushing forward the 'consumer revolution' in urban China.

Rise of the new 'propertied' middle class

In his keynote address marking the eighteenth anniversary of the Chinese Communist Party (CCP) on 1 July 2001, the former Chinese President and Party Secretary Jiang Zeming announced that the CCP will now admit 'outstanding elements' from the 'new social stratum' of private entrepreneurs, business people and capitalists. This new social stratum, widely touted as embodying the skills and virtues of the 'most advanced productive forces' in Jiang's self-proclaimed Three Represents Theory (the other two represents refer to the CCP's advanced culture and representing the interest of the majority of the people), was subsequently written into the Party's Constitution at the Sixteenth Party Congress, despite reservations from some of the party hardliners and conservatives. Significantly, as some scholars have observed, by bringing (capitalist) class back into the party, the CCP leadership has been perceived as trying to engineer the transition of the party (and by extension China) to a post-Marxist–Leninist party-state (Zheng, 2004: 282).

Since economic reform began in 1978, Chinese society has been experiencing a widening of income gaps, resulting in the formation of class differentiation and social disparity, most acutely seen in China's big cities, which receive huge influxes of poverty-stricken migrant labourers searching for jobs in the city. In Shanghai alone, this floating population is estimated to be more than 3 million people. According to the United Nations Human Development Report 2004, the Gini coefficient in China is beyond 0.447. At the same time, the gap between the annual incomes of the poor versus the national average has also been widening – from a ratio of 1:2.45 in 1992 to 1:4.12 in 2003 (*People's Daily*, 9 July 2005). Amidst the income and social polarization, the emergence of an upper stratum of new rich, petty bourgeoisie and new middle class not only has transformed and unsettled the formerly homogeneous and stable social structure in China but also poses some interesting challenges for researchers who are trying to understand the nascent development of class politics and social stratification in the country. As A. Chen (2002: 409) points out, given the lack of income taxation data, it is often difficult to determine precisely the real size of China's class structure. In many party-state documents and officially censored social science publications, the richest social stratum is often referred to as 'private entrepreneurs' (*seying qiyezhu*), 'individual business households' (*geti gongshanghu* or *getihu*) or, more broadly, the 'middle classes' (*zhongchan jiecheng*). These blurred references and deliberate mixing of the categories add much perplexity to the reading of the relevant statistics, and they compound misunderstanding of class differentiation in China.[9]

Although the nascent class structure in China proves to be difficult to pin down, scholars such as Tomba (2004: 5) have traced the emergence of the affluent class (or the 'new rich') to four generations of 'people who got rich first' (*xianfu qunti*). These four generations are the hard-working agricultural entrepreneurs in the late 1970s; entrepreneurs in rural township and village enterprises in the early 1980s; successful entrepreneurs in speculative activities such as construction and the stock markets in the 1990s; and the high-achieving urban professionals and highly skilled workers in both public and private sectors that rose through the ranks in the late twentieth century. For David Goodman (2008), the new middle class in China, far from being the product of (Western-style) liberal market capitalism, is in fact a social stratum that is closely linked and, in part, owes its existence to the ruling Communist party-state. These middle-class urban elites are either managers transferred from previous senior administrative positions in now defunct state-owned enterprises or businessmen who are the descendants of leading political cadres who built their business on social networks or relationships cultivated through the influence of their parents or grandparents. For these 'princelings' and well-connected entrepreneurs, their direct or tacit relationships with the party-state allows them cost-free access to resources and effectively subsidized income not available to others. As Goodman (2008: 24) further contends, these 'new rich categories of entrepreneurs are less the new middle class than a future central part of the ruling class'. Fundamentally, they are quite unlike the nineteenth-century European bourgeoisie in the extent to which they have emerged from and retain close relationships with the established political system.[10]

Within China, on account of its loaded political connotation and sensitivity, the term 'middle class'[11] (*zhongchan jieji* or *zhongchan jiecheng*) has seldom been used until recently. (For the subtle distinction between *jieji* and *jiecheng*, see Zhang, 2008.[12]) Following Deng's call to allow some of the Chinese people to 'get rich first' and later Jiang's endorsement of the 'advanced productive forces', the term 'middle class' has suddenly become a popular label that serves as a status signifier for aspiring Chinese citizens. In particular, 'middle class' has often been used interchangeably with other terms such as 'new rich' (*furen*), 'new rising social stratum' (*xinxing jiecheng*) or, more broadly, 'successful people' (*chenggong renshi*). In a recently published book detailing the rise of the new middle class in China, the authors observe that:

> In the minds of [the Chinese] people, the 'middle class' is an attractive label that is closely tied to the relatively well-off (*xiaokang*) and affluent (*fuyu*) segments of the society, and their ability to consume high-end goods such as wine, villas, apartments and cars . . . In a word, to be middle class is a sign of being wealthy (*fuyu de xiangzhen*), a mark of high taste (*gao pingwei*) and a fashionable lifestyle (*shishang shenghuo*).
>
> (G. R. Chen and Yi, 2004: 1)

The authors then went on to identify at least eight types of middle-class occupational categories in China including the professional managerial group; information technology (IT) experts; intellectuals; private entrepreneurs; white-collar workers; CEOs of companies; communications media and entertainment industry; and sports stars. In a report in the official *China Daily* newspaper (27 October 2004), the middle class was further defined as referring to those groups of people 'with stable incomes who are capable of purchasing private houses and cars, and can afford the costs of education and holidays'.

In his study on the changing social structure in China, Zheng (2004: 286) further notes that several strata can be identified in China's emerging middle class. The first stratum comprises managers of large enterprises and private capitalists. These managers of large enterprises or 'red capitalists' constitute about 1.5 per cent of the total population and contain three subgroups: first, cadres in large state-owned enterprises (SOEs) and collective enterprises; second, managers of large private enterprises, who may not be the owners of these enterprises but are hired by the owners; third, managers of *sanzi* enterprises (i.e. equity joint venture, contractual joint venture, and wholly foreign-owned enterprises). In addition to the managerial elites, the middle class also includes owners of small enterprises (private capitalists or entrepreneurs) and high-level professionals. The last group, which had increased from 3.48 per cent in 1978 to 5.1 per cent in 1999, is increasingly significant in managing the state and society thanks to their professional training and experiences. For other researchers, further distinctions are being made between middle-class and upper-class bourgeoisies in China. A. Chen (2002), for example, identifies middle-class household as those with an annual income between 100,000 and 700,000 yuan, a group numbering around 35–45 million people and constituting around 9–11 per cent of the urban population (but not exceeding 4 per cent nationwide).[13] On the other hand, the bourgeoisie – owners of relatively large capital, the wealthiest private entrepreneurs or the millionaires (*baiwan fuwong*) – number around 3 million or fewer than 0.25 per cent (approximately 1 per cent including family members) of the Chinese population.

Concurring with the above reports, a three-year study on social and economic stratification by the sociologist Li Chunling at the Chinese Academy of Social Sciences (CASS) finds that the group that most people think of when asked about the middle class – managers, professionals, skilled technicians and service workers earning US$2,500–$10,000 a year – constitutes considerably fewer than 5 per cent of the national population or fewer than 65 million people (*China Daily*, 27 October 2004). Another CASS sociologist, Sun Liping (Sun *et al.* 2004: 57), further argues that, since economic reform, China has been faced with serious problems with social equity issues due to the uneven distribution of resources and benefits (*liyi fenhua*), with high-income earners benefiting at the expense of the lower strata of the population. Yet, in other more optimistic reports in the *People's Daily*, it was stated that China's middle class in 2003 accounted for 19 per cent of the country's population. In another study done by the CASS, the middle class in China is expected to make a startling leap to 40 per cent of the entire Chinese population by 2020, based on an annual growth of one percentage point (*People's Daily*, 27 October 2004). Admittedly, these diverging reports and statistics not only point to the problematic concept of class (specifically the lack of standardized criteria for identifying and measuring class sizes) but also reveal the tendency for state-controlled publications to exaggerate the size of China's middle class for political reasons. The rationale behind the state's intention to expand the middle class stems from several concerns, the most important of which is the dominant idea among the ruling political elite that the existence of a large middle class is able to improve the social and political stability of the CCP rule. A second rationale for the need to promote the middle class is linked to the policy to stimulate consumption and sustain domestic economic growth. In the attempt to boost consumption demand, the government has implemented several policies including increasing the salaries of public employees, approving housing mortgages and easing credit lending rules. All in all, the middle- and upper-class elites with considerable spending power have been incessantly encouraged by government policies to increase their consumption through the purchase of big-ticket items such as cars and houses.

Although a detailed theoretical discussion on the middle class in China is clearly not within the scope of this study, it is important to emphasize that the concept of the middle class in this study aligns itself with Weber's idea on (middle-)class position as being determined less directly by its relations to the 'means of production' (selling labour or owning capital) than by its relations to the market and consumption practices – in this case the ability of privileged social groups to buy into private gated communities and lifestyles as the defining trait of class membership. In addition, the study also avoids making too fine a distinction between the different classes or social composition of residents in Shanghai's gated communities, taking heed of Leichty's (2003: 64) insights that class categories (like pointillist paintings) are best, or at least most clearly, seen from a distance. The more closely one looks at a class group, the more its boundaries dissolve and its supposedly distinguishing features blur into a haze of contrasting and conflicting detail. On the other hand, it is also important not to overlook the diversity of social groups within gated communities and treat them as an undifferentiated whole. Nevertheless, there are many significant commonalities among residents of gated communities in Shanghai. For example, most of these residents share a relatively new experience of home ownership, are generally highly educated and put substantial resources into education, and are largely employed in positions that imply some levels of responsibility, managerial, technical or administrative. They have in common a relatively well-defined consumer identity and share the benefits of privileged access to the real estate and awareness of the rights that this brings. In an attempt to cultivate their newly minted class status and sensibility, the urban middle class in China's cities from Shanghai to Kunming are busy *learning* to become respectable members of the group by comparing and competing with their peers on *appropriate* types of consumption befitting their class status. These include lavish club membership, car ownership and other forms of conspicuous consumption traits such as enrolling their children in expensive private schools for early training in golf, ballet, music, horseback riding, etc. or indulging for long hours in speciality salons offering high-end manicure services, facial treatments and 'foot-soaking' for the 'leisure women' – ladies from wealthy families who stay at home and have plenty of free time (Zhang, 2008: 37). As Tomba (2004: 4) further observes, although the middle-class group appears to be rather amorphous and may lack the cohesiveness required by the traditional definitions of class, its members appear increasingly to shape their status and collective identity through their modes of consumption, most conspicuously seen in their housing preferences and desires to buy into the exclusive lifestyles associated with commodity housing enclaves. In this respect, up-market commodity housing enclaves in China have become prime sites of and for the learning and cultivation of middle-class habitus or disposition, judging from the numerous expensive salons, restaurants and club houses found in these gated enclaves. In Shanghai's Vanke Garden City, for example, the estate boasts of two members-only club houses, several hairstyling and beauty shops, an English-language tuition centre run by foreigners and even a golf shop and a pet-grooming salon. The estate management office also offers in-house programmes such as wine-tasting, Western culinary classes and jazz dancing, and frequently organizes car shows with automobile companies in an effort to 'educate' residents on how to 'appreciate and enjoy the finer things in life'. The next section will now examine in closer detail the emergence of gated communities in Shanghai and how they are transforming the urban social fabric of the city.

Emergence and distribution of gated communities in Shanghai

The emergence of gated communities in China, as pointed out in the preceding discussions, should be understood within the context of China's economic reform and urban restructuring, more specifically the housing commodification polices, the intensification of social stratification and class differentiation, and the liberation of urban consumption forces (see also Y. P. Wang and Murie, 1999; Li 2000; F. L. Wu, 2005). With the introduction of the land sales programme and private housing market in the 1980s and 1990s, privately developed commodity housing enclaves have proliferated in Shanghai both within the city centre and in the suburban areas.[14] As Wu (2005: 241) observes:

> [T]he commodification of housing has led to a new type of residence: pure commodity housing estates. These estates are developed by real estate developers and managed by property management companies. To promote an image of high-quality life, the entrances to these estates are often marked by magnificent gates, sometimes in the style of elaborate baroque facades. Some estates adopt so-called 'enclosed property management' which is becoming very popular. Because residents have been filtered through housing affordability, the estate is created as an 'enclave' of those with similar socio-economic status.

Although enclosed housing complexes are certainly not new in China, there are important distinctions to be made between the 'old' and 'new' forms of gated residences. Unlike commercially developed gated communities that select residents based exclusively on income and lifestyle, older forms of enclosed residential developments such as work-unit compounds and retrofitted old housing complexes typically contain considerable diversity and a mix of income groups.[15] In addition, gated communities in China also differ from those in the United States in several aspects. As Miao (2003) observes, Chinese cities generally have densities about five to ten times higher than in the United States.

> While the mainstay in U.S. urban housing types is the low-rise, single-family home with about 12–15 families per hectare, the buildings in a Chinese residential quarters are primarily high (ten or more stories) and mid-rise (six storey walk-ups), with 120–180 families per hectare and a floor area ratio of 1.2 to 1.5.
>
> (Miao, 2003: 48)

In this respect, gated communities in China tend to be more densely packed and spatially compact than their North American counterparts. However, developers of up-market gated communities in China are beginning to build low-density housing estates in the suburbs with extensive green fields surrounding the residential development. In many of these gated enclaves, the proportion of green spaces (*lühua lü*) can reach up to 50 per cent and above.

Although there are currently no statistics on the number of gated communities in Shanghai, the figures can be inferred from the number of newly built and sold villa housing and high-end apartments (most if not all of which are extensively gated). According to the *Shanghai Statistical Yearbook 2004*, there has been a dramatic increase in the number of such high-end gated housing. In 1995, the accounted for by private villas and high-end apartments sold in Shanghai was approximately 1.6 million square metres. In 2000, the figure had increased to about 5.3 million square metres; in 2002, to 18.2 million square meters; and, in 2003, the quantity of private villas and high-end apartments sold reached a staggering 21.7 million square metres. In other words, between 1995 and 2003, the number of high-end villas and apartments sold had increased by approximately 13 times! These new commercial housing estates built by property developers and targeted at upper- and middle-class housing consumers as well as foreigners are developed along the lines of exclusive lifestyle enclaves with condominium facilities such as swimming pools, club houses, restaurants, tennis courts, etc. These gated communities are built on leased land demarcated by the city government where developers are allowed to define the physical boundaries of their housing project and separate it from the rest of the city (F. L. Wu, 2005: 243). Yet, despite the reforms, the Chinese state retains the power to appropriate land and relocate people by fiat. Even though private home-owners may be said to 'own' the houses, the land on which private property stands is only leased out for a period of between 50 and 70 years, with the state still being the de facto owner of the land.

Like fortified enclaves elsewhere, huge gates and walls enclose the entire housing estate, leaving the surrounding streets and pavements barren of urban activities and social life. Gated communities manifest a form of territoriality aimed at keeping out non-residents. As will be shown in the later chapters, residents and real estate management companies rely on various territorial strategies such as erecting walls and fences, installing high-tech surveillance equipment and employing a legion of private security guards to control and restrict access to the gated enclaves. Territoriality of gated communities reflects not only the real estate trend towards gating up privately developed commodity housing estates but also the exclusivist housing aspirations and desires of middle-class residents, who often demand that their privacy and 'private property rights' be enforced and respected. The design principles of gated communities are, however, often antithetical to the basic elements that constitute modern urban life such as the openness and transparency of urban structures, primacy of streets and the free circulation of people and vehicles (Caldeira, 2000: 306). Miao (2003: 45), for example, observes that in the vicinity of gated communities located outside Shanghai's inner ring road:

> The walls keep going on and on, sometimes as long as 500 meters, and are only occasionally punctuated by a gaudy gate decorated with copies of Greek statues and private guards dressed like police officers. Between the gates you find nearly empty sidewalks in a city of citadels.

To be sure, gated communities in Shanghai are designed as physically isolated fortresses that are oriented inwards with walls and gates that offer little or no gestures towards external street life. As Miao (2003: 52) further argues, not only are these gates and walls ineffective protection against crime, they also generate various 'structural conflicts' in the daily life of urban residents in China. First, gated communities in Shanghai drastically reduce social activities in public streets by enclosing huge tracts of urban spaces and streets within walls and gates, hence denying public access and pedestrian activities within these enclosed spaces. The gates and walls create both physical and psychological barriers for urban residents and discourage activities in the contiguous spaces and streets, as evidenced by the often deserted pavements outside gated communities (see Figure 3.3). 'These empty sidewalks spell wasted resources and lost opportunities because the high density in Chinese cities, along with Chinese residents' traditional dependence on public space, could easily support more social setting on these currently underused sidewalks' (Miao, 2003: 53). Even in city centres with traditionally dense street grids, government-sponsored urban renewals often close up many existing minor streets to create gated communities of larger blocks. For example, 10 such streets disappeared in 1997 in Shanghai's inner city. In addition, gated communities also cause great inconvenience to people's daily life by creating obstacles and closing off streets, leading people to take long detours. Such inconvenience can sometimes be deadly, particularly during times of emergency. In Shanghai's Hongkou district, for instance, it was reported that an injured elderly man died while waiting for the ambulance, which was delayed by blocked entrances and the complicated layout of the residential complex (*Shanghai Daily*, 16 November

Figure 3.3   Deserted pavements outside a gated villa estate in Shanghai's Hongqiao/ Gubei District. (Source: author's photograph, 2005.)

2004). According to the residents, some of the entrances into the residential compound were replaced by revolving doors and were later blocked with concrete walls for security reasons.

Besides road blockages, gated communities also create social disjuncture and undermine the provision of public infrastructure and amenities by 'locking up' the much needed facilities inside the gates for the exclusive use of affluent residents while the majority of poor neighbourhoods in the city are often deprived of even the most basic amenities such as children's playgrounds or parks. Not only do gated communities contribute to the dearth of street life and dwindling public infrastructure, they have also progressively 'colonized' dwindling farmlands in the suburban areas, pushing agricultural communities and other poor neighbourhoods further to the outskirts of the municipality. Statistics show that, from 1997 to 2004, 5 per cent (6.7 million hectares) of the country's total arable farm land was lost to industrial and new town development and housing construction. In Shanghai, the cultivated farmland per rural person decreased from 800 square metres in 1978 to 669 square metres in 2003. In absolute terms, the area of cultivated farmland decreased by about 30 per cent from 3.6 million hectares in 1978 to 2.5 million hectares in 2003 (*Shanghai Statistical Year Book 2004*). As gated communities proliferate in the suburbs, socio-spatial polarization and urban segregation are now evident in many districts in Shanghai, where differences in class, status and lifestyles are increasingly being marked out spatially. Juxtaposed against the new gleaming residential enclaves are run-down living quarters of the urban poor and disenfranchised migrant workers, who are displaced further and further into the outlying areas with poorly developed urban amenities and infrastructure.

On the whole, the 'quartering' of the city into private fortified enclaves represents a dramatic departure from the relatively homogeneous and standardized housing landscape that predominated during the socialist period, when urban housing was largely subsumed under the monopolistic and integrated structure of the comprehensive work-unit system (of course, this is not to say that the former socialist city in China was a perfectly egalitarian one, as social differences did exist; for example, some favoured work-units had better facilities and were accorded preferential treatment over others). Yet the demise of such a standardized public housing system in favour of the 'neoliberal' private development segmented along the lines of income, lifestyle and class exemplifies what Graham and Marvin (2001) term the 'unbundling' of urban infrastructure and the formation of a 'splintering urbanism'. As Graham and Marvin (2001: 138) point out: 'central to all this is an understanding of how unbundled infrastructure networks more intensively and actively connect valued places [and social groups], while at the same time progressively withdrawing and disengaging from other less valued places [and social groups]'.

In Shanghai, the unbundling of public housing infrastructure has led to a reconfiguration of social and spatial relations in the city. What has emerged is a pattern of urban segregation and spatial polarization in which prestigious gated neighbourhoods (correlating to residents' status and income) have fragmented the cityscape into multiple nodes of 'high-class' enclaves. Within the central city area (see Figure 3.4), a clustering of expensive neighbourhoods concentrated in a few select areas can now be seen.[16] Among some of the most sought-after

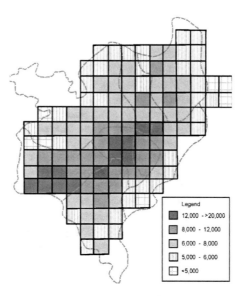

Figure 3.4 Distribution of commodity housing prices in Shanghai's central city area (calculated in yuan per square metre). (Source: data collated from author's own survey and various sources including real estate reports, commercial brochures, magazines and interviews with property agents.)

neighbourhoods are the Pudong Lujiazui area; Xujiahui area in the Xuhui district; Huaihai Middle Road in the Luwan district; and Hongqiao Road in the Gubei New Area (these areas also have a high concentration of foreigners and are all within the inner ring road, which has easy access to the city centre).

In the inner and outer suburbs, such as Minhang, Jiading and Songjiang districts, large-scale master-planned gated communities and high-end commodity housing enclaves have also flourished, taking advantage of cheaper land prices and larger land areas. For example, an entire 'German' new town (Anting New Town) spanning 1 square kilometre has been built in the Jiading district. Numerous other 'foreign-themed' housing developments and new towns are now dominating the suburban landscapes in Shanghai, offering an idyllic retreat for home-buyers who want to take advantage of the cheaper housing prices and sprawling land. (Gated enclaves in the suburban areas are typically larger in scale than those found in the city centre on account of the scarcity of land in the city area.) It is also not uncommon for many financially well-endowed individuals or families to own two properties, a smaller apartment in the central city area and a villa in the suburbs. Increasingly, many of these new suburban areas have become much sought-after residential 'retreats' for the urban middle class, desperate to get away from the congested and polluted city centre. According to King and Kusno (2000), traditionally in Chinese spatial hierarchy, the closer one gets to the centre, the greater is one's social status; and, inversely, power and prestige diminish as one moves towards the periphery. It is interesting to note that the emergence and growing popularity of these gated suburban enclaves and new towns in contemporary Shanghai may in time challenge such traditional notions of urban centrality and prestige. With rising private car ownership and the construction of transportation networks and highways into the outskirts of the municipality, well-heeled urbanites may soon be trading in their small downtown apartments for the grand villas, townhouses and green lawns in the gated suburbs.

Summary

As has been emphasized in this chapter, the development of gated communities needs to be understood within the changing context of Shanghai/China's economic transition and reform policies. In particular, the state through its housing reform policies has created a new category of commodity housing; many instances of this took the form of gated community developments. Although enclosed residential style is certainly not foreign to the country, what needs to be further examined is precisely how the functions and meanings of gating have actually changed and, more specifically, how gated communities in contemporary Shanghai ultimately represent for the middle class the lure of an elusive good life – a privileged lifestyle and a secure living environment that rely ultimately on the spatial sorting of class, income and lifestyles. The next chapter will now turn to examine how representations of the good life have been packaged and sold to buyers of gated communities.

4 Imagineering suburbia

Contested representations of the Chinese dream home

Advertising nourishes the consuming power of men [*sic*]. It sets up before a man the goal of better home, better clothing, better food for himself and his family. It spurs individual exertion and greater production.

(Winston Churchill, quoted in Ellis, 1993: 124)

I mean, there were 1 billion people living without any real sense of lifestyle . . . My dream was to bring aesthetics to Chinese society . . . Chinese [people] have a lot of money now . . . But they need inspiration on how to spend it tastefully. That's where I come in.

(The late Chen Yifei, one of China's most commercially successful artists and founder of *Layefe Home*, a fashion and home concept company, quoted in *Time Magazine*, 11 November 2002)

Introduction

Tucked behind the freshly laid adobe brick walls, first-time visitors to Rancho Santa Fe – a luxurious gated community in Shanghai's Hua Cao County southwest of the city centre – will be struck by the startling sight of palm trees, orange-stucco houses and miniature barnyards juxtaposed against the dwindling farmlands and ramshackle houses nearby, where Chinese farmers can still be seen tilling the soil and tending to vegetable plots. Located near the Shanghai-American International School, the exotic and romanticized landscapes of 'Spanish-American home-stead' in the estate, complete with verdant greenery and foreign-sounding street names such as Monterey Avenue and Del Mar Street, is part of Vanke property developers' attempts at imagineering an ostensibly 'Southern California lifestyle' enclave (Figure 4.1). 'Welcome to Rancho Santa Fe, Shanghai's premier Southern Californian-style suburb', a gigantic billboard announces to passers-by in both English and Mandarin. According to the developer's brochure, Rancho Santa Fe or *Lanjia Shenfei* is a place where there are 'no city's noise' and 'no traffic jams', 'where life is so beautiful and happy' and 'full of rurality and sunshine' – at least for those well-heeled urbanites who can afford to buy into the much coveted 'villa lifestyle' (*bieshu shenghuo*), where each villa unit costs at least 450 million yuan.

To the extent that these new exclusive enclaves in Shanghai are underwritten by an explicit marketing script dominated by the emerging trope of middle-class

Figure 4.1   Interior of Rancho Santa Fe with orange stucco houses and miniature barnyards doubling as parking garages. (Source: Author's photograph, 2005.)

privilege and conspicuous consumption, this chapter provides a 'grounded' analysis of the place-marketing strategies and advertising rhetoric that have been assembled in the marketing and selling of gated communities in Shanghai. By grounded analysis, it is implied that the meanings of the advertisements do not reside directly in the texts and images but are inferred from a socially and historically grounded process of interpretation. Such an approach not only yields a context-sensitive understanding of the changing housing aspirations and appeals of gated living in Shanghai but also sheds light on the broader dynamics of urban social and cultural transformations in reform China. Recent works in cultural geography have further highlighted and stressed the importance of approaching the study of landscape *practically* and *relationally* by attending to their performative roles rather than merely decoding their underlying meanings (Thrift, 1996).[1] As David Matless (quoted in Bunnell, 2006: 28) indicates in his work, the geographical study of objects/landscapes is 'less through an assumption that hidden relations are concealed in a finished form which thereby requires dismantling, than by considering that finished form as one significantly congealed state with a wider field of relations of which it is an effect'. To this extent, Thrift (1996: 8) further reminds us that 'representational effort is always firmly embedded in a contextually specific process of social negotiation'. Thus, it is not merely the landscape-text and its encoded meanings that this chapter is interested in but also the wider social field in which these images and meanings are embedded in as well as their *practical effects* and active roles in shaping individual subjectivities and desires. As the following discussion will evince, the 'cultural pragmatics' (Alexander, 2004) of housing consumption that brings together complex meaning structures, contingency, power and material interests can be seen to work towards (per)forming the collective class consciousness and identities of Shanghai's nouveau riche home-owners.

In Shanghai, the ideal dream home packaged for private consumption in housing advertisements offers home-buyers a 'phenomenology of the future' (Dovey, 1999: 139) – an ideal living environment where middle-class housing desires and aspirations will be fulfilled and performed. The dream home in gated communities thus acts as a mirror that reflects and reproduces a neoliberal dream world of a good life attainable simply with the purchase of a commercial home in a gated community. Drawing on data gathered from a survey of housing advertisements published in real estate magazines, marketing brochures and newspapers, and further supplemented by fieldwork observations and interviews with housing agents, residents and researchers, this chapter critically examines how territorial representations of the good life (*xingfu shenghuo; meihao shenghuo*) are being shrewdly packaged, sold and consumed by residents of gated communities who eagerly appropriate these signs as 'symbolic capital' that bestows upon their owners 'a reputation for competence and an image of respectability and honorability' (Bourdieu, 1984: 185). Such representations of the good life draw explicitly on a repertoire of ideas about an idealized residential landscape that reflect and reinforce the exclusivist middle-class housing aspirations and private visions of gated communities. The good life, in this sense, is defined in neoliberal terms of a desirable and alluring gated private lifestyle that is separate from the rest of society.

This chapter is organized into five sections. Following the introduction, the next section examines the symbolic significance of the house and home in the construction of the self and family life in contemporary Chinese society. The third section will then demonstrate how housing developers have attempted to create a sense of 'awe' and 'admiration' in their place-marketing strategies by associating their housing projects with grandiose architectural images and extravagant lifestyles of the elites. In turn, the fourth section will map out the recurrent themes, rhetoric and symbols that are used to represent the neoliberal good life in gated communities. As will be pointed out, often embellished in these housing advertisements is the spatial 'imagineering' of foreign ('Western') suburban lifestyles that centres on the consumption of 'Western-style garden mansion' (*huayuan yangfang*) and villas – the exclusive housing forms of Shanghai's expatriate communities and urban elites during the bygone Concession era. The final section argues how these exotic foreign suburban models and garden mansions in Shanghai's gated communities are ultimately territorial expressions and symbols of modernity and conspicuous consumption that attempt to establish the purported linkages between gated lifestyle and social distinction.

House as a symbol of self and family

According to Amos Rapoport (1977), the home is a form of 'codified culture', a patterned set of cues and 'system of settings' that channel social actions and meanings. The meaning of houses and home, as Dovey (1985) further notes, is founded upon a series of linked dialectic oppositions: home/journey; familiar/

strange; inside/outside; safety/danger; order/chaos; private/public; and identity/
community. For Bachelard (1964: 17), a house 'constitutes a body of images that
give mankind proofs or illusions of stability'. To the extent that the home provides
an ontological security for the individual, home spaces are also encoded with
multiple social meanings and cultural significations that have profound influences
on the well-being of urban life and the community. Marcus (1997) further sees the
home as an elaborate façade of the self that not only reflects wider social relationship but also symbolizes social status and differentiation. As a corollary to this,
the home and its physical landscape can then be considered as constituting a form
of 'symbolic capital' and habitus (Bourdieu, 1984, 1990) that are actively sought
and cultivated by home-owners intent on creating an aura of distinction and status for themselves. In her study on luxury housing advertisements in São Paulo,
Caldeira (2000: 263) observes that:

> The home crystallizes the important symbolic systems and shapes individual
> sensibilities. Residence and social status are obviously associated, and the
> home is a means by which people publicly signify themselves. As a conse-
> quence, the construction or acquisition of a home is one of the most important
> projects people undertake. The home makes both public and personal state-
> ments as it relates the public and domestic. In creating a home, people both
> discover and create their own social position and shape their intimate world.

Although a full examination of the role of the home and family life in China
lies beyond the scope of this study, a brief discussion helps to highlight the significance of home advertisements in China. In post-reform Shanghai, the overhaul of
the socialist housing institution has seen the emergence of a burgeoning group of
status-conscious housing consumers who readily subscribe to conspicuous consumption practices that help enhance and affirm their newly acquired middle-class
status (anxiety?). The house has effectively become a hotly sought-after consumer
good in Shanghai and a prime locale for the articulation of personal distinction,
taste and status. In contradistinction to the mass welfare housing system of the
past, the ability to own a newly built commercial home (*shangpingfang*) is now
considered a prime status symbol. A recent editorial (7 April 2005) in *Shanghai
Star* (one of the city's leading English-language newspapers) points out:

> If a man in Shanghai is going to propose to his girlfriend, the most important
> thing he should prepare is not a candle lighted dinner, a bunch of roses or a
> diamond ring . . . The grand finale should be something that will make the
> woman hold her breath and even move her to tears. What kind of thing has
> such magic? If our male readers ask their girlfriends, they should expect the
> answer: 'a key' that opens the door of an apartment in the city. Many young
> men might be knocked back by my words, but this requirement has come into
> favour among Shanghai women. One of my friends once said seriously that
> her Mr. Right must own an apartment. She especially stressed that the house
> should not be on mortgage . . . This may be labelled as more solid evidence

that Shanghai women are shrewd . . . [but] the price of real estate in Shanghai has rocketed dramatically lately. The prices of some houses, especially in the downtown area, have tripled and even quadrupled. No wonder the possession of an apartment has become the most appealing criterion for a young man to prove his ability and economic status . . . Owning a house is the most effective way for a young man to offer his beloved one a feeling of security.

If the family is often considered the bedrock of Chinese society and social life, the home can be described as a prism that reflects the multiple social, political and economic relations between people and places, home and power. For many people, owning a home is more than just having a roof over one's head. It is a powerful symbol of the self and at the same time fulfils many needs such as a venue for self-expression, an abode or refuge from the outside world, and a hearth that offers security and affection. Conversely, not having a stable home is seen as deviant and even a socially undesirable trait. As Marcus (1997: 2) notes, a person without a fixed abode is viewed with suspicion in our society and often labelled as a 'vagrant', 'hobo' or 'street person' (see also Cresswell, 2001). The same can be said about Chinese society (more on the theme of vagrant in Chapter 6).

For most Chinese, the house represents 'the material symbol of having a family and has always been viewed as the source of safety and happiness in Chinese life' (Tong and Hays, 1996: 625). To a great extent, the family is synonymous with the home (*jia*), which almost always necessarily implies having a house.[2] From the time of Confucius, the family, not the individual, was seen as the basic unit of society. The ideal Chinese family based on Confucian principles, which accord the utmost significance and importance to harmonious family relations, is considered essential for building and maintaining a stable society. Since housing reform, developers and place entrepreneurs have engineered elaborate marketing plans aimed at capturing the hearts and minds of home-buyers with ostentatious signs of modernity and elite lifestyle. For example, real estate advertisements promote the idea of urban elites enjoying a 'new lifestyle' in 'new concept housing' (*xin zhuzai linian*) that rests on seductive images of the home and the pursuit of the good life. By buying into these housing developments, Chinese consumers are seen to create for themselves and their families a superior quality of life and a 'stylish lifestyle' (*shishang shenghuo*) that set them apart from the common masses.

To the extent that housing design seems to shape and influence the decisions of Shanghai's home-buyers, it will be worthwhile in the rest of the chapter to engage in a close-up analysis on the themes contained in some of these housing advertisements. Before proceeding further, two caveats must be sounded. First, we need to be careful not to treat Chinese home-buyers as cultural dupes who respond uncritically and naïvely to the effects of glitzy real estate advertisements. In my interviews and interactions with home-buyers and property agents, it is evident that pragmatic concerns such as housing quality (*zhiliang*), location (*didian*) – whether the property is within Shanghai's inner or outer ring road or close to subway stations and highways – availability of neighbourhood facilities and amenities (*peitao sheshi qiquan*), property prices and potential for investment returns are still important considerations when making housing investments. Nevertheless, these pragmatic considerations are not the *only* factors influencing housing decisions. In particular, home-buyers are often swayed by the 'branding' and design appeal of housing properties. As a home-buyer quoted in a *Xinhua News* report (12 September 2005) opined:

> The quality of the housing is certainly a priority in buying a home, but I also think the name of the real estate is important. If I buy a home inside a real estate block bearing a nice exotic name, other buyers may think my home should be more grandiose than theirs.

A household survey of residents living in Vanke Garden City further reveals some of the reasons and motivations for moving into the gated community (see Figure 4.2). Forty-eight per cent of the residents surveyed indicated that the brand and reputation of the housing developer were the prime motivation for moving into Vanke Garden City. Other respondents also felt that sound estate management and safety (11 per cent), convenience (10 per cent) and the availability of green spaces (10 per cent) were prime factors influencing their decisions to move into Vanke Garden City. In the interviews and interactions with residents in Vanke Garden City, it was also evident that, although the branding of housing development and the developer's reputation are important, pragmatic concerns such as maintaining the property values of the housing investment are also important considerations. In fact, as will be shown later, pragmatic factors and the branding of real estate are in many cases very much intertwined. Second, it must also be noted at the outset that this chapter is not so much concerned with exposing the gap between marketing rhetoric of real estate advertisements and reality. Rather, to echo Gold and Gold's (1994) contention, the gap between 'reality' and 'rhetoric' does not mean that the latter should be dismissed pejoratively as a distortion. Instead the

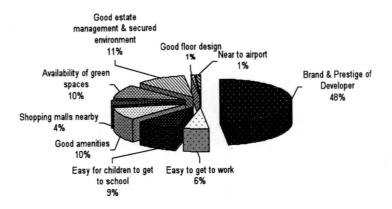

Figure 4.2   Reasons why residents moved into Vanke Garden City. (Source: Vanke Garden City, 2004.)

criterion for evaluating these advertising images should be not the measure of their 'authenticity' but rather their ability to grasp, reflect and reinforce the housing aspirations and dreams of consumers.

Advertising luxury gated enclaves: landscapes of privilege and lifestyle of distinction

Advertisements, as Fraser (2000: 29) points out, are about the construction of dreams and alternative realities. These 'fables of abundance' mediate between the perceptual reality of the everyday life and the imagined reality of a better world that offers commodity-based solutions to social dissatisfactions. In addition, advertising also provides possible models for consumption and potential configurations of social identity that result from purchase. It is the potential implied by advertising that is designed to resonate with readers' imaginations. Through the careful manipulation of housing landscape, architectural codes and symbols, housing developers mediate between the aspirations and desires of housing consumers and the production of the housing landscape. In these new commercial housing enclaves, images derived from an actual or fictional history provide the basis for giving a visual identity to suburban space in order to represent the coherence of a community and its distinctiveness as a marketable place (Brain, 1997: 260). Overall, the organization of architecture and design in these newly produced residential spaces reflects the self-conscious efforts by developers to create a 'scenographic enclave' (Crilley, 1994) through incorporating a pastiche of architectural forms and the stylized representations of exotic lifestyles, yielding a visually stimulating and aesthetically pleasing real estate package meant to entice housing consumers with alluring images of the good life and a privileged middle-class lifestyle.

One of the most common advertising tactics deployed by developers is the 'strategy of awe' and 'admiration' (Laswell, 1979) by associating the housing projects with grandiose images and extravagant lifestyles of rich and powerful elites. Take for example the advertisement for Summer Villa: home-owners are compared to modern-day royalty in the marketing slogan 'The King Returns' (*wangzhe gui lai*). Like a king who has returned to his palace, the advertisement strokes the ego of the potential home-owner, who is cast in an enchanting world of regal fantasy where he too can 'live like a king' by simply moving into Summer Villa. In other advertisements, home-owners are referred to as 'celebrities' (*mingliu*), 'successful people' (*chengong renshi*) or 'bourgeois nobility' (*daguan guiren*). Remarkably, what were formerly considered 'class enemies' (capitalists, bourgeoisies, etc.) in Mao's China have now become the new valorized role models of the country, supplanting the long-held position of 'model workers' (*laomuo*), who have been praised in the past for their selflessness in serving the party and state.[3] In contrast to urban young people of the 1980s, who were often searching for life's meaning, contemporary youths are success oriented and openly seek the good life by becoming eager consumers in the global market (Rosen, 2004). To this extent, images of upwardly mobile home-owners or yuppies have often been depicted in many housing advertisements, in which the notion of individual betterment and the upgrading of one's home and living environment serve as a constant reminder and yearning for the masses.

The housing developer's strategy of awe and admiration is further extended to the marketing of architecture and the built environment in gated communities. Architecture, according to Crilley (1994: 233), has once again become a form of advertising as city government, powerful corporations and redevelopment agencies show a renewed interest in manipulating the built environment proactively to attract business and investments. In the advertisements for the Shimao Riviera, an upmarket gated community in Pudong, the towering apartment blocks were pictured next to 'world-famous' landmarks such as Paris's Eiffel Tower and London's Big Ben clock tower. In the advertisement for Shanghai Gardens, the futuristic-looking Jinmao Building and the Oriental Pearl TV tower loom large in the background of the housing development, lending an aura of prestige to the housing development.

In the 'political economy of sign' (Baudrillard, 1981), the choice of the architectural icons is of course not incidental but deliberately selected to generate a feeling of admiration and awe among the audiences regarding the 'comparative worth' of the housing development. Commenting on the role of home advertisement, interior decoration and the generation of envy in urban China, Tang (2000: 299–300) notes how '[t]he sign value of objects enforces a logic of differentiation and establishes, through display and conspicuous consumption, a distinctive hierarchy of taste, status, and identity'. King and Kusno (2000: 44) further observe that, 'just as socially marginal subjects get themselves photographed in the company of prominent personalities in the expectation of raising their own status, developers adopt the same strategy with their buildings'. In the advertisement, developers seek to persuade buyers the virtues of their housing products by imbuing them with meanings drawn from already understood cultural codes. In relocating these developments onto one imaginary global plan, the expectation is that the accumulation of signified meaning, attached to familiar signs, will in some way drain off into the one that is less well known.

Another way in which a sense of awe and admiration is generated in the place-marketing is through the sheer size and scale of the housing project. For example, Shimao Riviera Garden calls itself 'the largest scale super high riverscape deluxe residential building in Shanghai'. Another housing development (Vanke New Town) states that the gated enclave holds a sprawling recreation zone with an 8,000-m² gigantic club house and fitness centre. Through the ostentatious display of what Tafuri (1979) calls the 'metaphysics of quantity', the physical prominence of housing development is purportedly translated into its dominance in the real estate market. In the highly competitive real estate market, design strategies emphasizing the distinctive architectural facades or spectacular urban designs (the biggest, largest, tallest) are considered to be essential in helping these developments 'get noticed' and capturing a 'semiotic advantage' over rival places (Griffiths, 1998: 44). According to a property manager interviewed:

The key to selling a property is to make it talk of the town. It doesn't matter how many people are actually buying it, as long as you've attracted plenty to come and see it, you have half the battle won.

Besides getting noticed, spectacular architectural design also placates the 'edifice complex' of its owners. As Deyan Sudjic (2005: 10) notes:

Architecture feeds the egos of the susceptible. They grow more and more dependent on it to the point where architecture becomes an end in itself, seducing its addicts as they build more and more on an ever-larger scale. Building is the means by which the egotism of the individual is expressed in its most naked form: the Edifice Complex.

The crossover of architecture into advertising and place-marketing is further demonstrated in the selection of 'brand name' architects by housing developers. Like designer labels in consumer apparel, houses designed by culturally conse-crated architects function as a form of symbolic capital, signifying the cultural nobility and good taste of their inhabitants and owners (Crilley, 1994). In the advertisement for Palm Spring Estate, the bold typeface announces that the hous-ing project is the product of an 'acclaimed Harvard architect'. In other housing projects, home buyers are told that their exclusive housing estates are the unique masterpieces of architects and planners with professional qualifications from Berkeley, Yale and other reputable universities. In these advertising schemes, it is hoped that the prestige associated with 'brand name' architects and institu-tions will somehow be grafted onto the housing project. Since reform and the opening up of the Chinese cities, Chinese developers have eagerly courted 'world-renowned' foreign architects such as Paul Andreu and Rem Koolhas to bestow an aura of prestige and legitimacy on their development projects.[4] As Sudjic (2005: 10) observes, despite a certain amount of pious rhetoric in recent years about architecture's duty to serve the community, to work at all in any culture the archi-tect has to establish a relationship with the rich and powerful.

Whereas 'awe' and 'admiration' constitute the general leitmotif behind the place-marketing schema of luxury commodity housing enclaves, some recurrent themes and symbols have also emerged in the analysis. Collectively, these real estate advertisements weave together several marketing themes that commodify family life and home as a site of/for conspicuous consumption through selling its family-oriented atmosphere, security, privileged lifestyle and exclusive 'natural' scenery (*fongjing*) behind the gates. Each housing advertisement, as Fraser (2000: 28) notes, constitutes to a greater or lesser degree a visual context for domestic life, a chart for the urban imagination. Each one is a panel of fantasy, within which is embedded the mosaic of commercialized dreams. In this sense, the commercial-ized dream of the good life is defined in terms of an enviable lifestyle that can readily attract the attention of middle-class consumers who aspire to distinguish themselves from the rest of society. As a manager of a property firm quoted in the *Shanghai Real Estate Guide* (Fall 2004: 22) elaborated:

All our properties are named around themes . . . It not only represents a recognizable corporate brand, but also speaks for a certain lifestyle or an idea. It's like an advertising slogan that automatically attracts a group of people who can respond well to this particular lifestyle or idea.

The next section will examine the lifestyle marketing strategies and representations of the privatized and exclusive good life in gated communities.

Neoliberal representations of the good life

Gated communities and the commodification of family life

Along Shanghai's busy Nanjing Road, a prominent billboard advertising the 'Happy Family' housing mortgage loan from CITIC Industrial Bank (one of the five largest banks in China) displays the photograph of a young boy in a baseball cap standing at the edge of a lake, looking pensively into the horizon. Printed over the photograph is a bold caption in Chinese stating: 'Own a house, a car, and greater love' (see Figure 4.3). The message of the advertisement unequivocally suggests that the material possession of a house and car will presumably bring about greater domestic happiness in family life. By targeting the family and home as a site for consumption, the advertisement demonstrates how commercial institutions and housing developers attempt to capture the spending power of China's urban middle class. In contrast to the 'extreme asceticism' of Chinese family life under Mao, the commodification of family life has now become an important theme that has been exploited by developers since the liberation of consumptive forces in China.

Figure 4.3   A billboard along Shanghai's popular Huaihai Road espousing the virtues of owning a house and car and enjoying blissful family life. (Source: Author's photograph, 2005.)

Typically, housing advertisements often rely on conjugal vocabularies and the rhetoric of happy domestic life and the family benefits that flow from private home ownership in a gated community. The private homes are often described as a 'love nest' and a 'cocoon' (*anle wo*) that shelters family members from the outside world. In the advertisement for Green Springdawn housing enclave, middle-class families are depicted in an idyllic scene that evokes the 'endless possibility' of a blissful domestic life behind the gates. The advertisement further shows small nuclear families (the targeted consumer group) partaking in various leisure and domestic activities. In the advertisements, the families depicted are usually young to middle-aged couples with one child (usually a boy) – reflecting China's one-child policy and the preference for male offspring. References to the friendly and family-oriented atmosphere are also common features in gated community advertisements. Developers of gated communities have also been quick to replicate the cosy 'old neighbourhood feeling' through marketing a sense of community in their advertising strategies.

Marketing brochures often portray gated communities as cordial places where residents are able to socialize easily and make friends. One advertisement even claims that security guards in the gated community know everyone by name. Yet, despite the apparent conviviality and friendly atmosphere that pervades gated communities, the social environment is often characterized by social homogeneity. In the advertisement brochures, phrases such as 'to be among equals', 'meet others just like you' and 'congregation of like-minded people' have been used to describe the gated community. The promotional materials for Vanke Garden City, for example, state:

> A community is a circle of like-minded people living together. After 10 years of successful development, Vanke Garden City has attracted close to 20,000 high-calibre people (*gaosuzhi renqun*) or 5,000 families. Residents are all friendly and polite, well educated and knowledgeable professionals from all over the world.

Even when homogeneity is not featured in the text, it is powerfully portrayed through images that conform to the ideal residential profile: young to middle-aged couples; 'middle-class' professionals, affluent and sophisticated looking; well dressed and stylish. These advertisements provide insight into the advertiser's notion of the ideal family. Invariably, the 'typical Chinese family' portrayed in the advertisements is a young Han Chinese family (none of the advertisements I came across addresses minority audiences) with an urban(e) and youthful demeanour. Even when social diversity is suggested, the advertisements typically appeal to a narrow band of expatriate residents, instead of the genuine diversity of social groups found in the city. The term 'international community' (*guoji shequ*) has also become a popular label for gated communities that claim to have a diverse group of foreign residents of different nationalities residing in them.

Explicitly gendered messages are also common in the housing advertisements. As Deborah Davis (2002) notes in her study, the featured customer in real estate advertisements is invariably a glamorous man in his thirties who carries a small boy on his shoulders as he strolls through a field. The large caption describes him as 'the New Age man who loves his family and home'. The husband is shown as a man of substance, as befits one who has both the income and the security of employment to secure a housing loan. The wife is depicted as demure and welcoming, the traditional housewife and mother. Overall, these advertisements designate the male as the targeted customer and the home as the female object of desire. Another interesting theme closely related to the family is the notion of the vulnerability of children, who need nurturing and protection in secure environments. In China, young children are increasingly the target of marketing because of the increasing amount of money they spend themselves and the influence they have on the expenditures of their parents (and grandparents). The presence of a child in an advertisement can cash in on people's perpetual yearning for family harmony and, in turn, make the commercials more touching and effective. As Gold and Gold (1994: 88) note in their analysis of English suburban home advertisements during the interwar years, the most interesting symbolic element is the figure of the young girl, who was intended as a symbol of gentleness and defencelessness. The sight of her playing happily and safely in the back garden symbolized the opportunities available to provide children with a secure and healthy environment in which to grow and flourish. It also subtly reinforced the idea that it was up to the father, who would normally be the sole bread-winner, to provide such an environment in order to give a child 'a decent start in life'. In a similar vein, the advertisements in contemporary China sought to portray and reinforce the idea of middle-class gated communities as the ideal safe haven to raise families.

Walls of security and privilege

Quite expectedly, the scripting of advertisements for gated communities is often underpinned by a strong preoccupation with security and territorial exclusivity of the housing compounds. The advertisement for Shanghai Western Residences, for example, boasts of a 2.5-metre-high wall that surrounds the house, guarding the exclusivity and security of its inhabitants. In Shanghai Garden, the advertisements further claim that residents are protected by 'walls more than five meters high in classical style' and 'delicate metal gates dotted with fine sculpture of flower pattern'. Like fortified enclaves elsewhere, these advertisements advocate a new concept of 'total security' in which absolute protection and fortification of the housing enclaves are necessary for ensuring not only total isolation and security but also happiness, harmony and even freedom (Caldeira, 1999, 2000). In particular, security measures include the erection of fences and walls, with private security guards donning paramilitary uniforms.

Some gated communities also boast an impressive array of high-tech security gadgets ranging from biometric scanning devices and centrally controlled intelligent building programmes to infra-red surveillance systems (now mandated by law for all newly built residential estates). Along with basic forms of fortification such as walls and fences, gated communities with their arsenal of high-tech security gadgets increasingly exemplify the 'militarization' (*junshihua*) of neighbourhood life that is justified on the grounds of improving security. This obsession with security is not just about enhancing safety in gated communities. It has also become a source of prestige and a status symbol for those living in gated communities. In particular, the presence of high walls and closely guarded entrances suggests the importance and exclusivity of the inhabitants. As Mike Davis (1990) notes, market provision of security has become a 'positional good' defined by income, access to private protective services and membership of exclusive neighbourhoods.

> As a prestige symbol – and sometimes as the decisive borderline between the merely well-off and the 'truly rich' – security has less to do with personal safety than with degree of personal insulation, in residential, work, consumption, travel environments, from 'unsavoury' groups and individuals, even crowds in general.
>
> (Davis, 1990: 224)

The scripting of the advertisements for gated communities also considers fortification as necessary for the taming of the hostile external urban environment. The home in gated communities is portrayed as a luxury retreat behind the gates, a separate 'city within a city' and a private universe that sets itself apart from the rest of the society. In the advertisements, home-buyers are invited to escape into gated communities behind the walls of privilege where a life of total luxury and convenience awaits them. 'The advertisements present the image of islands to which one can return every day, in order to escape from the city and its deteriorated environment and to encounter an exclusive world of pleasure among peers' (Caldeira, 1999: 120). The advertisements often depict gated communities as 'middle-class playgrounds' that come complete with private swimming pools, golf courses, fitness centres and club houses, an environment that is specially customized for the active lifestyle of modern-day elites. In the advertisements, residents of gated communities are pictured relaxing by the swimming pools, working out in the fitness centres and having fun with families in the private playgrounds and parks. In addition, the restaurants and shops located within the gated communities ensure that residents can enjoy all of the city's conveniences without having the step out of the gates. In Vanke New Town, residents are promised a life of total convenience with over 200 shops located right at their doorsteps in the gated estate. In Vizcaya, another gated community designed with a Mediterranean theme, the manager (quoted in the *Shanghai Real Estate Guide*, Fall 2004: 22) revealed that:

> The image of Vizcaya is in line with our vision for our property. We envisage a comfortable and leisurely lifestyle. Vizcaya will be the choice of urban elites who have finally retreated to simplicity – although this simplicity is built upon absolute comfort through the services and facilities we provide.

Overall, these advertisements suggest a private and exclusive world in gated communities that is clearly distinguishable from the surrounding city – a life of total security, comfort and prestige that is befitting of the middle-class inhabitants.

'Natural' scenery and the garden landscape

Another prominent theme in the selling of gated communities is the marketing of 'nature' and the 'natural scenery' (*fongjing*) through appropriating ecological discourses (green areas, parks, lakes) to entice home-buyers with alluring images of a healthy and wholesome living environment. Advertisements for gated communities often introduce the housing environment in a naturalized setting where residents are able to consume 'nature' and pristine natural scenery in their own private backyards. Housing projects with a high percentage of green spaces (*lühualü*) are touted to offer a salubrious environment that will bring health benefits to the residents. In the advertisements for the City of Charming Sun, an enclosed commodity enclave in Shanghai's suburb, home-buyers are promised a 10,000-m^2 'bio-ecological lake' that provides a peaceful lakeside living for all those who can afford the hefty price of private home ownership. Similarly, in Oasis Riviera, the development boasts of 55 per cent green coverage with large green belts where residents are able to enjoy private and 'gracious living' (*youya shenghuo*) that is at the same time 'close to nature' (*qinjin da zhiran*). In other housing advertisements, the depiction of clear sky, fresh air and sunlit scenes in gated communities further emphasizes the regenerative and recuperative powers of nature, which is fast becoming a rare commodity in Shanghai's increasingly polluted urban environment. Set against this background, the selling of nature in gated communities takes on an enhanced meaning with scenes of privileged families enjoying 'nature' and its nurture in lush green spaces, contrasting with the situation outside, which by comparison is dirty, crowded and insalubrious.

Also emphasized in the advertisements is the Chinese landscape notion of 'mountain and water' (*shanshui*) that is typically depicted in classical poetry and paintings. As Tuan (1995: 128) notes, since antiquity, a cosmic aura of awe and intimation of the sacred has been attached to the Chinese landscape idea of *shanshui*, as have vestigial beliefs in fertility and potency. By the third century AD, landscape had become essentially a beautiful–sublime concept and a world that the viewers would want to and could enter through its physical manifestation in garden design, poetry and painting. Thus, by invoking these ancient symbols of *shanshui*, the advertisements strive to encode the gated communities with traditional conceptions of the Chinese nature-aesthetic to further enhance the value of the property development. On the whole, as Fraser (2000: 27) argues, 'oasification' commodifies green pleasant aspects of a constructed nature to create a buffer zone between the individual apartments and houses and their larger social and spatial context. As a marketing tool and conceptual relationship in urban design, oasis reverberates across social strata with its promise of respite, greenery and peace.

Like gated developments elsewhere, the garden landscape as a symbol of a cultivated 'nature' lies at the centre of the marketing rhetoric. Here, we can detect significant differences between Chinese and European conceptions of the garden. Tuan (1995: 26), in particular, observes that:

> In China one speaks of 'building' a garden whereas in Europe one may speak of 'planting' a garden. The difference suggests that the Chinese, unlike Europeans, are more ready to admit the garden's artifactual character. Because artifice connotes civilisation to the Chinese elite, it doesn't have quite the negative meaning it has for Europeans brought up on stories of prelapsarian Eden and on Romantic conceptions of nature.

To the extent that the garden connotes civilization to the Chinese elites, private gardens are a further sign of privileged status and wealth. Traditionally, private gardens in China were spiritual shelter for men of letters and high standing – a place closer to nature and one's own heart, while far away from their real social lives (see Lin, 2004). In ancient China, withdrawal to a secluded place in the midst of nature first gained popularity when the vast and sophisticated Han Empire was in turmoil (Tuan, 1995: 130). The Mandarin gentry who were the empire's scholar-officials fulfilled their ambitions at court, but they also found life there constraining, vexing and sometimes dangerous. Many were torn between the splendour of the city and the Taoist–Buddhist allure of the countryside. Some disdained official life altogether and aspired solely to the virtue and charmed life of the artist-recluse. For them, the solution to having the urban amenities and the enjoyment of solitude was the garden.

For the modern-day urban elites in Shanghai, the private gardens (*sijiayuanlin*) in gated enclaves, besides offering a peaceful retreat for families, also project an air of power, artifice and importance that speaks of a highly privileged lifestyle. Real estate advertisements explicitly compare their interior landscaping to the classical Chinese gardens such as the Lion Forest Garden (*shizhilin*) and Humble Administrator's Garden (*zhuozhenyuan*), both famous landmarks in Suzhou, a historic city in Jiangsu province that is well known for its elaborate gardens built by elites in seclusion during the Ming and Qing dynasties. The advertisement slogan for Celebrity Villa further proclaims that: 'Every world-class celebrity deserves a world-class garden of his own'.

To be sure, the appeal of these Chinese gardens goes beyond just their aesthetic attractions. These gardens are also powerful symbols of prestige and class distinction that are increasingly bound up with neoliberal ideologies and exclusionary spatial practices. By offering a secured environment with shared aesthetic/sensory pleasures, gated communities thus serve as 'pedagogical' sites where middle-class sensibilities and identities are being cultivated (see Pow, 2009a). As a homeowner in an up-market gated community explained to me:

> In the past [the feudal period], only the rich gentries had private gardens in their own homes. There were very few public parks available for ordinary people to enjoy. So to be able to have a private garden in your own backyard is seen as an elite status symbol. That is why now you see so many upscale

developments attracting home-buyers with all kinds of exclusive garden landscapes.

Private gardens in Shanghai's gated communities are thus encoded with dual messages: first, as a cultivated 'nature' that provides residents with a refuge away from the polluted city; and second, as a territorial symbol of an elite lifestyle. In summary, this section has demonstrated how real estate advertisements, by appealing to ecology, health, leisure and security, present gated communities as the antithesis to the chaos, dirt and danger found in the city. The next section will extend the analysis by examining the foreign and exotic appeal of 'Western-style' gated communities.

Selling 'foreign chic': Western-style suburbs as symbols of modernity and lifestyle distinction

> Shanghai still very much looks to the Western flair; the rule of the thumb is every-
> thing with a foreign flair sells.
> (a villa sales manager quoted in the *Shanghai Real Estate Guide*, Fall, 2004: 22)

Whereas luxury commodity housing enclaves have become hotly sought-after real estate in Shanghai, the image that confers the ultimate status symbol on home-buyers (and arguably the most seductive) is the Western-style gated communities. In recent years, exotic suburban home models including German and English towns, Australian homes and Southern California suburbs have sprung up all over Shanghai's suburban landscape. Real estate advertisements often portray romanticized notions of 'Western' suburban lifestyle by reproducing alluring and idealized images of 'Western' residential landscapes. An important component in the imagineering of these foreign-inspired suburbs is the incorporation of various Western pastoral aesthetics in their place-marketing tactics. Phrases such as 'Tudor cottages', 'English manor houses' and 'country gardens' are used extensively in the advertisements to evoke bucolic images of a charming rurality set in an exotic Western context. In addition to the quest for comfort and security, the lure of these Western-style gated communities lies in the pursuit of a modern (often conflated with Western) lifestyle. These suburban gated communities are advertised as homes of superior quality and comfort that are imbued with a Western aura of modernity. As Duncan and Duncan (2003: 50–52) elaborate:

> [Place] advertising spins narratives that relate an object for sale to a whole constellation of places, practices and objects. In order to be efficacious, these narratives draw upon culturally ingrained symbolic systems that resonate with the consumers.

To this extent, advertisements for Shanghai's Western-style gated communities rely heavily on various cultural/national stereotypes to sell their products.

For example, in the Australia Home villa estate, national icons such as kangaroo sculptures are used to signify the 'Australian identity' of the housing development. Home-buyers are invited to experience 'living in this elegant community in Shanghai, [where] you will feel like [you are] living in the sunshine of Australia'. Furthermore, Australians' supposed 'love for nature and the great outdoors' is also reflected in the design of green open spaces and parks bearing the names of the country's famous cities such as 'Sydney Garden', 'Melbourne Garden' and 'Adelaide Garden'. In Hopson Town, a British-inspired gated community designed with an 'English old town flavour' complete with manicured English gardens and Tudor-style cottages, home-buyers are invited to 'discover UK in Shanghai' (see Figure 4.4). Housing compounds in Hopson Town are divided

Figure 4.4   British-inspired Hopson Town (top) and 'Australia Home' (bottom) in Shanghai's suburbs. (Source: Author's photograph, 2005.)

into four main sections that are marked as Northern Ireland, Scotland, Wales and England. Familiar British icons such as Buckingham Palace and the River Thames further grace the cover of the promotional brochures.

As a report in the *Xinhua News* (12 September 2005) noted:

> Buyers of homes inside real estate blocks bearing fancy exotic names and 'fake landscape' might get a substitute satisfaction . . . so real estate developers try hard to attract consumers to buy commercial apartments by widely promoting an idealised Western-world and satisfying the need of the public in pursuit of an exotic life without getting one step away from home.

These Western-style gated communities in Shanghai strive to distinguish themselves as 'modern' lifestyle enclaves that offer the nouveau riche middle class in the city a superior living environment and a high quality of life that can 'match up to modern Western living standards'.

To be sure, these foreign-inspired suburbs in Shanghai are in part the product of a local hegemonic imaginary that utilizes the discourse of transnational modernity to legitimize elite spaces and lifestyle. In particular, Chinese developers are capitalizing on local consumers' growing hunger for status and foreign products by building on the gated community's inherent qualities of prestige and safety while at the same time cultivating the flair of contemporary foreign chic. According to Ong (1999: 35), representations of (Western) modernity in developing countries are constituted through different sets of relations between the state, its population and global capital; these representations are specifically constructed by developmental elites who appropriate 'Western' knowledge and re-present them as truth claims in their own countries. In the same way, developers of gated communities acting as the 'purveyors' and 'arbiters' of the good life have transformed the Chinese residential landscape in the image of modern Western suburbia and represented the Western standards of living to the local consumers.

Often embellished in Shanghai's housing advertisements are the imagineering of foreign (Western) suburban lifestyles that centres on the consumption of the 'Western-style garden mansion' (*huayuan yangfang*) and other accoutrements of 'modern Western lifestyle' such as the garage, Western-style kitchen and modern home appliances. For King and Kusno (2000), Western urban artefacts such as suburban villas and mansions (alongside other archetypes like skyscrapers and apartment buildings) constitute what they call the 'metaphors of modernity' that are invested with transnational meanings by developmental elites. Specifically, the term 'villa' came into the English language as a response to a renewed interest in the classics during the seventeenth century. The term and architectural idea of the villa first spread from Italy into the fashion-conscious vocabulary of the *beau monde* (fashionable society) in England from the second half of the eighteenth century and became synonymous with all that was chic, petite, *à la mode* or *dernier cri* (King and Kusno, 2000: 55). According to architectural writers of the time, the villa was seen as being suitable for the social and economic category of a 'gentleman of moderate fortune'. By the early nineteenth century, the notion of the villa with that social connotation had become fully absorbed into the social, experiential and architectural vocabulary of the nascent suburban bourgeois class.

In China, the villa (*bieshu*) is both transplanted and translated as an idea and architectural style and is now often used interchangeably (and sometimes loosely) with other terms such 'Western mansion' (*yangfang*), garden house or townhouse, the last also known as 'terraced villas' or 'economic villas' (F. L. Wu, 2004). Despite its varied housing styles, the defining characteristic of a villa or mansion in Shanghai is its location in an area of relativley low-density housing and the provision of a private garden in front of the house.[5] As Wu (2004: 230) notes:

> The town house is in fact a terraced or semi-detached house designed to high standards. Thus, local property agents explain that townhouses are 'terraced villas' or 'economic villas'. Most townhouse projects are located in the suburbs. The townhouse is called a villa because it is built at low density, in contrast with high-rise commodity housing.

What is important here is not the accuracy of local consumers' conception of a particular architectural style or genre but rather the encoded meanings and social signification that comes with being identified as a villa/mansion home owner. In Shanghai, European and US-style villa houses are considered as symbols of prestige that enhance the social status and distinction of their inhabitants. These transnational urban spaces follow a 'cut and paste' logic in which foreign architectural forms are 'cut' from the particular historic urban experiences of some societies and cultures, 'pasted' into another society and culture, and then 'edited' in order to help constrict new, though not necessarily seamless, transnational spaces (King and Kusno, 2000). In practically every new suburb in Shanghai, one can easily find newly developed gated communities with transplanted Western-style villa houses or mansions. To boost their authenticity, developers in collaboration with foreign architects construct projects that mimic Western housing designs and motifs, and even go to the length of adopting foreign names for their roads and buildings. By adopting foreign designs and nomenclatures of European- and American-style houses, developers hope to infuse their housing projects with the enchanting qualities of an imagined 'Western' suburban lifestyle and transnational modernity.

The villas and mansions, like the townhouses, are designed for those who want to own a plot of land under the feet and a piece of sky overhead, and the ownership will bring them 'land, sky, garden, and garage' (F. L. Wu, 2004: 230). Through the appropriation of these transnational spaces, foreign 'exotic' housing designs serve as symbolic capital that bestow upon their owners 'a reputation for competence and an image of respectability and honorability' (Bourdieu, 1984: 185). In this way, aspiring upper- and middle-class home-buyers may attempt to establish for themselves their own habitus by which they can be identified and with which they can identify (McCann, 1995: 227).

However, Western-style villas and mansions are not entirely novel urban forms if we take into account the context of Shanghai's complex urban history. As

Anthony King's (1984) landmark study on the cultural history of the 'bungalow' (a housing form that first originated in colonial India and was later exported to Britain, the United States, Africa and Australia) reminds us, the development of specific urban forms and the multiple meanings attached to them are not accidental but historically inflected. In a similar vein, the origins of villas and mansions in Shanghai can be traced back to the 'Western-style garden houses' (*huayuan yang fang*) that first appeared in Shanghai during the Concession era in the late nineteenth century. These garden houses were then the preferred housing of Shanghai's expatriate communities and urban elites. As the native Shanghai historian Hanchao Lu (2000: 111–112) notes, in early twentieth-century Shanghai:

> Western-style, or foreign-style houses (*yangfang*), as the name implied, referred to European-style detached, multifloor homes with a front garden. Hence, this type was also known as a 'Western-style garden house' (*huayuan yangfang*). This was by far the most luxurious type of housing in Shanghai; many such houses were truly extravagant homes elsewhere in the world, and like extravagant homes elsewhere in the world, they often served as proud symbols of the city.[6] They were, however, largely irrelevant to the lives of ordinary people.

Given this, the process of imagineering and transplanting these foreign housing forms (metaphors of modernity) and the transnationalism that pervades Shanghai's gated communities today can hardly be considered as simply the product of contemporary globalization. Rather, its global and transnational origins could be traced back to several colonial and post-colonial modernization projects that preceded the onset of present-day economic/urban reform in Shanghai. Specifically, many scholars have argued that (transnational) modernity in fact arrived in China much earlier in the form of the violence of the Opium War (1839–1842) in which China suffered a humiliating defeat at the hands of the foreign powers led by imperial Britain. The Opium War and the subsequent Treaty of Nanking eventually led to the ceding of port cities such as Shanghai and Hong Kong to the American, French and British forces, spearheading the development of China's first 'modern' city ports (Lee, 1999). Within treaty ports such as Shanghai, transnational influences are strikingly palpable as Western architectures jostled for dominance with traditional Chinese buildings. As Lee (1999: 8–9) observes:

> The harbour skyline [in Shanghai] was dotted with edifices, largely British colonial institutions, prominent among which were the British consulate (the earliest building, 1852; rebuilt in 1873), the Palace Hotel, the Shanghai Club (featuring the 'longest bar in the world'), Sassoon House (with its Cathay Hotel), the Customs House (1927), and the Hong Kong and Shanghai Bank (1923) . . . [M]ost of these British edifices on the Bund were built or rebuilt in the neoclassical style prevalent in England beginning in the late nineteenth century, which replaced the earlier Victorian Gothic and the 'free style' of the arts and crafts movement.

P. Rowe and Kuan (2002: 30) further note that:

> Within the treaty ports and other foreign concessions and missions, foreign
> architects designed mostly in an eclectic variety of the revivalist styles
> fashionable in the West and elsewhere during the last half of the nineteenth
> and early twentieth centuries, strongly reflecting the architectural ambitions
> of their colonial patrons and providing architectural familiarity. After all,
> these ports and concessions were effectively foreign states or administrative
> units within the border . . . consequently in places like Shanghai and later in
> Qingdao, they were sites of Western city building and architecture.

After the collapse of the Qing dynasty, foreign influences, particularly in the
city's architecture, continued unabated. In 1880, there were very few foreign
architectural practices in Shanghai; the number rose to seven by 1893 and 14 by
1910 (P. Rowe and Kuan, 2002: 41). In 1912, the foreign architectural firm Palmer
and Turner established its first branch in Shanghai. One of its most prestigious
commissions was for the Hong Kong and Shanghai Bank in neoclassical style.
Other architectural firms followed suit and pushed in the directions of orthodox
modernism, International Style and later Art Deco 'moderne' style. From the late
1920s, multistorey buildings taller than the colonial edifices on the Bund also
began appearing in Shanghai's urban scene as a result of the diffusion of modern
construction materials and techniques from America. These were mainly bank
buildings, hotels, apartment houses and department stores – the tallest being
the 24-storey Park Hotel designed by the famous Czech-Hungarian architect
Ladislaus Hudec, who was associated with the American architectural firm of
R. A. Curry before he opened his own offices in 1925. The transnational influence
and impact on the city was so profound and entrenched that by the late 1930s the
commercial centre of Shanghai along the Bund had well and truly become modern
and high-rise, earning the city the sobriquet 'the New York of the Orient'.

Alongside the glitzy commercial buildings, Western villas and housing forms
were also transplanted into Shanghai, with New England-style houses, French
villas and English country houses dominating the Concession-era housing architecture, along with the 'compradoric' style mansions – the latter referring to the
sometimes outlandish amalgam of Western and Chinese motifs. As P. Rowe and
Kuan (2002: 38) remark, the so-called compradors were the go-betweens who
were necessary to effectuate trade between China and West. These compradors
became wealthy as a consequence and sought to express their newfound economic status through their residences and establishments. In addition, wealthy
local elites commissioned Western architects to build their homes, such as the
Zhou House (1930) and Wu Residence (1933) designed by Hudec, which were
overtly modernist projects using contemporary materials with clean lines and
symmetrical facades. Even the traditional *shikumen* housing is a hybrid combining the Western terrace house tradition with the Chinese courtyard-style house.
As H. C. Lu (2000) further observes, in the Republican era Shanghai elites built
urban villas surrounded by walls and gardens. The Western-style mansion with

front garden was the residential form preferred by the city's foreigners and local Chinese elites. Examples include the mansions of the government official and banker Song Ziwen and revolutionary leader Sun Yat-sen, which are located in the French concession. However, Lee (1999: 13) reminds us that:

> To the average Chinese, most of these high-rise buildings (and other Western places) are, both literally and figuratively, beyond their reach. The big hotels largely catered to the rich and famous, and mostly foreigners. A Chinese guidebook of the time stated: 'These places have no deep relationship to us Chinese'.

Evidently, the transnational influences visible in Shanghai's suburban landscapes are not entirely 'foreign' or novel. To the extent that the meanings and symbolisms of these urban forms are historically inflected, the selective representation and appropriation of the meanings and messages of these imported foreign ('Western') residential landscapes and symbols represent, in part, attempts by Shanghai's developmental elites and privileged urban class to 'recover' the 'glamorous' side of the city's history in order to enhance and legitimize their newfound status and social standing. In post-reform Shanghai, villas and mansions are currently being reinvented and packaged as high-end real estate products in gated communities for the consumption of those who aspire to high social status. For example, the Shanghai Greenland Group (one of the largest property conglomerates in the country) advertises its new villa houses as 'Shanghai people's new Western-style garden houses' (*shanghairen de xinhuayuan yangfang*). In 'Shanghai Garden', an up-market gated community in the Pudong New Area, the properties are marketed under the tagline of 'old Shanghai culture' (*laoshanghai wenhua*), capitalizing on the nostalgia and 'old world charm' of Shanghai in the late nineteenth and early twentieth centuries (see Figure 4.5). In the advertisement brochures, home-owners are drawn to the explicit comparisons between 'old' Concession-era Western houses (*laofangzhi*) and the 'new' Western-style garden houses (*xin huayuan yangfang*) (see Table 4.1). The latter not only inherit the original 'Olde Shanghai' culture and flavour but are remodelled for modern-day living convenience and comfort. According to the advertising brochure, these new garden houses are equipped with elevators and employ 'state-of-the-art' building technologies and modern construction materials.

Yet, despite their modern appeal, home-buyers are reassured that these houses have not lost their 'nostalgic charm' and 'old world flavour'. Such 'nostalgia for the future', as H. C. Lu (2002) argues, celebrates the return of the city's once celebrated Western influences. But unlike most nostalgia, which is commonly negative, dispirited and withdrawn, the Shanghai nostalgia is positive, spirited and receptive – at least for those who can afford to indulge in such nostalgia. In addition, the designs of many of these new garden mansions and villas are also 'localized' with features such as a Chinese kitchen (in addition to a full-scale Western kitchen for display and admiration) and internal housing layout that follows Chinese geomancy or feng shui principles to ensure a harmonious energy

Figure 4.5   Olde Shanghai – replication of 1920s Concession era Western-style garden houses in a Pudong gated community. (Source: Author's photograph, 2005.)

flow within the homes. Such feng shui injunctions dictate that bedrooms are to be designed to face south to catch the sunlight, stairways must not be visible from the front entrance and the main doors should not directly face the street.

In recent years, housing developers in China, at the behest of the government, have begun to adopt more 'sinicized' names for their housing projects instead of blindly copying exotic Western ones. A critic was quoted as saying: 'On the one hand, Chinese citizens take westernisation for modernisation and refer to the Western lifestyle as an example, and on the other hand, real estate developers [have to] cut down signs suggesting the Western world to cater to the tastes of some local consumers' (*Xinhua News*, 12 September 2005). In Shanghai, overtly foreign and exotic property names are often accompanied by more sinicized names. For example, La Cité Jardin, a relatively up-market commodity housing enclave jointly developed by the Chinese property developers Dahua and Forte Group, also has a more localized Chinese name *yihehuacheng* (literally 'Yihe Chinese City'). From my interviews with residents and property agents, it was also apparent that most Chinese consumers referred to their properties by the Chinese names rather than the more superfluous foreign-sounding ones. As a housing agent revealed: 'The European-sounding names are there to create an impression of Western exoticness [*yangqi*]. On a daily basis, most of us only use the Chinese names, which are easier to pronounce and also more meaningful.'

Clearly, such attempts at localizing real estate products in Shanghai should not been seen as efforts to repudiate Western or foreign influences. Rather the localization of these transnational dynamics and the conspicuous consumption of foreign (Western) culture play a pivotal role in legitimizing the new middle class in Shanghai as 'modern' and 'cosmopolitan'. The ability of locals to consume foreign imported products thus becomes a mark of status differentiation and social

Table 4.1 Comparisons between old and new Western-style garden houses

Characteristics	Old 'Western-style garden mansion'	New 'Western-style garden mansion'
Location	Mostly concentrated in districts such as Luwan, Xuhui, Jing'an, Changning and other areas in the former Concession territories and the city centre	New Shanghai Centre–Lujiazui CBD (as well as outlying suburbs)
Scale of development	Small-scale, usually stand-alone unit	Large-scale high-class enclave
Residential environment	Quiet and peaceful neighbourhood; exclusive private spaces	Quiet and peaceful neighbourhood; exclusive private spaces
Architectural style and design	'European style' (oushi fongge)	'European style' with added contemporary designs for modern-day comfort
Green landscaping	Low density; large green spaces	Low density; large green spaces
Building materials	Mostly wooden structures and outdated construction materials	Uses advanced state-of-the-art building technology and modern construction materials including glass for illumination
Amenities and services	Relies mainly on shared amenities in surrounding vicinity supplied by the municipal government	Private club house facilities for residents only; high-end services provided by professional property management company
Internal housing design	Some parts of the house may not be suitable for modern living; dark and wet in some areas of the house	Modern housing layout with well-lit interior; heightened privacy and total comfort for its inhabitants
Security features	Relies mostly on basic protection measures such as gates and padlocks	Comprehensive protection using modern intelligent security management system; employs professional security personnel and infra-red surveillance system
Parking facilities	Few or limited parking spaces	Underground parking facilities; garages with ample parking spaces
Lift	No lift	Houses fitted with lifts connected to underground parking garage
Overall atmosphere	'Old Shanghai' culture and flavour; but old housing layout may not be suited for modern living and comfort	Inherits the original 'Old Shanghai' culture and flavour but suited for modern living and comfort; housing development able to display the gracefulness (youya) and nobility (zungui) of its inhabitants

distinction. In my interviews, many residents were eager to appropriate tropes of transnational modernity to legitimize their new-found status. For example, a resident in a villa estate expounded:

> Shanghai was already a very modern and internationalized city [*guojihua chengshi*] in the late nineteenth and early twentieth century. Foreign houses and lifestyles were already very common in those days. Of course, at that time, only those with power and money [*youshili*] could afford to stay in these Western-style villas and houses. Now it's like we are like returning back to those heydays days of the 1920s and 30s!

Another villa owner exclaimed:

> We bought this villa because we like the design very much; it has a very classical [*jingdian*] style and a grand aura [*qipai*]. The houses are reminiscent of the old Western houses [*lao yangfang*] in the Concession era! You can still find them [the old Western houses] in the city centre but they are all old and needed extensive renovation, unlike the modern villas you fin here. When our friends visit us, they always envy how we are now leading a villa lifestyle [*bieshu shenghuo*].

Just as Shanghai's urban elites in the late nineteenth and early twentieth centuries consumed foreign imported goods as a mark of prestige and social distinction, middle-class residents in present-day Shanghai attempt to establish their own status and class signifier through the consumption of foreign housing styles and their purported modern lifestyle. With their emphasis on the consumption of imported goods and lifestyles, the reforms of the 1990s did not simply produce a new transnational urbanism but were founded upon what was in fact a pre-existing discourse of (post-)colonial modernity and its relation to an 'elsewhere' – more specifically, its exclusion from and desire for a First World modernity and the good life to which most of the middle-class residents in contemporary Shanghai now felt an entitlement. In this sense, the past, both real and imagined, becomes a source of prestige and social status for those who can claim connections with it. As Hogan and Houston (2002: 258) in their study on gated communities in Jakarta noted: 'the design of these estates and housing styles and the appropriation process by their occupants is anything but a simple unilinear process of metropolitan promotion and colonial emulation and consumption'.

Having said that, one needs to be careful not to overstate the totalizing influences and design appeals of private homes in gated communities. As the following section will elucidate, although not everyone is totally sold on the marketing rhetoric of the developers, with some residents even expressing dissenting views, the appeal of the good life associated with private gated living in Shanghai nevertheless presents an alluring image even though it is not always easy to disentangle the overlapping influences of marketing rhetoric and pragmatic concerns.

Ambiguities and resistances

Indeed, for many home-buyers, beyond the glitzy images and rhetoric produced by the property developers, practical considerations such as house location, price and quality of housing construction remain prime considerations. Although the branding strategies of the developers and the superlative marketing rhetoric may initially draw the consumer's attention to a particular housing development, people are still ultimately concerned about how well their housing investment can fulfil their practical needs and long-term personal interests. As one developer revealed during an interview:

> Investing in a property is a huge decision. Rarely would anyone just buy a property for the sake of the name alone or because of clever advertising slogans or marketing gimmicks. However, once we succeed in attracting customers through our front door, keeping them committed will require the housing product to live up to its name. Chinese consumers are not ignorant . . . We need to show proof to them that our product and brand name is good value for their money [*wuyoushuozhi*].

In fact, the branding and reputation of developers may also translate into economic terms. For example, over half of the residents interviewed in Vanke Garden City stated their preferences for buying commodity houses from established and branded developers because they are able to guarantee their housing investment in the long term. As one home-owner who had bought a property from Vanke Corporation remarked:

> Vanke Corporation is a 'golden brand name' [*jingzhi zhaopai*] developer. You can't go wrong with them. Their houses are well designed and built with great style [*qipai*] that appeals to the high tastes of the sophisticated Shanghai consumers . . . Just look at those properties Vanke Company has built, their prices have appreciated at least by 30 to 50 per cent!

In this sense, economic motivation thus becomes intertwined with the branding strategies of developers and their housing projects, with practical and symbolic forces mutually reinforcing one another.

Yet, far from producing hegemonic consensus amongst the local urban residents, gated communities have often generated various ambiguities and symbolic resistances. Caldeira (2000), for example, has illustrated how wealthy enclaves and enclosed condominiums in São Paulo and their associated codes of social distinction are actively resisted and even subverted by different social groups as they engage and negotiate with these fortified spaces on a daily basis. In Shanghai, overt forms of resistance against gated communities can range from minor acts of transgression such as trespassing in gated neighbourhoods by non-residents to vandalism such as graffiti and spray-painting on the gates and walls (see Figure 4.6). Even though these transgressive acts do not pose a direct chal-

Figure 4.6 Migrant workers hanging their laundry on the ornamental fences of a gated community, much to the chagrin of the middle-class residents who complained about the defilement of the aesthetic facade of their estate. (Source: Author's photograph, 2005.)

lenge to neighbourhood enclosure, they can nevertheless be read as purposeful acts of opposition that could potentially destabilize the codes of distinction and neoliberal (aesthetic) regime that underpin fortified urban landscapes in Shanghai (Pow, 2009a).

Beyond overt forms of resistance, dissenting views and symbolic discontent are also centred on the ostentatious 'vulgar' design and 'undesirable' social elements behind the gates. Many of the local residents I spoke to are clearly critical of the Western-style houses in gated communities, regarding them as unrefined, pretentious and fake. In one instant, an overzealous home-owner in Vanke Garden City had illegally remodelled[7] his house by building and extending a 'New England-style' porch in his front yard, complete with an outdoor dog kennel and an al fresco dining area (see Figure 4.7). Clearly at odds with the surroundings, the owner came under fire not only from the estate management office for 'unlawful construction' (*weijian*) but also by his neighbours, who lambasted the home-owner for his decidedly 'boorish taste'. Such 'taste wars' not only reflect the rupture and disjuncture in residents' aesthetic codes and landscape views (see, for example, Mitchell, 1997) but also emphasize the often differentiated and fragmented usage and consumption of gated communities. One interviewee, for example, remarked:

It's quite laughable . . . some of the new rich [*baofahu*] would spend huge sums of money investing in expensive villas and renovating their homes with upscale fixtures, thinking that their social standing will be transformed overnight. But in reality, their backward behaviours and uncouth habits haven't

Figure 4.7   Illegal extension of a house in gated community with 'New England style' porch (right) and outdoor dining area (left). (Source: Author's photograph, 2007.)

quite caught up with their new living environment. Worse still, the designs of some of these houses are so vulgar with huge Western sculptures and ornate gates to flaunt their wealth.

What her remarks also reveal is the opinion that social behaviour in modern Shanghai often lags behind material improvements, a phenomenon that has been evidenced in other 'Third World' contexts as well (see, for example, Bunnell, 2002). In a similar vein, some of Shanghai's luxurious gated communities and their purported high-class lifestyles have also come under social disapprobation from civic-minded local residents. Not only are gated communities criticized for their elitist and antisocial tendencies, local people have also come to associate some of these gated communities with illicit or immoral affairs. For instance, it is well known amongst the locals in Shanghai that many private gated estates (bearing fancy high-class names such as Rotterdam Park and Paris Garden) in the expatriate areas of Gubei New Area often serve as the rendezvous for wealthy overseas Chinese businessmen from Taiwan and their Shanghainese mistresses (*ernai*), the latter also known colloquially as 'golden caged birds' (*jingsiniao*).[8] Interestingly, the reference to these 'kept women' in gated communities as caged birds not only reveals the gendered and sexualized politics dominated by 'masculine transnational business agenda' (Shen, 2005) but also reveals some of the negative perceptions associated with some of the high-class gated communities in Shanghai.

Summary

This chapter has critically examined the advertising themes and rhetoric that were assembled in the place-marketing of gated communities in Shanghai. Collectively, these neoliberal representations of the good life both reflect and reinforce the exclusivist housing aspirations and privatized lifestyle of middle-class residents of gated communities. As this chapter has further argued, these alluring real estate images and their socio-spatial codes do more than just represent visions and symbols of the good life behind the gates but also *present*, shape and help constitute (middle-)class distinction and subjectivities. Put in another way, the cumulative meanings and social-cultural significations associated with these housing images and architectural codes thus help to constitute the 'space of lifestyles' (Bourdieu, 1984) for the emerging middle class in Shanghai. The house, as a physical foundation for the personal and social life of its inhabitants, actively mediates and constructs one's social identity in a community. Like fortified enclaves elsewhere, the advertisements in Shanghai all elaborate and thrive on the myth of a new concept in urban(e) living that rests on the articulation of images of prestige, security, isolation and homogeneity. Inherent in the pursuit of the good life behind the gates is also the desire for private seclusion and privacy. The next chapter will examine the rise of privacy and the privatization of domestic life in gated communities and their implications for communal living.

5 Seeking privacy and seclusion

Private property, individualism and neoliberal subjectivities

Conceiving house and home as *private*, therefore, and everything and everyone not belonging to this realm as *public*, one theme that requires treatment is the way people live together in this place, that is the protection that a private place provides for relationships, for families. What then emerges is that in spite of the long tradition of this separation and the institution of private relationships and the family, the modifications characteristics of our present-day understanding of the term can be traced on the one hand to the emergence of liberalism and on the other hand to the emergence of the bourgeois family in the nineteenth century.

(Rossler, 2005: 143)

Previously, Chinese people didn't pay much attention to the protection of privacy because in accordance with Chinese traditions, we had almost no privacy . . . After being silent about privacy for so many years, Chinese people tend to the other extreme, which leads to excessive privacy.

(a sociology professor at Fudan University, quoted in *Shanghai Star* 21 November 2002)

Introduction

A reader of one of Shanghai's most widely read local newspapers, the *Xinming Evening News*[1] wrote in to complain (12 September 2004) about what he considered to be an infringement of his family's privacy by over-zealous security guards employed in his gated neighbourhood. According to the writer, a Mr Wang, the security guards at his new commercial housing estate keep a close watch on the people and vehicles entering and leaving the housing compounds, a standard practice in many commodity housing estates in Shanghai. Even though such security measures were initially welcomed by Wang, he had been rather perturbed lately when some of the security guards started to 'update' him on the daily movements of his family members. For example, on his way out of the main gate one morning, a security guard on duty casually mentioned to Wang that his wife had just gone to the nearby shopping mall and that his daughter had just left for school an hour ago. While such 'friendly surveillance' meant no malice and may even attest to the vigilance and 'professionalism' of the security guards, for Wang, it posed an uncomfortable threat to his sense of privacy (*yinsi*).

Far from being an isolated case, Wang's letter is indicative of a much broader set of social changes occurring in contemporary Shanghai. Although there are limited rights to privacy in the Chinese constitution (see *Privacy International*;[2] *Constitution of the People's Republic of China*, 2004), private life and privacy[3] have become increasingly important dimensions in the life of urban residents in China (Pellow, 1993; McDougall and Hansson, 2002). Books on privacy can readily be found in commercial bookstores and public libraries, and discussions in state-run newspapers, on television and radio programmes and in internet discussion forums frequently feature issues related to privacy protection for individuals. In December 2002, the Sixteenth Congress of the Chinese Communist Party approved a new draft civil code that guaranteed 'legal protection to human dignity', including the right to privacy and rights to private as well as public property.[4] In 2004, the Shanghai municipal government's proposed bill to extend privacy rights to minors (those below 21 years of age) further elicited wide-ranging debates such as whether concerned parents who pry into their children's diaries are violating privacy rights and if schools should publicly disclose the academic results of students (*Shanghai Daily*, 26 November 2004).

Prior to economic reform and the opening up of mainland China in the 1980s, privacy rights of citizens and private life were seldom invoked, and rarely debated in the open. Barely two decades later, there is now a heightened awareness of and general 'demand' for respect of people's privacy rights and the emergence of a relatively autonomous private/domestic sphere that is, to some extent, free from the interference of the state (Yang, 1994; D. Davis, 2000; Read, 2003; Tomba, 2004). Yet what do the terms 'public' and 'private' mean in the context of Shanghai and how are spatial practices of the public and private conducted in the daily life behind gated communities? More significantly, how do middle-class residents of gated communities construct a new private lifestyle enclave that departs from traditional communal living arrangements and in the process challenges and unsettles hegemonic state controls in China? And to what extent can we frame our understanding of the Chinese resident's quest for privacy, autonomy and individualism in terms of the emergence of liberalism and bourgeois/middle-class families, as referred to by Rossler (1995) in the opening quotation?

Contrary to Anglo-American literature, in which gated communities are typically cast in a negative light and often depicted as the bulldozing of public spaces by private interests (M. Davis, 1990; Blakely and Snyder, 1997; Caldeira, 1999, 2000; Low, 2003), this chapter offers a more nuanced interpretation by arguing that Shanghai's gated communities are potentially sites where greater household autonomy and personal freedom may be negotiated and realized *away* from the hegemonic control and interference of the Communist party-state. Although the notion of an autonomous private sphere in gated communities may hardly be a novel observation in the context of Anglo-American cities, it will be interesting to examine how the shifting dynamics in reform Shanghai have presented an opportunity for urban residents to live away (albeit partially) from the control of the state in these newly built private housing enclaves. Furthermore, it is important to clarify at the outset that it is not the intention of this chapter to undermine the complexities of the public and private life in contemporary Shanghai. (Arguably, the political and social conditions in China today are far more complicated than the simplistic depiction of a dominant Communist party-state versus the oppressed private citizenry.) Rather, the aim here is to show how spatial practices of the public and private operate in a specific non-Western context – in this case Shanghai's gated communities.

Communal spaces in Shanghai

The lack of personal space and privacy is a common refrain that one frequently hears when urban residents in Shanghai/China talk about social life in traditional communal neighbourhoods. With a per capita living space of less than 10 square metres, it is hardly surprising that personal space and privacy was a scarce resource in the pre-housing reform days. Although it has been reported that housing consumption has significantly increased in recent years as a result of economic/housing reform and the real estate boom, not everyone can afford to move into the spacious new apartments and houses, given the escalating prices of commodity houses in the city (Y. Huang, 2003). Crowded housing conditions with two or three generations of family members living under the same roof in crammed housing conditions are still common in old neighbourhoods and migrant housing quarters in Shanghai (Pellow, 1993; H. C. Lu, 2000; T. Y. Huang, 2004). In many of these old neighbourhoods, the typical housing type is the old *shikumen* or stonewall houses, a particular building type in Shanghai that is derived from the traditional courtyard housing style and is arranged on a narrow grid of lanes (see Figure 5.1). Each *shikumen* building contains several apartments housing multi-

Figure 5.1 Crowded *shikumen* homes in Shanghai with many households living in the same building. (Source: author's photograph, 2005.)

ple unrelated families living under the same roof and sharing communal facilities such as the kitchen (usually on the ground floor) and washing tap and basins.

As Pellow (1993) observes, the *shikumen* buildings are not particularly spacious. A seven-apartment *shikumen* building with a total of 194.3 square metres is shared by 28 people, averaging out at 6.9 square metres per person. It is not uncommon for an entire family to live in a small room of less than 10 square metres. In the crowded *shikumen* houses and to a lesser extent in relatively newer work-unit apartments, the lack of personal space for intimate activities has necessitated various coping mechanisms. For example, the main room serves the functions of sleeping, eating, dressing, reading/studying, playing and entertaining visitors. Since these activities are conducted at different times of the day, it requires the functional redefinition of the same room/space throughout the day. In *shikumen* houses, residents have further adopted creative means to deal with privacy and lack of space by building lofts in houses with high ceilings or using furniture to demarcate personal spaces (see Pellow, 1993: 406).

As a result of the crowded living environment, domestic and commercial activities often 'spill out' onto the streets. As is the case in contemporary post-reform or post-*doi moi* Vietnam (see Drummond, 2000), the use of public streets and pavements for personal and commercial purposes is also rampant in Shanghai, especially in the traditional neighbourhoods in the downtown area near Yuyuan, where many traditional *shikumen* houses may be found. A common sight in these traditional neighbourhoods is the temporary appropriation of public walkways and pavements by itinerant street vendors, barbers, food and vegetable hawkers, etc. Often, these vendors will lay out their wares along the pavements and streets during the early morning and, depending on the nature of the business, clear out by noon or mid-afternoon. There are also semi-permanent stalls that belong to families who run their businesses from the frontage of their *shikumen* homes. Like the stall owners documented in Drummond's (2000) Vietnam study, proprietors in Shanghai understand that they are not supposed to 'colonize' the public streets and walkways, but appear to feel that they need to use the space in order to conduct commercial activities as long as they do not get caught or the penalties are not too harsh.[5]

Besides commercial activities, private/domestic tasks in communal neighbourhoods are often conducted in full view of the public because of cramped housing conditions. What are typically considered as private activities necessary for social reproduction (eating, sleeping, cooking and even washing up) are often conducted in full public view. In these communal neighbourhoods, people seem perfectly at ease consuming their meals on the streets outside their homes. As a result of the spatial arrangement of *shikumen* housing, the shared kitchen is located on the ground floor. For this reason, cooking activities usually spill over to the streets and pavements in front of the houses. It is also common for families to prepare their meals outside the confines of the small kitchen, cooking over coal stoves that are placed in semi-public lanes and walkways. On account of poor air circulation in the crowded *shikumen*, it is also not uncommon to see residents relaxing or taking afternoon naps in fold-up beds and chairs along the pavements and lanes (Figure

5.2). In the activities highlighted above, the spilling out and encroachment of public streets and lanes for private uses have blurred the conventional boundaries between public and private spaces. In recent years, however, the Chinese state, in an attempt to spruce up the 'modern' image of the city, has tried to clamp down on the indiscriminate hanging of laundry in public streets. According to the Shanghai Municipal City Appearance and Environmental Sanitation Administration, from April 2002, anyone found drying their washing along main roads or close to parks, cinemas and other tourist sights will face a fine of 20 yuan (this rule is seldom enforced).

As noted earlier, a distinctive feature in China is the 'state-hegemonic public sphere' (Kraus, 2000), with the Chinese Communist Party (CCP) attempting to reorganize modern Chinese society to create a public sphere over which it can hold power. In socialist China, the totalitarian party-state has effectively hijacked the 'public' and transformed society into a massive bureaucratic structure under the rule of the CCP in which society is organized under a nationwide administration of 'collective housekeeping'. In everyday life, the state's attempt to control the use of public spaces extends even right down to managing the 'proper' behaviours and dressing of urban residents in public spaces. For example, the wearing of pyjamas outdoors, a common practice for many middle-aged and elderly Shanghai residents, is frowned upon by officials. According to the state's rationale, the wearing of 'personal' clothing such as pyjamas should be reserved for the confines of one's home and it is inappropriate for pyjama-clad residents to be seen in public spaces. As the *Xinming Evening News* (13 August 2002) reports: 'People, especially housewives, in their sleepwear go shopping in supermarkets, go to hospitals and even take buses. This does not conform to the task of civiliza-

Figure 5.2 Residents resting and eating on the pavements. (Source: author's photograph, 2005.)

tion.' In addition, the state has also launched a series of initiatives and a public education campaign aimed at eradicating some of the 'backward' and 'uncivilized' social practices such as spitting on public streets, talking too loudly or spewing vulgarities in public spaces (more on the contested notion of 'civilized' practices in Chapter 6).

Besides controlling the use of public spaces, the state also interferes in the domestic sphere, particularly in the private realm of reproductive activities, marriage and practically all major aspects of the citizen's private life through the work-units and the household registration (*hukou*) system that determines where people can stay. In the sphere of reproduction, the state's 'one-child' policy, which strongly advocates compulsory family planning, is strictly enforced by the work-unit and monitored by grassroots organizations such as residents' committees. Until recently, couples registering for marriage had to seek permission to marry from their work-units or neighbourhood committees and had to undergo a compulsory 'pre-marriage health check' (*hunjian*) to ensure that there would be no defective offspring (see Diamant, 2001). But, since reform, the state has gradually retreated from micro-managing domestic life and allows greater freedom in selected areas of private life. For example, pre-marriage health checks are no longer compulsory (though calls to reinstate the health checks have been made recently); as a result of economic restructuring citizens can now seek employment in private and foreign firms instead of being assigned to traditional work-units; and people are now free to live anywhere in the city (or wherever they can afford) independent of their work-units, which no longer build homes for their workers. On the whole, although the state continues to exert considerable influence in the personal lives and private sphere of the people, the declining influence of the work-units and the devolvement of the state from public housing provision have invariably opened up a semi-autonomous private space in the form of the commodity housing enclaves. As will be shown later, in these privately developed and managed residential enclaves, where the main criterion of entry is no longer work-unit affiliations but income, residents enjoy greater freedom and autonomy that is to some extent independent of the state's control.

To summarize, what could be observed about Shanghai's traditional neighbourhoods is the frequent blurring of public/private boundaries that prove to be fluid and routinely transgressed even as the state tries to impose certain forms of control over the 'appropriate' use of public space as well as intervene in the private sphere. Personal/intimate spaces also seem to be lacking in many communal neighbourhoods, largely because of the housing constraints and spatial arrangements. This situation is, however, not unique to Shanghai. The dynamic interplay and appropriation of public and private spaces/spheres are common in Asian and Western cities (see D. Mitchell, 1995; Lee, 1999; Drummond, 2000; Law, 2002). What is distinctive here is how the urban conditions reflect the particular context of Shanghai/China, which is undergoing rapid economic and social transformation. In the newly built commercial housing enclaves, not only are residential compounds within gated communities highly regulated by developers' housing codes and zoning policies that adhere strictly to the demarcation of public and private boundaries, but the personal spaces and privacy of residents in these gated communities are also zealously guarded and protected. The following sections will illuminate how private/personal spaces are defined and valued within private gated communities and how this has reconfigured the territorial organization of space and social life in the city. As will be shown later, in these privately developed and managed residential enclaves, residents enjoy greater freedom and autonomy that is to some extent independent of the state's control.

Buying the concept of privacy and 'interiority' in gated communities

The word for private/privacy in Chinese (*si* or *yinsi*) literally means something hidden, something that is protected from anyone knowing and often carrying a pejorative connotation, but *si* may also be used in a positive sense in certain contexts, especially in compounds with words such as *jia* (family) (McDougall, 2004: 2). In particular, embedded in the second meaning of privacy is also an elitist notion of privacy that is tied to power and status. Although rarely scrutinized, power relations are inherent in privacy, existing asymmetrically between those who have and those who lack the power to intrude on others' privacy as well as to protect their own privacy against intrusion (see Yan, 2003: 126). For example, in ancient China, high-ranking officials and wealthy merchants were known to build high walls around their private property (courtyard homes) to shield their private lives from the prying eyes of the public. High walls generally signified the wealth and high status of the inhabitants (see Moore, 1984: 223). In this sense, the concept of privacy may be seen to be closely tied to status and power.

Although heavily criticized and devalued in Maoist China, both privacy and private property have been re-evaluated in the post-reform era, giving rise to a new appreciation of privacy functions and values. In post-reform China, the ability to enjoy privacy and seclusion has become a mark of social status and a fashionable 'lifestyle concept' that are eagerly sought after by residents of gated communities. As Feuchtwang (2002: 216) notes: 'The privacy of domestic space has been made materially more thick, substantial and excluding. It has, moreover, become a space of consumer goods.' It is thus significant to note how private lives and privacy, once highly taboo and undesirable during Mao's reign, have now been turned on their heads and elevated to a level of public respectability and prestige. The idea of privacy as a privileged lifestyle concept is not unique. As Duncan and Duncan (2003: 53) note in their study of an up-market North American suburb, 'privacy is also a mark of wealth, for in the relatively densely populated New York metropolitan region, privacy is a scare and costly commodity'. In densely populated Shanghai, privacy is similarly a prized commodity. Residents buying into gated communities are not only living the new dream of private home ownership and an exclusive lifestyle behind the gates, they are also expressing their subjectivity and individualism through the reconfiguration of personal spaces and interior of their apartments. To this extent, privacy is also intimately linked to the concept of interiority. As Tang (2000: 311) argues in his analysis of a home advertisement in China: 'Home reads as a perfect example of how effortlessly a cluster of once politically sensitive ideas such as individuality, self expression, privacy and interiority can be grafted onto a commercial advertisement targeted at a new managerial class.'

As middle-class residents move out of communal neighbourhoods to live in commercial apartments and private houses in gated communities, they also acquire new private spaces and a sense of interiority. In particular, the idea of interiority correlates to the much-contested notion of 'subjectivity' that connotes the idea of freedom. One of the reasons for the controversy over 'subjectivity' was the political implications of the term in the harsh political climate of collectivist uniformity and a hegemonic public sphere in Maoist China. After more than a quarter-century during which the idea of a private home was systematically erased and interior design became an alien concept, city dwellers are now investing a great deal of money and time in decorating and remodelling what they can claim as their own living spaces. Affluent urban residents in China have been known to splurge on the interior decoration of their homes, spending anything from a few thousand to more than 30,000 yuan to deck out their new homes, sometimes in outlandish designs and styles. In 1996, residents in Shanghai reportedly spent an average of 10,000 yuan (about US$1,230) modernizing their bathrooms, even though the typical bathroom is no larger than 4 square metres (Tang, 2000: 309).

According to a report in the *Shanghai Star* (14 January 2000), expenditure on interior decoration of a 50-m² apartment in Shanghai ranges from 40,000 yuan (US$4,837) to 90,000 yuan (US$10,883). Taking the minimum expenditure as 40,000 yuan per household, the report estimates that total expenditure on interior decoration in the city is at least 10 billion yuan (US$1.2 billion) every year. The report further notes that the general trend is moving towards higher-grade and more lavish remodelling costing upwards of 100,000 yuan (US$12,092) with some spending as much as 400,000 yuan (US$48,368). In particular, consumers generally prefer imported goods such as aluminium and wood windows from the United States, frameless windows from Austria and heat-absorbing curtains from the Netherlands even though these cost three or four times the price of local goods. The deputy secretary with Shanghai Interior Decoration Association was quoted as saying:

> The Socialist era of white walls and dark red floors are gone for ever. Now Shanghainese pursue diversified styles of decoration. A scholar usually focuses on his study room; a businessman likes a luxurious living room; while a new couple would choose romantic decoration, with warm colours and chic ornaments.
>
> (*Shanghai Star*, 14 January 2000)

In many apartment showrooms, interior designers are available to help home-buyers conceptualize their new interior home concept (*linian*). A sense of individuality and uniqueness in doing up personal space is a crucial element of interior design. Thus, as Tang (2000: 208) argues, Chinese cities are at the stage 'when people's lives will have to be systematically interiorized and interiority imaginatively engineered and expanded so as to create more fantasies and needs'.

Why then are affluent Shanghai urban residents spending so much money in remodelling their homes? Since reform, with the purchase of commercial housing, people are eager to create a unique sense of identity in their own personal spaces. What home-owners want is more than just a comfortable home; they are also after a more fulfilling private world, a new experience of interiority, engendered by new personal spaces and expressive interior design. Deborah Davis (quoted in Fraser, 2000: 43), for example, argues that interior design in Shanghai homes often serves as a vehicle for self-expression outside or in opposition to the claustrophobic control of the Communist party-state. According to Fraser (2000: 27):

> When people buy private housing, they acquire not merely a domicile but also a personal, private terrain that fosters a greater sense of individual entitlement that is often expressed through consumption. The new lifestyle repudiates the severe constraints on personal life imposed in earlier decades by the Maoist work unit or *danwei*.

In the words of Tang, interiority could be viewed as a defence of 'negative freedom, the right to resist the hegemonic control of the state by escaping and turning inward' (Tang, 2000: 304).

Privacy in the post-reform era has to a large extent been transformed into a marketable lifestyle concept, a mark of social status (especially in gated communities) and a vehicle for self-expression and autonomy (when connected with the concept of interiority) that is integrally linked to the interior transformation of individual's homes. In the next section, I will examine how privacy functions and is valued in the everyday life in gated communities. As will be shown below, there is not only a greater sense of privacy in gated communities but also the idea that one is entitled to private spaces and privacy (having paid a premium for it). This is in part linked to rising individualism, consumerism and greater autonomy of the individual and household away from the state.

Private life behind the gates

In Peter Wilson's (1988) work *The Domestication of the Human Species*, he argues that a major watershed in human history was the development of relatively stable and permanent partitions or walled-in structures within a community or settlement that allowed people to be part of a community yet to stay apart, to be connected yet disconnected. Whereas nomadic hunters and gatherers live a relatively 'unbounded life' and have a 'focus-oriented' spatial framework (Bushmen 'territories', for example, may centre on particular water holes that define their sense of place belonging), domesticated people have a 'boundary-oriented' framework in the forms of walls and architecture that profoundly altered human behaviours, ideas and thinking. According to Wilson (1988: 176):

[T]he development of domestication 'meant,' among other things, the construction of technology that simultaneously enhanced the opportunities for concentration by erecting physical barriers against intrusion and interruption; reduced the chances of distraction; and hindered the free-flow capacity of people to pay attention to one another as an undifferentiated feature of the routine of everyday life.

Thus, when cultures develop more permanent partitions, or when humans become 'domesticated', we find not only an increase in the differentiation of groups into subgroups, but also an increase in the individual sense of the self. Tuan (1982) further shows that, when societies become more segmented as places multiply and are progressively 'thinned out' and specialized, the members of the societies are able to develop a fuller and deeper appreciation of the self as an individual. These segmented places in which individuals could withdraw out of view from everyone else and become to some degree detached and differentiated from the rest are what make gated communities significantly different from communal neighbourhoods in Shanghai.

During my fieldwork and interviews, many of my respondents were quite at ease with using the Chinese term *yinsi* to describe their sense of privacy. Yet, as McDougall (2002: 2) warns, whereas it is easy to locate instances of privacy in China, it is considerably more complicated and difficult to find evidence of the conceptualization of privacy, for example as a value. In the following, I will first sketch out a 'common sense' understanding of privacy among residents in gated communities to examine how domestic spatial and social relations have been transformed. By examining the everyday spatial practices and experiences of residents in gated communities, I hope to tease out how privacy functions and is valued as well as the spatial strategies and rhetoric of privacy and private property that are being mobilized by middle-class residents of gated communities.

I will primarily be interested in spatial privacy or what Rossler (2005) calls 'local privacy'. In particular, Rossler (2005: 5) compares the practice of privacy to an 'onion' model with different layers of control and access corresponding to different scales. At the centre is the realm of personal or bodily intimacy and privacy, in contrast to which everything else is regarded as 'public'. The second layer comprises the classic realm of privacy of the family, as opposed to the outside world of society and the state that constitutes the public realm. Adopting this multilayered view of privacy in the analysis, I will show how different layers of privacy operate and function in gated communities, starting first with 'primary' territories within the home/household and then proceeding to more 'secondary' territorial zones within the neighbourhood where social interactions between neighbours and the wider community take place.

Privacy of individuals within the household

Local privacy or privacy of the home/household constitutes one of the most basic dimensions of privacy in modern liberal society. As Rossler (2005: 144) explains:

When we say 'this is my room' (or house), we mean by this that we can determine who is and is not allowed to enter it and when. We also mean that in it we can do or not do just what we want, unobserved, undisturbed. And we mean that this room (or house), just as it is, is mine, made for me, for my needs, my requirements, my habits, my history, my predilections, and my interests.

Unlike in communal neighbourhoods, where personal spaces and privacy are scarce commodities, newly built commodity housing enclaves place a greater premium on ensuring and protecting the privacy of their inhabitants through a number of changes in housing design. First, commercial apartments have much larger living spaces than old *shikumen* houses and communal flats, thus allowing domestic chores and activities to be contained well within the private spaces of individual homes. Usually, the average size of commercial apartment in gated communities is from 100 square metres (for a basic two-bedroom apartment) upwards, more than twice the average size of communal flats and several times larger than *shikumen* rooms. Whereas sharing of the communal kitchen and other housing facilities is common in old neighbourhoods, new commercial apartments and private houses are equipped with their own private bathrooms and kitchens. Thus, domestic activities no longer spill over into the public arena and are kept behind closed doors, thus ensuring greater privacy and convenience for residents who no longer have to endure the public gaze.[6] The spacious commercial apartments also mean that residents do not have to deal with noise or interference from neighbours.

According to Saunders and Williams (1988), the house has a central role in the reproduction of social life. It is the setting that makes interaction meaningful and predictable, linking intimate emotional and sexual life to economic and political life. In this regard, the housing plan and layout thus act as important signifiers of both the semantics and the syntax of domestic space. Examining homes in Australia and California, Dovey (1999: 141) argues that a general housing 'genotype' or pattern dominates housing design through the primary division of domestic spaces into different zones such as a formal living zone (incorporating the living room, dining room, entrance, etc.); informal living zone (kitchen, nook); master suite (master bedroom, bathroom, dressing room, etc.); and minor bedroom zone (children's and guest bedrooms, recreation area). These housing genotypes engender a set of structured relations between primary clusters of space or division of domestic space that mediate relations between inhabitants and visitors, and between different generations and familial activities within the house.

In Shanghai, the new genotype of commercial apartments typically consists of models with two or more bedrooms (usually featuring a main master bedroom (*zhukuo*), a study room (*shufang*) and a children's room) with a living room (*keting*), a kitchen (*chufang*), dining area (*fanting*), store room and balcony. In contrast to the crammed housing conditions in communal neighbourhoods, where different activities often take place within the same space, functionally separate and segmented domestic spaces within commercial apartments suggest that domestic activities are now structured around specific and formalized settings and spaces that are dedicated to different activities as well as the privacy needs of each family member. For example, the main bedroom usually reserved for the head of the household or elderly family members is primarily a personal space for resting and sleeping. Dining activities usually take place in a separate dining area adjacent to the living room or sometimes in the kitchen. The living room is usually reserved for entertaining guests and for relaxation by family members. (Until recently, children often slept in the same room and even on the same bed with their parents until 10 to 12 years old.) Overall, the housing genotype of commercial apartments places a huge premium on protecting the personal spaces and privacy needs of individual members of the household and functionally separating different domestic activities and spaces.

In practice, the observance of privacy among family members is often lax and frequently transgressed. Parents and children, for example, enter each other's rooms quite freely. Room doors are also seldom closed or locked. In general, parents do not seem to mind children going into their rooms except when they close their room doors, which suggests that privacy is needed. Many adult respondents also stated that it is the responsibility of the grown-ups to secure their own privacy at home rather than assuming that privacy is to be taken for granted (see Pellow, 1993). The most frequent justification for lax privacy at home is that 'We are all one family' – implying that between family members there is no need for strict observance of privacy as 'there are no secrets' in the family. Even though there are separate bedrooms, children as old as 10 years still continue to sleep with their parents in the same room and often on the same bed. Thus, according to M. Whyte and Parish (1984: 80), 'The Chinese architectural standard is that children will sleep in the same room with their parents through age twelve.' On the other hand, even though privacy among family members is generally lax, teenagers often complain about parents 'snooping' on their privacy even after they have moved into their own independent rooms. A common refrain among Chinese adolescents is the interference in their privacy by parents, who often enter their rooms at will, opening their drawers and reading their diaries or letters, on the pretext of checking on their homework. Although some families I interviewed claimed to emphasize the value of privacy within homes, on the whole, privacy among family members, especially that of children, is seldom observed strictly, partly on account of the enduring paternalistic Chinese family culture. For example, when a new privacy law on minors was passed in Shanghai in 2004, it generated great discontent among parents. As a parent revealed: 'I don't think the law will be accepted by most Chinese parents, who take very good care of their children and consider it their responsibility to check on their letters' (quoted in *Shanghai Daily*, 26 November 2003).

Privacy and autonomy of individuals and households from state control

Unlike in the old system of work-unit-based housing and in traditional residential estates, where state surveillance and grassroots control were relatively strong, commercial housing estates in contemporary gated communities are built and managed by property developers, real estate management companies and private home-owners' associations, which are primarily interested in protecting the housing investments of private home-owners. In tandem with the development of private gated communities, the rise of home-owners' associations coupled with the commodification of housing services has also supplanted some of the traditional functions of government-linked grassroots organizations such as residential committees.[7] As the private housing market expanded, relations between the state, property developers and private home-owners become highly complex. In many up-market gated communities, the residential committee's traditional roles (for example providing welfare assistance, family planning, promoting government propaganda) have been sidelined and are often considered irrelevant by the residents. In some commodity housing estates, privately employed property management companies have even taken over certain state-delegated functions of the residents' committees such as the household registry system, much to the chagrin of the local government (Read, 2003: 54). As F. L. Wu observes (2005: 245):

> In the estates of commodity housing, the homeowners association becomes the more powerful organization, replacing the residential committee because members of the homeowners association are often successful businessmen and the political elites. In these communities, governance has experienced the transition from administrative dominance by the residential committee to self-governance led by the homeowners association.

Although activist home-owners' associations asserting their property rights (*weiquan*) and collective control or self-government (*zizhi*) over their private residential estates may at first sight appear to be rather unorthodox and depart radically from traditional state-dominated neighbourhood/urban organization structure, the (legal) power of home-owners' associations in China remains ill-defined and is in many respects heavily circumscribed by state institutions such as the Ministry of Construction as well as the local district governments.[8]

Nevertheless, it is undeniable that residents within private gated communities are indeed able to lead a more private and autonomous life.[9] For example, personal satellite television dishes that receive programmes from Hong Kong, Taiwan, Japan and even the United States, Russia and Europe are commonly found in the private homes in Shanghai's gated communities (see Figure 5.3). According to Yang (1994: 299), in the early 1990s, many private Shanghai homes were equipped with satellite dishes (most of them made in China by rural factories hoping to profit from this highly valued product) even though state regulations forbid the setting up of personal satellite dishes at home, except for those work-units dealing with international business, foreign embassies and government-approved hotels. The Public Security Bureau and the State Administration of Radio, Film and Television (SARFT) mounted periodic raids in Shanghai to confiscate these private dishes, but after a while the dishes went back and the police sometimes

Figure 5.3 Illegally installed satellite television dish outside a home in Vanke Garden City. (Source: author's photograph, 2005.)

chose to ignore them. In particular, the enclosed and secluded compounds of commercial housing enclaves make it difficult for the authorities to detect the illegal installation of satellite dishes in private homes. During my stay in Vanke Garden City, almost every household in the estate had a satellite dish protruding from its windows or balconies. Every week, my mailbox was filled with commercial flyers advertising different satellite television packages (with prices ranging from 3,000 to over 6,000 yuan for the dish installation).

Most residents in my estate subscribed to channels that allowed them to watch Hong Kong and Taiwan media productions such as the Hong Kong-based Phoenix TV Channel.[10] When I enquired whether installing the satellite dishes is illegal in Shanghai, residents at Vanke reassured me that, even though it is against the law, the authorities don't normally enforce the rules; some residents even remarked that, since this a private estate, it is difficult for the authorities to enter and conduct checks on every household. One feisty resident even suggested to me that, 'even if the authorities come knocking on your door, just don't open it or hide the satellite dish until they have left'. As Yang (1994: 297) contends: 'what we find in post-Mao China is a new, complex political economy in which state and capital both converge and diverge at different moments'. On the one hand, it is the state that initiates and sustains the new market-oriented policies such as economic reform and housing privatization and eagerly lays out the welcome mat to capital. On the other hand, the state also finds that the new market forces that it has unleashed often have a logic quite threatening to its own desire to retain absolute control of society.

Besides satellite television dishes, government officials have also encountered difficulties in enforcing family planning policies in up-market gated communities. On the 'China Family Planning Association' website,[11] for instance, several articles have highlighted that government officials and local residential committee members have been denied entry into some private gated communities. According to another news report (*Dongfang Morning Post*, 18 January 2005), grassroots officials also face difficulties soliciting census information from residents in gated communities who want to protect their own privacy. In more extreme cases, even the police have been denied entry into some gated communities (F. L. Wu, 2005). According to some of the residential committee officials I spoke to, the problem lies largely with the enclosed housing management styles of gated communities that put residents physically and administratively 'out of sight' from close monitoring and surveillance by grassroots organizations such as the residential committees or the street offices. The problem is further exacerbated by the 'uncooperative' attitudes of property management companies, which often refuse to provide government officials with information on tenants residing in the neighbourhood on the basis of protecting the privacy of the residents. Another difficulty with the enforcement of family planning policy lies in the social composition of the gated community residents. As most residents residing in gated communities belong to the affluent and well-connected middle- and upper-class strata, local officials and residential committee members often find it difficult to make these 'high social status people' comply with rules and regulations. This is also compounded by the fact that, since housing reform, both locals and foreigners are free to purchase or rent commodity housing without much restriction.

Evidently, residents in commodity housing enclaves are able to lead a more autonomous and private life away from the state's direct interference and control. It would be unrealistic to suggest that the state has entirely withdrawn from managing the private lives of the citizens. Nevertheless, as Deborah Davis (2000: 1) notes, 'even though the political regime remained intact, [the] relationship between agents of the state and ordinary citizens had changed' as the market unleashed forces that nurtured individual desires and social networks that sometimes challenged official discourse and conventions. As is evident in Shanghai's gated communities, the commodification of housing and the increasing privatization of the domestic sphere have provided middle-class residents with a new-found level of autonomy, privacy and private space for self-management that was unavailable in the past under the work-unit housing system. As Ong and Zhang (2008: 7) further argue, privatization in China encompasses more than just the dismantling of state enterprises or the spread of private property but is accompanied by a new kind of self-consciousness and self-optimization that liberate citizen-subjects and induce them to pursue a range of self-managing goals in their daily life. With the distancing of the state regulations in what Ong and Zhang (2008) term 'socialism from afar', the proliferation of self-governing practices such as those found in private gated communities is widening the space between the socialist state and everyday activities that are now increasingly under individual control.

Privacy between neighbours and households

In so far as privacy has emerged as an important value in private housing enclaves, the changing social relations between neighbours in gated communities further reflect the prevailing trend and desire for greater seclusion. In commodity housing enclaves, it is common to hear that residents are no longer as close-knit as before in communal neighbourhoods, as residents now retreat into their own private apartments and homes after work. The once common practice of visiting or dropping by neighbours' houses (*chuanmen*) during the daytime or after dinner is no longer prevalent in commodity housing enclaves, as many residents now do not even know how their neighbours are, unlike in older neighbourhoods, where residents are mostly co-workers employed by the same work-unit. As Pellow (1993: 421) notes:

> Neighbouring has changed as the ideal type of housing has changed from *shikumen* to new apartments. Previously, Shanghainese had close relations with their neighbours. They knew each other, cared about each other – even though they also quarrelled with one another about sharing the water tap or kitchen. At dinner time, one could casually drop by a neighbour's house, rice bowl in hand, and be fed. If one were ill, he/she could depend upon neighbours for help. The children always played together. Housewives did their domestic tasks side by side, talking, bragging about their families, laughing at one another. Now in new apartments with private toilets and kitchens, people need not see one another. It is not uncommon to live in the same building for a number of years and not know neighbours' names.

Unlike the convivial atmosphere observed in the traditional old neighbourhoods, residents in gated communities mostly keep to themselves as family life becomes more reclusive and privatized. Like most commodity housing enclaves, the houses in Vanke Garden City are buffered by a small plot of green spaces that marks out the private territory of individual homes. Typically, residents also like to plant short trees and shrubs in their yards and balconies to shield the interior of their homes from public view. Another popular practice is to use curtains and tinted windows to secure the privacy of the interior. In some cases, white picket fences have been constructed to demarcate the private turf of the home from the public streets and to prevent people from trespassing into the yards.

As in most gated communities, residents in Vanke Garden City all close their doors promptly upon reaching home and seldom interact with the neighbours (this is distinct from the 'open-door' policy commonly found in traditional neighbourhoods in the past). In fact, during my one-year stay at Vanke estate, my neighbours usually kept to themselves and most of them did not know who lived next door (see Zhang, 2008, for similar observations on the obsession with privacy and lack of social interaction in Kunming's up-market gated community). In a household survey conducted by Vanke estate management company, none of the residents surveyed indicated 'close neighbourhood relations' as one the most satisfying aspects of living in Vanke; neither are residents concerned with good neighbour-hood relations when they decide to move into Vanke Garden City (Vanke, 2004). In a survey of 1,821 families living in large cities (including Beijing, Shanghai and Guangzhou), it was revealed that only 10 per cent of urbanites actually stay in close contact with their neighbours, whereas 44 per cent of those surveyed said they didn't know the names of the people living next door (*Shanghai Daily*, 25 September 2003). In addition, people also feel that there is a general decline in neighbourhood life and community interaction. One major reason for this decline is that people are now moving into independent apartment units, hence reducing the opportunity and the need to interact with neighbours. But what is more inter-esting is that it was also suggested in the survey that younger-generation urbanites generally enjoy the privacy (and freedom) they have from not knowing the people next door. Although this survey did not target gated communities specifically, such trends are even more pronounced in private gated residences, where a huge premium is placed on privacy. As one respondent revealed in an interview: 'It's quite natural to shut my door immediately after returning home from work, which gives me the feeling of freedom and that I won't be interfered with by others' (quoted in *Shanghai Daily*, 25 September 2003). The same situation was observed by F. L. Wu (2005) in his study on gated communities in Beijing. In particular, he found that anonymity is seen as essential to gated communities in urban China, where the idea of achieving anonymity is 'equivalent to liberation'. For the nou-veau riche in the midst of rising social inequality, the retreat into an anonymous life has even become a necessity, to avoid incurring jealousy and trouble (F. L. Wu, 2005: 248).

When I enquired what having privacy means to residents of gated communities, most of them expressed their sense of privacy in terms of practical advantages or utilitarian values such as more convenience, freedom, and in general improving one's 'quality of life' (*shenghuo shizhi*). One respondent explained that privacy for him simply means that 'I can do what I like to do and be myself' (*zizai*). Another respondent expressed that privacy means that 'I don't have to let other people know the things that I don't want others to know.' Some respondents also emphasized the value of privacy as the need for physical and mental space: 'I can have my own private space' (*siren kongjian*). Many respondents also described privacy as necessary for personal fulfilment and self-development as well as mutual respect and dignity (see also McDougall, 2001). A resident who recently moved into Vanke Garden City commented:

> In my old neighbourhood, everyone knows about even the most private mat-ters about one another. For example, where I grew up, my neighbours know how well I scored in my school exams, whether my family has bought new furniture and even what we cook for dinner. In my own apartment now, I do not have to face nosy neighbours who query endlessly about your private life.

Another resident in Vanke elaborated that:

In the old neighbourhoods, the elderly folks would just sit along the lanes and alleyways to observe and gossip about everything that goes on in the neighbourhood. They have no concept of privacy. If they want, they can know about your whole life. This is one thing that I detest most about living in the old communal neighbourhoods.

Overall, the general decline in social relations and neighbourliness in gated communities reflects the desire for residents to retreat into their own private spaces, unencumbered by the interference of others ('the nosy public'). In contrast to communal neighbourhoods, where each family's life is like an 'open book', residents who move into new commercial housing enclaves clearly welcome the greater sense of privacy, independence and autonomy. However, this new sense of privacy is not always regarded favourably. As Wilson (1988) observes, in many societies, spatial segmentation also brought along with it the possibility of the 'unknown' and suspicious behaviour, hence creating tensions within the community. In particular, when individuals of a community are out of view, it arouses suspicion that they could do things that are out of the ordinary and even threatening to the rest of the group. In a somewhat disapproving tone, Xu, a professor at the Police Officers' Academy at Beijing (quoted in Dutton, 2000: 224), commented that:

In the single-storied multi-family residences of communal neighbourhoods, it can be said that each family's secret is revealed for their lives are like open books. As residents come and go, they all see one another and it is even said that their conversations can be heard between walls and their manners known. Everything is heard and everything is there to see. This quite often leads to these places operating as sites of mutual control. But when they move into the multi-storied apartment buildings, things change. Each family's life becomes a private affair. The comings and goings of people, as well as their activities, becomes difficult for others to know. Why is it that so much of the uncultivated, unhealthy and sometimes even obscene materials and activities, all of which are prohibited, can be discovered and are even popular in these large apartment buildings? These have a lot to do with the way family lifestyles have become private affairs. It has also a lot to do with the fact that other people have no way to keep an open eye on them.

Interestingly, it is precisely this lack of mutual control and concealment from the 'prying eyes of the public' that residents of gated communities found most liberating about their new-found freedom and private lives in gated communities. With the compartmentalization and concealment of private residential spaces, residents of gated communities are able to withdraw into their own private spaces to enjoy a greater sense of autonomy and freedom. As the next section will illustrate, this sense of privacy is further extended to other neighbourhood spaces and is linked to the protection of private property.

Privacy of the neighbourhood and private property

At the entrance of every gated community in Shanghai, the ubiquitous 'Do Not Enter' sign serves as a constant reminder to passers-by not to encroach on private property or disturb the privacy of residents (see Figure 5.4). In Oscar Newman's (1972: 63) terms, these important legible symbols that define clear spatial boundaries marking transition from public to private spaces serve 'to inform that one is passing from a space which is public where one's presence is not questioned through a barrier to a space which is private where one's presence requires justification'.

If the signs are not sufficient deterrent, privately employed security guards that stand guard outside the gates further ensure that trespassers do not enter the estate. Residents of gated communities often stressed the need to preserve the serenity and security of the neighbourhoods but also the greater desire to uphold the 'private status' of their properties by keeping out those who are not part of the community. Unmistakably, these comments not only reflect the concern for privacy but also evince the 'proprietary attitudes' of the residents that revolve solely around 'the owner and that which he owns set against those who might threaten those entitlements' (Blomley, 2004a: 619). At the same time, many also

Figure 5.4 A 'No Entry: Private Residence' sign outside Vanke Garden City. (Source: author's photograph, 2005.)

stress the need to protect their private property and investment. A resident who lives in Pudong New Area insisted that:

> This is a private neighbourhood. Non-residents should not be allowed to walk in and out as and when they like, even though they may not be criminals or pose security threats. They didn't pay for the maintenance and the upkeep of the place and they certainly don't have the right to enter the private estate or make use of the parks and gardens. These belong to the common property of paying residents only.

Another respondent justified the view that that they had 'paid a premium to live in this gated estate. Why should we allow people to come in and intrude upon our private life?'

Residents of gated communities also framed their responses in more legalistic terms, stressing that they are the 'rightful owners' and therefore have the legal right to protect their privacy and investment. By mobilizing the language of private property and the discourse of privacy, residents of gated communities not only are expressing their strong desires to secure the private spaces in their neighbourhoods, but are also actively affirming their proprietary status ('we are the owners') and individual property rights. To be sure, such territorial claims and assertion do not always go unchallenged. For instance, the *Xinhua News* (30 April 2005) reported a conflict between residents of two adjacent gated estates in Shanghai's Baoshan District. Reportedly, residents in the two estates were at odds over who had the right of way over common properties such as the roads and common access areas straddling the two estates. One resident, for example, protested that: 'Even though the residents on the other side had bought a commodity house, they only own their houses but not the road. Why should they have exclusive right to the road?' (quoted in *Xinhua News*, 30 April 2005). In recent years, disputes over access to streets and urban amenities in gated communities have also increasingly surfaced in Shanghai (*Xinmin Evening News*, 8 August 2004; see also Miao, 2003).

Many of my respondents residing in gated communities also assert a sense of individualism by insisting that they are exercising their individual right to protect their private property and private life. As Deborah Davis (2004: 302) notes, when the Chinese leadership relegitimized private ownership and enthusiastically created the new hybrid of market socialism, they opened the way for private real estate development and created the conditions for a new logic of entitlement defined by rules of individual property rights and private ownership. Private ownership has now become the norm (at least for those who can afford it) and the legal system consistently stands on the side of individual property rights as the party-state is pressing for greater monetarization of goods and services. In China's post-socialist property regime, hegemonic discourses on market-based individual property rights seem to prevail as residents of private gated communities deploy the language of private property to assert their prerogatives as 'rightful' property owners and to protect their own immediate interests. In this sense, a market-based logic of entitlement underlines property and exclusionary social relations that are defined in terms of the separation between owners/residents and non-owners/non-residents (*yezhu/fei yezhu*), as well as public/private, self/others. Private property ownership in Shanghai's gated communities is used as a territorializing device that signals proprietary status, ownership and belonging. As such, the lure of private property rests on its promise of exclusivity, individuality and certainty that in turn manifests in a particular set of spatial representations – the gated community being a prime example.

By linking privacy with the defence of private property, I am not subscribing to the 'sceptical' or 'reductionist' view[12] that rejects the inherent value of privacy by reducing it to another value (in this case, the value of property ownership). As Scanlon notes (1975: 318), '[property] ownership is relevant in determining the boundaries of our zone of privacy, but its relevance is determined by norms whose basis lies in our interest in privacy, not (just) in the notion of ownership'. Nonetheless, privacy and property rights are intimately linked in so far as the integrity of privacy rights also depends largely upon the protection of private property rights. In Shanghai's gated communities, privacy stems from the individualist and property-oriented notion that an individual is the sole proprietor or possessor of his or her own private property, independent of others and even the wider society. Privacy in this sense is inherently territorial and characterized by an individualist and possessive right and conception of private property that finds its clearest expression in Shanghai's gated communities. It will be worthwhile in the next section to examine more closely the emergence of such an individualist and possessive view of privacy and how residents in Shanghai's gated communities think about and act in relation to their private property.

It is important to qualify at the outset that individualism in the Chinese context does not necessarily mean the growth of liberal individualism or Western notions of individual rights. Indeed, as Ong and Zhang (2008: 12) argue, in China's evolving neoliberal configuration, economic liberalism has flourished without political liberalism and market individuation has thrived without political liberalism. As will be shown later, whereas individualism was vilified in Maoist China, a selective appropriation of individualism was promoted during the reform era to stimulate economic growth by priming the entrepreneurial powers of the private self through private capital accumulation, self-promotion and property ownership.

Private property, individualism and neoliberal subjectivity

As the preceding discussion has shown, private property ownership as a 'territorializing device' (Blomley, 2004b: 617) in Shanghai's gated communities has enabled residents to lead a relatively secluded and private lifestyle, away from unwanted public interference. Spaces of private property within gated communities thus instantiate notions of private property rights through the territorialization of social–spatial relations, underpinned by the central notion of private property ownership as being unambiguous, individualized and definite (as commonly espoused by neoliberal pundits such as Hernando de Soto, 1989, 2000). Yet, to be sure, the desire for privacy and seclusion in gated communities also reflects the rising trend of individualism and privatism in contemporary urban China, which is consonant with the formation of the neoliberal subject (Larner, 2000; Bondi, 2005; Rofel, 2007). As Blomley (2004b: 614) has pointed out, neoliberalism is, in part, a hegemonic language of property that locates private property as the foundation for individual self-interest and optimal social good (see also N. Smith, 2002). With urban housing reform and the rise of private property ownership in China, it is interesting to note how everyday discourses and proprietary attitudes on private property now revolve around neoliberal ideas about individual ownership centred on the self (and by extension the immediate family) that are ultimately oriented towards the gratification of individual desires via market opportunities.[13]

Like other scholars studying the politics of social transition in contemporary urban China (see, for example, X. Y. Wang, 2002), I am not suggesting that neoliberal values such as individualism and privatism shape or characterize every member of the Chinese urban middle class, just as not everyone in Mao's China fully embodied Communist values such as selflessness and loyalty to the party-state. Rather, the point here is to examine 'the subjectivizing aspect of privatization as a mode of thinking, managing, and actualizing of the self' (Ong and Zhang, 2008: 3) and how individualism and privatism have come to be the defining modes of neoliberal subjectivity in contemporary urban China. Recent scholarship on neoliberalism has examined the transformations in the relationship between capitalism, governance and subjectivity. More than just a political philosophy or economic ideology, neoliberalism when deployed as a form of governmentality[14] makes normative rather than ontological claims about the pervasiveness of market rationality and disseminates these market values to all institutions and social actions. In the process, citizen-subjects are reconfigured as entrepreneurial, rational and calculating individuals whose moral autonomy is measured primarily by their capacity for self-care and personal gain. Yet the emergence of neoliberal subjectivity and values is not without its specific geohistorical context. The ensuing discussion will illustrate how individualism, private property and privacy rights come to intersect in contemporary China.

Possessive individualism

According to Yan's (2003) notable study on rural transition in northeastern China, he notes that post-reform village life reflects the historical trend in the evolution of private life, whereby the family has become more privatized, family life revolves around the husband–wife union, and family members have become more aware of their individual rights, hence demands for their personal space and privacy.[15] In Xiajia, ordinary villagers' quest for privacy has led to the reconstruction of domestic spatiality; at a deeper level, this reflects a growing sense of entitlement to individual rights in private life (Yan, 2003: 39). Similarly, in Shanghai's gated communities, individualism and privatism are often reflected in the residents' claims for individual property rights. In contrast to old communal neighbourhoods, residents in gated communities clearly enjoy a greater sense of privacy and personal spaces. Private spaces in commodity housing enclaves are clearly demarcated, with residents now retreating into their gated enclaves and spending far less time mingling with others. Yet to what extent can the decisions of gated community residents to withdraw into their own private enclaves and their demands to protect their own privacy and private property be considered as acts of individualism?[16] More specifically, how can we understand the relationship between privacy, the rise of private property relations, individualism and neoliberal subjectivity in Shanghai?

After the housing reform, urban residents were no longer 'supplicants' to the state (D. Davis, 2003) in that they are now not beholden to the government for a roof over their heads. Except for the very poor, individuals are largely left to their own devices to secure the best form of housing they can afford. In contrast to public/communal housing provision in the past, housing reform in China has spawned a new commodity housing market and competitive individualistic consumption, whereby the most capable and successful people (*chenggong renshi*) are able to secure for themselves and their families the most expensive and luxurious housing they can afford in exclusive private neighbourhoods. During my interviews with residents of gated communities, new home-owners often pride themselves on having made it to the ranks of the new 'propertied class' in Shanghai through the acquisition of private property – the 'quintessence of individualism' and a sign of personal success. Fraser (2000), for example, notes how commodity housing advertisements often entice buyers with the label of being successful through the slogan 'buy a home and become a boss'.

Buying a home (preferably in a commodity housing enclave in a prime location) is thus a fundamental concern for anyone wishing to climb the ladder of social status and is often considered a 'life-changing experience' (Tomba, 2004: 20). One often heard comment by home-owners is how they have capitalized on market opportunities and made 'a killing' in their housing investment. In local media reports, the housing market is often likened to a 'war zone' and, as one property agent counselled me during an appointment: 'You have to watch the property market very closely (*kanzhun shiji*), do your own preparation ground work (*zuohao zhunbei gongzuo*) and enter the market to seize the day!' Clinching a hot property deal is thus often described in euphoric terms like winning a war that is pitted against other fellow home-buyers eyeing the same lucrative property. In particular, one of the first things that home-owners often tell me during interviews is how the prices of their houses have appreciated many times as a result of their astute investment foresight. On account of the high prices of real estate in Shanghai, many of the residents often used a combination of personal savings and extended family network resources to finance their homes. This includes tapping into the state-mandated Housing Provident Funds (*zhufang gongjijin*)[17] (which are often insufficient), personal and family savings, loans from banks and, most commonly, selling or renting out apartments that either they or their parents had bought earlier at substantial discounts during the initial phase of housing reform. Having purchased the commodity housing and a new private lifestyle through their own 'resourcefulness' as well as family networks, residents of gated communities are often zealous in protecting the privacy of their neighbourhoods. A common attitude among middle-class home-owners is a new-found sense of economic freedom and the relentless pursuit of the good life, often realized through the material possession of the dream home, car and other consumer products. Most of them also feel a sense of entitlement to the good life that comes with private property ownership, having 'worked hard' to capitalize on their skills and market 'talents' in the brave new world of economic reform. As one respondent proudly proclaimed to me:

> We worked hard to own what we have now . . . the apartment, the car, etc. . . . Of course, we were also lucky to buy the property when the prices were not sky-high like now but it's not always about luck, we worked hard and also do our research on the [real estate] market before plunging in. Don't ever think that it is easy, we were practically on our feet visiting newly listed properties every weekend and public holiday when we are not working. It's sheer hard work you know . . . At the end of the day, you really have to rely on yourself to get the best deal.

The economic freedom to pursue a privileged lifestyle brought about through economic reform, however, also feeds into a culture of isolated individualism amongst the middle-class residents in Shanghai's gated communities. In seeking seclusion and privacy behind the gates, residents have largely justified their privileged lifestyle as an entitlement that they rightly deserve through their own hard work and sheer capabilities. The preoccupation with and fixation on defending the exclusivity and privacy of gated communities often reflect a form of 'possessive individualism' in urban China that is tied to private property ownership and the pursuit of self-interests. To some extent, the situation in China may be said to converge with (and diverge from) Western notions of individualism (see, for example, Yan, 2003).

In the (Western) political theory of possessive individualism, society is presumed to consist of relations among independent owners, and the primary task of government is to protect owners against illegitimate incursions upon their property and to maintain conditions of orderly exchange (the recent amendment of Article 13 in the Chinese constitution to protect private property rights of individuals is a case in point; see Chapter 3). The notion of ownership here also draws upon an understanding of property as private and exclusive, entailing the right of owners to exclude others and to use or dispose of their property as they choose. This version of individualism is ultimately justified on the grounds that it is congruent with human nature, for human beings are portrayed as 'bundles of appetites' (the Hobbesian view) that are, in principle, unlimited and not subject to rational scrutiny. 'A social world organized around individuals as owners will, it is said, maximize the satisfaction of such desires' (Carens, 1993: 2). For Macpherson (1962), the ethos of possessive individualism states that the human essence is freedom from dependence on the wills of others, and freedom is a function of possession. Society thus comprises 'free equal individuals' related to each other as proprietors of their own capacities and of what they have acquired by their exercise and diligence. In this sense, society consists of 'relations of exchange between proprietors', and the foundations of an autonomous life lie largely in the concept of ownership whereby the self and the individual dominate (Macpherson, 1962: 3).[18]

But, one might ask, how did such presumably Western notions of individualism and neoliberal subjectivity take root and evolve in China, a country often thought to be steeped in the traditions of communalism and collectivism? As Yan (2005) critically points out, individualism as a value in contemporary Chinese society is often misconstrued by the locals for historical reasons. Whereas individualism was portrayed as a corrupt value of dying capitalist culture in Maoist China, the evil image of individualism was suddenly turned on its head during the post-Mao reform era of the 1980s, because it was rediscovered to be one of the engines of modernization in the West, stimulating individual incentives and economic growth. Yet there has been no serious effort even amongst the Chinese intellectual circles to explore what individualism actually is and how it works in Western culture (Yan, 2005). The moral and ideological vacuum created in the wake of economic reform also meant that individualism for the majority of Chinese denizens is still a self-centred, ultra-utilitarian and hedonistic morality that places self-interest above the needs of others and leaves no room for the consideration of the wider good of society. In Wang's (2002) analysis of the 'post-communist personality' in reform China, she argues that the regime's intention to promote a competitive ethos and to develop a market economy that would promote rapid economic development has resulted in an unintended consequence that aroused a burning desire for individuals rushing 'to get rich first', in the absence of a comprehensive, internally consistent ideology.[19]

Although such a pragmatic notion of individualism appears to emphasize the proprietary and atomistic social relations that define the new private lifestyles of the middle class in Shanghai's gated communities, the efflorescence of such (possessive) individualism expressed by Shanghai's urban middle class should not be conflated with Western/American-style liberal individualism or seen to be diametrically opposed to state rule. As Ong (2008: 183) astutely observes in her penetrating study on 'self-fashioning' urban elites in Shanghai, the individualizing logic and Chinese version of self-proprietorship is not the product of political liberalism but is fostered by conditions produced by the intersections of market freedom and political authoritarianism. In Shanghai's commodity housing enclaves, the middle-class residents know only too well that their newly acquired privileged lifestyle and private properties are as much a product of their own enterprising selves as the privatization opportunities underwritten by the (erstwhile) socialist state. To put it another way, the implicit social contract that exists between the middle-class home-owners and the state ensures that while the former get to live up their 'Chinese dream' of acquiring a nice home (along with all the trappings of the urban good life), the latter, by providing opportunities for that realization, can enhance its legitimacy of rule and count on the support of the emerging propertied middle class, at least for the time being. However, the elusive sociopolitical construct of achieving the elusive 'Chinese dream' is clearly not meant for everyone. As the next chapter will further illustrate, Shanghai's gated communities, built on exclusive consumption rights and exclusionary spatial practices, often rely on a narrowly defined model of 'community' that is centred on the 'rightful' owners and proprietors. Spaces of private property thus become more than simply functional demarcation of property ownership but are also embedded in a moral spatial order that sets apart owners versus non-owners, insiders/residents versus outsiders/non-residents.

Summary

This chapter has provided an analysis of how social–spatial practices of public and private life function and operate in the city, focusing specifically on the transformation of domestic and social life from communal-based neighbourhoods to the 'private lifestyles' in middle-class gated communities. Existing alongside the expansion of these autonomous personal spaces, what is also apparent in contemporary urban life in Shanghai is the increasing privatization of urban neighbourhood spaces as middle-class families retreat behind privately developed and managed commodity housing enclaves where access is based primarily on income, class and lifestyle. For its inhabitants, gated compounds provide a safe haven and create a non-porous private space/sphere that engenders a distinct form of middle-class territoriality.

Whereas gated communities around the world are typically cast in a negative light (such as the bulldozing of public spaces by nefarious 'private' interests), this chapter offers a more nuanced reading of Shanghai's gated community as potentially sites where greater personal and household autonomy and freedom may be negotiated and to some extent realized away from the hegemonic control of the state. The right to privacy in gated communities also mirrors neoliberal claims on individualized property rights and privatism as well as the prevailing ethos of possessive individualism and consumer citizenship. In Shanghai, what is apparent now is the increasing privatization of urban neighbourhood spaces as middle-class families retreat behind gated communities where access is based primarily on income and class. Although this prevailing trend will no doubt exacerbate urban conditions of residential segregation and sociospatial polarization in the city, what needs to be further investigated is precisely how middle-class territoriality and exclusionary processes work in these spaces. This will be the focus of the next chapter.

6 Maintaining order and civility

Purified spaces and the paradox of gated living

> [S]patial boundaries are in part moral boundaries. Spatial separation symbolizes moral order.
>
> (Sibley, 1995: 39)

Introduction

In the autumn of 2004, the local property grapevine in Shanghai was abuzz with news about an impending legal feud between residents of an up-market gated community and a property developer. Reportedly, the residents of Shanghai Spring City – a commodity housing enclave located southwest of the city – were infuriated that the developers had reneged on an earlier promise to fully enclose the entire private housing estate and had taken the developers to court (*Dongfang Morning Post*, 30 November 2004). According to the plaintiff, the developers had broken their contract by allowing several publicly accessible commercial shops and restaurants to operate within the estate's compounds. Among some of the concerns cited by the residents were the loss of neighbourhood exclusivity and security as a result of the developers' actions as well as worries that the 'unruly public' might trample upon and destroy the private facilities in the estate, echoing the classic 'tragedy of the commons' argument. As one resident (quoted in the news report) commented, the shops might encourage outsiders of 'inferior quality' (*di suzhi*),[1] especially migrant workers, to enter the housing estate:

> We are very worried about outsiders entering our neighbourhood, even if they are just here to patronize the shops. Once the shops are opened, all kinds of people will enter our estate and disrupt the order and peace . . . and spoil the image of the neighbourhood.

In a separate incident, when a kindergarten was planned to be built in a private gated community near Vanke Garden City, residents there were worried that the influx of outsiders would lead to a loss of the exclusiveness of their neighbourhood, bringing down the property prices and destroying the pristine environment in the housing estate. The thought of *ah yis* (nannies or domestic maids, usually from rural provinces) with their 'uncouth' manners and 'unhygienic' habits swarming into their neighbourhood with their young charges was enough to turn the residents off the idea of having a child care centre in their private estate, despite the convenience it would bring for some of the families. In addition, some residents I spoke to also expressed concern that the cars and school buses ferrying the children in and out of the neighbourhood would generate significant daily noise and air pollution.

In the cases cited above, a strong moral undertone is palpable in the residents' responses and complaints, coupled with a sense of indignation that their private enclaves were being threatened by the intrusion of 'uncivilized' outsiders. In particular, gated communities manifest a distinct form of territoriality that operates to keep out outsiders by securing private territory as a means of exercising social control. Residents and real estate management companies rely on various territorial strategies and spatial tactics such as constructing high walls and fences, installing high-tech surveillance equipment and employing a legion of private security guards to control and restrict access to these gated enclaves. As Sibley (1988: 416) observes, with the 'social sorting involved in the creation of residential submarkets, the likelihood of encountering difference and otherness is minimized, by the same token, when such encounters do occur, the greater is the likelihood that a moral panic will ensue'.

Residents often expressed fear and worry about outsiders trespassing and 'invading' their private territories and defiling the pristine environment; their concerns were invariably targeted at the hordes of migrant workers that are now flooding the city in search of a living.[2] As this chapter will later demonstrate, gated community residents' anxieties and concern over the looming physical presence of migrant workers and their potentially dangerous and pollutive bodies critically mirror an emergent neoliberal biopolitics that seeks to 'problematise the "quality" (*suzhi*) of China's rural migrant population' as 'the corporeal value of the rural masses is increasingly found wanting' and is often considered out of sync with the new demands of the global economy as well as the sophisticated urban(e) middle-class lifestyle (Ong and Zhang, 2008: 14).

Overall, a strong moral order seems to pervade Shanghai's gated communities where the moralities of places and communities – in Durkheim's (1984 [1893]) sense of a social collective or collective consciousness – are defined in large part against the 'constitutive others', a notion that is fixated on the outsider/migrant worker as an immanent threat and intruder. On the other hand, private property in the form of commodity housing enclaves is held up and valorized as a modern and progressive form of housing arrangement and living environment befitting its cultivated middle-class residents. In so far as the moral order and territorial boundaries of urban places are seen to overlap with boundaries of class cultural distinctions (cf. Bourdieu, 1984),[3] this chapter critically examines the contested moral geographies of gated communities by demonstrating how territoriality, social exclusion and residential segregation in Shanghai's gated communities are underpinned by a strong moral rhetoric that controls and frames spaces according to the purported 'civilized' values of the middle-class residents. By mobilizing a repertoire of morally charged stories, the normative framing of space is, however, not politically neutral or innocent as it excludes those (namely the poor migrant workers) who are deemed not to fit into the civilized landscape visions of gated communities. In this chapter, I argue that these values constitute the moral–spatial order that shapes and structures territoriality and social life in gated communities. By inscribing and mapping the moral–cultural logic onto urban spaces, residents of gated communities thus attempt to 'soften' and 'naturalize' the exclusionary territorial landscape by reconstituting it as the pristine civilized spaces befitting Shanghai's 'cultivated' middle class. At the same time, these moral–spatial discourses are also shaped and inflected by contemporary urban conditions as well as historically rooted ideas in China regarding the 'city' (*cheng*) and the 'countryside' (*xiang*) – between the civilized lifestyles of cultivated urban(e) elites and the rustic and 'uncultured' ways of the peasants and migrant workers (the outsiders) who lead an uneasy existence with the privileged urban class in Shanghai's increasingly segregated spaces.

In the following, I will first examine the moral spatial order underpinning Shanghai's gated communities where the process of 'moral othering' is constituted through the social and ideological construction of migrant workers as uncivilized, dirty and dangerous. Specifically, I want to show how these negative and pathological representations of migrant workers are both invented at particular junctures in China's recent urban reform and transition but also historically embedded in enduring ideas and 'ways of thinking' about 'peasants' (*nongmin*), the mobile or 'floating population' (*liudong renkou*) and 'outsiders' (*waidiren*). In the third section, I will examine how invocations of moral order through the rhetoric of 'civilized modernity' motivate, shape and structure the territorial practices and residential life in gated communities. In particular, it is argued that territoriality in Shanghai's gated communities is constructed and enforced via a moral–spatial regime that is fixated on the subject of the migrant worker/outsider as threat and intruder. Yet just how effective are gated communities in keeping out these undesirable others? As the fourth section will elucidate, despite the housing developers' promises of 'total enclosure' (*quan fengbi*) and seclusion, the boundaries of gated communities are ultimately porous and in a constant state of flux as gated communities are themselves intertwined in a complex and dynamic 'social totality' (D. Mitchell, 2000: 140) in which outsiders/migrant workers play a crucial role in the territorial (re)production of the good life in these gated communities. Even though residents of gated communities may loathe and fear the presence of outsiders in their community, they have to depend invariably on this 'outside labour' to maintain and upkeep their privileged lifestyle in the civilized enclaves. In this sense, gated communities in Shanghai can be viewed as both 'open' and 'closed' spaces and, ultimately, paradoxical landscapes fraught with internal contradictions.

Gated communities as a moral spatial order

Like the suburbs documented in North American cities (Baumgartner, 1988; Jacobs, 1996; Duncan and Duncan, 2003), a strong moral order prevails in Shanghai's gated communities, where an air of tranquillity, harmony and civility seems to permeate social life behind the gates. Such a wholesome environment and social atmosphere are not to be taken for granted and are the results of the concerted efforts by residents and estate management companies to construct a civilized moral enclave that keeps 'undesirable outsiders' from trespassing in neighbourhoods and 'polluting' the pristine environment. In trying to maintain the wholesomeness of their living environment, residents often draw upon moralizing discourses to construct moral geographies of exclusion/inclusion that shape and structure territoriality and social life in gated communities. According to Matless (2000: 522), moral geography may be defined as how

the conduct of particular groups or individuals in particular spaces may be judged appropriate or inappropriate, and the ways in which assumptions about the relationship between people and their environments may both reflect and produce moral judgments.

Closely interconnected with the moral geography of place is the concept of moral order, described as the 'outcome of the operation of shared moral assumptions concerning right and wrong in human action' (Matless, 2000: 524). In George Lakoff's (2002) terms, the moral order describes who has 'moral authority' over whom and who is morally superior and thus possesses greater social power, prestige and stature. Reflecting on the 'political enemy of fear' and its pervasive discourse in contemporary urban policies and debates, Leonie Sandercock (2002) further points out that the 'stranger' and 'outsider' in the city, such as the rural migrant or social deviant, is often seen as a potential threat who will bring chaos into the moral social order of a society – from the imagined community of the nation to that of the familiar neighbourhood. Quoting the works of Ulrich Beck, Sandercock notes that, during unsettling periods of urban disorder and social upheavals, the desire for the logic of order and identity must be reasserted. ' "We" must secure our centrality and they, those who disrupt our homely space, must be pushed out from the centre. They (the strangers and outsiders) are not "like us" and therefore . . . are threatening' (Sandercock, 2002: 206).

To this extent, the moral order of Shanghai's gated communities may be said to be bound up in a cultural production of 'otherness' in which the perceived backwardness and cultural inferiority of outsiders/migrant workers as the 'other' becomes encoded in the moral and symbolic registers of urbanites. Inherent in this moral order is the distancing of the other in social and spatial relationships whereby, in the context of urban China, migrant workers are often cast in the light of abject difference. As Solinger (1999b) quotes:

The [migrants'] thinking, morality, language, and customs are all different, their quality is inferior. The places they inhabit are very likely dirty places . . . They lack a concept of public morality . . . so that behaviour that harms prevailing social customs occur time and time again. City residents are dissatisfied because they disturb normal life and livelihood.

(Wang and Hu, quoted in Solinger, 1999b: 3–4)

These negative views of migrant workers stem in part from the convergence of several official and popular discourses that construct 'peasant' migrant workers (*nongming gong*) as a culturally distinct and inferior category as well as more historically rooted fears about 'outsiders' and 'rootless people', who are often seen as threats to the stability of the traditional Confucian society. The strangeness and negative perceptions of migrant workers are thus products of 'ways of thinking' that are counterposed to the positive identification and valorization of urban(e) ways of life. Yet, as Cahoone (1996: 11) reminds us:

[T]he apparent identity of what appear to be cultural units – human beings, words, meanings, ideas, philosophical systems, social organizations – are maintained in their apparent unity only through constitutive repression, an active process of exclusion, opposition, and hierarchization. A phenomenon maintains its identity in semiotic systems only if other units are represented as foreign or 'other' through a hierarchical dualism in which the first is 'privileged' or favoured, while the other is deprivileged or devalued in some way.

Cohen (1993), in particular, demonstrates how modern intellectual and political elites had transformed China's rural population into the peasantry,[4] a culturally distinct and inferior 'other' that the new socialist state aimed to liberate. Elite representations of the 'peasant problem' often shore up notions of China's peasants as 'passive', 'helpless', 'unenlightened', in the grip of ugly and fundamentally useless customs and desperately in need of education and cultural reform. For the urban elites governing China, this image of the peasant confirmed their own moral claim to an inherently superior, privileged position in national political life (Cohen, 1993: 154–155). Ironically, the enduring legacy of this idea is in part attributable to the powerful reinforcement it has received since the establishment of the Communist government (whose power base is integrally built on the support of peasants and the working class). Under the Communist administration, incorporated into its official and administrative classification of China's population is the distinction between peasants and other categories of persons, such as *gongren* (workers) or *jumin* (urban residents). Even today, peasants in China have second-class citizenship, giving legal confirmation to the second-class culture they earlier had been identified with (Cohen, 1993: 159). As an editorial in the *China Daily* (4 April 2004) notes:

To those familiar with China, . . . [t]he term 'farmer'[5] carries quite different connotations in China from what it does in the West, where farming is a profession taken up by well-educated people and involves large-scale mechanical production. Also known as agricultural industrial workers, farmers have a social status equal to that of urban dwellers. In China, being a farmer is synonymous with low social status. Chinese farmers have a comparatively poor education and live on a small patch of farmland [per capita farmland is less than 1 *mu*, or 1/15 hectare]. Some farmers work in non-agricultural industries, or go to cities as migrant workers, but do not enjoy the same political rights and social guarantees as their urban counterparts.

The 'invented' peasantry in China, associated with growing rural–urban differentiation, is now found in a context of rapid economic development, especially in the cities, that is blurring the very rural–urban gap that encouraged the birth of the peasant idea in the first place. Nevertheless, in China, the idea of the peasant as constituting a distinct and backward cultural category shows no sign of losing its force (Cohen, 1993: 166). Arguably, such negative view of rural life is also the result of an urban bias in official policies under the Communist regime. Development strategies promoted urban industries with capital-intensive technology and established a rationing system to ensure low-priced foods and other necessities as well as guaranteed employment with benefits for most urban employees. Rural inhabitants, on the other hand, were confined to production units where they produced agricultural commodities under strict state planning. Surpluses emanating from the agricultural sector contributed to capital accumulation in urban industries and supported urban-based subsidies. Strict control of urban–rural migration reinforced the segmentation of urban and rural sectors. Not surprisingly, urban life is considered to be far preferable, and living standards and opportunities for such advantages as education are much better in the cities. This view is further entrenched after economic reform that opened up coastal cities, widening the gap and distinction between urban and rural. In the eyes of rural populations, the city and urban lifestyle is seen as the source of the good life whereas rural life, by both absolute and relative standards, is seen to be inferior and lacking. As Zhang notes (2001: 210):

[D]isplaced rurality is viewed as a form of social pollution and another source of illegality. In the discourse on Chinese modernization, peasantry and the countryside are regarded as lagging behind in the nation's march to modernity. Negative images associated with peasantry such as 'low class' (*cengci di*), 'low quality' (*suzhi di*), 'primitive' or 'unenlightened' (*yumei*), ignorant (*wuzhi*) and 'backward (*luohou*) are transferred to the construction of the floating population . . . These residual qualities, presumably derived from the impermeable, deep-rooted, 'dark and poor dispositions' (*liegenxing*) of the peasantry, are considered to be incompatible with the official vision of Chinese modernity and civility.

Furthermore, according to Zhang (2001), when peasant workers began appearing in cities in the early 1980s, they were generally seen by the urban public initially as temporarily displaced outsiders (*waidiren*) who would soon return to their rural origins. As more and more peasants poured into towns and cities, putting stress on urban infrastructure and resources, they came to be regarded as a social problem despite their enormous economic contributions. Spatially and socially detached from their home villages, rural migrants could no longer be directly reached by the rural authority in their places of origin; but at the same time they were considered outsiders by city officials. Hence, without a clear structural position in the reform Chinese society, migrants appeared detached from the existing social system and became a people of 'prolonged liminality' – belonging neither to the rural nor to the urban society (Zhang, 2001: 27). This liminal status in turn reinforces another set of disparaging discourses that cast rural migrant workers as outsiders and strangers who are out of place in the city. To compound the issue further, Fan (2002), in her study on Guangzhou's labour market segmentation, points out that temporary migrant workers often find themselves situated at the bottom of the occupation hierarchy in the city as a result of the unequal 'institution-based opportunity structure' that could be traced to the migrants' lack of urban residential status (*hukou*). As a result of their disadvantaged institutional positions, temporary migrant workers are often channelled to low-paying and undesirable jobs, thereby further reinforcing their marginal status as inferior outsiders (see also Roberts, 1997, 2002).

According to Yi-fu Tuan (1986), outsiders by implication belong to a lower order in many societies. They are strangers who have not submitted to local culture at its best. They are raw, unpredictable and dangerous. The existence of outsiders is a result of the prior existence of a classificatory system that inscribes familiarity and order in an otherwise chaotic world. The migrant worker in Shanghai is a case in point. In particular, migrant workers are often seen as outsiders who threaten the morality and social order of the city. This fear and suspicion of outsiders is an enduring theme that resonates in many historical studies on urban Chinese societies. For example, William Rowe's (1989) study on the port city of Hankow during the nineteenth century reveals how labourers, refugees, vagabonds and beggars were often denigrated as 'rootless people' who summoned up a 'pathology of fear' and distaste in the public consciousness of the port city's permanent residents. According to Rowe, the local hostility these rootless people attracted resulted in part from their unsettled status, which made them appear prone to criminal and deviant behaviour; basically they were outsiders who, by staying, had violated the rules of the game. In Hankow, more established citizens by no means welcomed the growing number of mobile and 'rootless' people, also termed *wu-lai* (literally 'having no place to turn'). As Rowe (1989: 217) notes:

> Owing allegiance to no man, without a guarantor or frequently even familial responsibilities to impel them to social respectability; *wu-lai* were flesh and blood hungry ghosts. Even had their conduct been exemplary, they were by definition a threat to stable Confucian society, urban as well as rural.

Drawing a parallel with urban life in early modern European cities such as Paris, Rowe further notes how a pathology of fear on the part of the city's established citizenry tends to label growing numbers of manual labourers as 'dangerous classes', 'as a race apart, a savage people more beasts than men and a growing confusion between predatory criminal elements and the urban lower classes' (W. Rowe, 1989: 243). This fear of outsiders is also reflected in Philip Kuhn's (1990) study on the Chinese sorcery scare in 1768, in which suspicions of sorcery, in particular 'soul-stealing' by allegedly clipping off the ends of men's queues (pigtails worn during the Qing dynasty by royal decree), were often targeted at wanderers, vagrants and mendicants, generally considered as people without roots, of obscure origins and uncertain purposes as well as people lacking social connections and hence 'out of control'. To the bureaucratic mind, wandering beggars of any sort threatened public security. People without homes and families were out of control and posed a threat to the stability of society and were a source of moral pollution. Kuhn (1990: 117) further observes that in a Chinese society fearful of strangers:

> [S]ocial outcasts gained a peculiar power, precisely because they themselves were already so polluted or so unlucky that they seemed neither for social 'face' nor for cosmological fortune. The mere 'touch' of the queue- or lapel-clipping beggar was enough to awaken fears of lethal pollution.

The fear of strangers, social outcasts and deviants is further explored by Sommer (2000: 96), who notes that during the Qing dynasty 'the bogey of the Qing judiciary was the marginal man, the "rootless rascal" or the *guang gun* (literally a bare stick) who stood outside of (and presumably opposed to) the family-based social and moral order that underpinned the late imperial state'. In terms of the semantic development of the term *guang gun*, Sommer interestingly notes that the word *gun*, which means a stick or a club, was applied metaphorically to a man who stands alone without roots or branches. The word thus implies both a lack of socializing ties and the roguery that resulted. The prefix *guang*, which means bare, naked and alone, emphasizes poverty and the lack of a wife. In sum, a *guang gun* was a man with no wife, family and moral order. This outside male was considered an aggressive penetrator in sexual and symbolic terms: 'he ruptured the boundaries of the household and threatened to violate the women (and young boys) within' (Sommer, 2000: 97). This sexual predator was moreover a subset of a more general stereotype of the dangerous male outsider that ran through Qing legal discourse and had been described variously as being 'violent' (*xiong*), 'wicked' (*er*), 'licentious' (*yin*) and a 'depraved rogue' (*diao tu*).[6]

In traditional Chinese society, transient populations were often considered dangerous, culturally and morally inferior, and a threat to the stability of the staunchly Confucian society. The preceding discussions have examined how prejudice and bias against outsiders and strangers in China are complex and stem from the convergence of several official and popular discourses. Just as the tramp was being 'made up' in the United States during the late nineteenth century as a product of *different* 'ways of thinking' (Cresswell, 2001), the same can be said about the perception of outsiders and strangers in China. In contemporary Chinese urban society, rural migrant workers are 'doubly marginalized', first by their ambiguous social position as outsiders in the city bearing no urban residential status or *hukou* and second by their inferior 'peasant' label. As will be shown in the following discussion, the discriminating attitudes against outsiders/migrant workers in the city persist unabated as migrant workers in Shanghai are treated with great suspicion by urban residents and even loathed and feared. An interesting parallel may be drawn here with Anderson's (1991) study on racialized processes behind the historical construction of Vancouver's Chinatown and the attendant moral/cultural domination of the Europeans. As the ensuing discussion will illustrate, just as the white majority in Vancouver came to understand Chinese people to be irredeemably different from themselves and regarded the ethnic landscapes of Chinatown as 'naturally unsanitary', middle-class residents of gated communities in Shanghai similarly constructed a moral geography of 'otherness' that puts migrant workers as well as places associated with them as morally and culturally inferior. A perennial concern among the urban middle-class residents in Shanghai's gated communities is the 'uncivilized' influence of migrant workers and the threats these unruly outsiders pose to the safety and orderly living environment of the community. Thus, residential landscapes in Shanghai's gated communities served to reaffirm a moral order of 'us' and 'them' (Anderson, 1991). Interestingly, whereas studies on social exclusion often focus on the discrimination of the 'racialized others', the case of China's migrant workers demonstrates how exclusionary practices and discrimination can also occur within same racial/ethnic groups and among fellow citizens. The next section will examine in detail how such exclusionary practices operate through the moral rhetoric of civilized order in gated communities.

Securing the good life within civilized enclaves

As the threat of invading hordes of peasant migrant workers looms large in the consciousness of many urbanites in Shanghai, securing a safe and wholesome living environment away from these threats takes on paramount concern and significance. By buying into gated communities, affluent middle-class people in Shanghai strive to establish themselves as refined residents living in civilized enclaves that are fortified against masses of 'uncultured' and dangerous outsiders. At the centre of this moral geography is the notion of being 'civilized' (*wenming*) or 'civilized modernity' (*xiandai wenming*), the buzzwords associated with urban modernity in contemporary China. In Shanghai, the importance of maintaining a civilized modern living environment is highlighted by an annual campaign in which residential estates throughout the city vie to be awarded the official title of 'Civilized Residential Quarter' (*wenming xiaoqu*) by the local district government (Figure 6.1).

Significantly, whether a housing development is enclosed and gated or not is an important criterion in deciding if a housing community is awarded the coveted title by district officials (Miao, 2003: 49). Practically all private gated communities I have seen or visited in Shanghai have been awarded the civilized title (almost by default). To be sure, the term 'civilized modernity' reverberates widely in commercial advertisements, newspapers, magazines and government propaganda

Figure 6.1 A 'Civilized Model Quarter' plaque awarded by the Shanghai municipal government outside a gated community in Shanghai. (Source: author's photograph, 2005.)

in Shanghai. All across the city, banners and posters promoting the building of modern 'spiritual civilization' (*jingshen wenming jianshe*) refer to the Communist Party's promotion of a code of public morality and etiquette that is aimed at serving economic modernization. Chinese citizens are further cajoled through endless government campaigns and public education to behave in the appropriate civilized manner befitting citizens of a modern nation-state (see Chapter 5). Selected government offices and institutions are also labelled as 'civilized units' (*wenming danwei*). In major cities such as Shanghai, municipal departments in charge of overseeing the modernization/civilization task (*wenming banshichu*) have also been set up. In a recent crackdown on Internet dissidents, the Chinese government announced that new steps to control information available on the Internet were implemented to foster 'healthy and civilized' news dissemination.

Although the political mobilization of the term 'civility' or being 'civilized' is often linked to social control and even political repression, the moral rhetoric of civility and civilized modernity in China encompasses a broader national/modernizing discourse that is aimed at building an orderly and socially cohesive nation.[7] Here, the discourse on civility in China may be compared with Norbert Elias's (1939/1982) study on Europe's 'civilizing process'[8] during its state formation period from the sixteenth to the eighteenth century. According to Elias (1939/1982: 5), the discourse of civilization serves to sum up 'everything in which Western society over the last two or three centuries believes itself superior to earlier societies or "more primitive" contemporary ones'. The concept of 'civilization' can refer to a variety of facts: the level of technology, the type of manners, the type of dwelling or the manner in which people live together. In this sense, civilization implies a progress along a scale from less civilized to more civilized and is often identified with (Western) advanced industrial nations, in comparison with which China is perceived as less civilized. In contemporary Chinese state, the civilized discourse through the concept of *wenming* has been strongly promulgated by the state as an effort to advance the Chinese people towards greater heights of civilization and modernity.

The Chinese concept of *wenming* also encompasses several related meanings such as when describing China's glorious historic past. For an old imperial formation such as China, civilization or *wenming* could be seen mainly as a process in terms of the spread of virtues from the moral centre (based in capital cities such as Beijing) to barbarians and people with 'depraved' customs (Duara, 2004). The notion of civility is also used in the (Chinese) Marxist distinction between material civilization (*wuzhi wenming*) and spiritual civilization (*jingshen wenming*). As such, the idea of 'civilized' is not entirely a foreign importation nor is it a recent invention in China. Another point worth noting is the flexible and often polymorphous character of the term 'civilized' that can be used to serve state policy in various ways (such as controlling the flow of dissident Internet information). As Brownell (1995: 172–173) contends, civilization is a concept in the name of which the state can invade the most minute actions of the citizen's body, because it is so polymorphous that 'there is almost nothing which cannot be done in a "civilized" or "uncivilized" way' (Elias, 1939/1982: 3). It provides a rationale for the state's permeation of everyday practice, which spirals out from Beijing, the centre of the civilizing process. In the name of civilization, the state can also appeal to feelings of nationalism and patriotism. The discourse of civilization is both inward and outward looking.

In urban China, the discourse on civility can be further traced back to the urban reform period between 1895 and 1937, when urban reformers in China sought to remake Chinese cities by promoting new types of orderly and productive urban community that drew from the Japanese concept of *bunmei* (civilization) or *wenming* in Chinese (Stapleton, 2000). Through urban reforms in the New Policies of the late Qing initiated in 1901 and later the City Administration Movement in the 1920s, reformers hoped to strengthen China by promoting civilized values and practices, such as improving public health, public safety, trade and civic pride in urban centres, thereby increasing the capacity of the state to harness the energies of the populace for national development. In a similar spirit, the moral discourse of civilized modernity found in gated communities in contemporary Shanghai reflects the desire to promote what are often considered progressive civilized values and an orderly living environment. More critically, the civilized discourse has also been mobilized by urban elites against the lower and 'morally inferior' classes, in this case against migrant workers.

If the civilized discourse in China is fundamentally a 'discourse of lack' and 'absence' that signals the failure of Chinese masses to embody international standards of modernity, civility and discipline (Anagnost, 1997: 76), the civilized discourses and 'labelling' that revolve around Shanghai's middle-class gated communities then symbolize the elite status of its inhabitants as having arrived at the threshold of a civilized modernity. To this extent, the moral discourses of civilized modernity in Shanghai constitute the core of the moral–spatial order that underpins and shapes territoriality and exclusionary practices in gated communities while valorizing those who reside in these civilized modern enclaves as being morally and socially superior. One important aspect of this civilized moral order in gated communities lies in the aesthetic production of landscape and the preservation of scenery, 'the look' of a place (*fongjing*). As Setten (2004: 399) points out, aesthetics are closely linked to moral considerations – landscapes should be tidy and clean and pleasant to look at, without things that don't belong there. This visual consumption of an aesthetically pleasing environment (*youmei huangjing*) and scenic landscape emphasizes the 'scenic morality' of place that revolves around various aesthetic features in gated communities such as the beautiful landscape gardens with man-made lakes and rivers, manicured lawns with exotic flowers, as well as grandiose Western-style architecture (see Figure 6.2).

Advertising brochures for gated communities often describe their internal housing landscapes using lyrical Chinese phrases that evoke the aesthetic/moral qualities of landscape such as *xiaoqiao liushui* (small bridges and running water) and *qingsan lushui* (green mountain with clear water). As Chapter 4 has highlighted, the marketing of the good life in gated communities often capitalizes on an aestheticized landscape that signifies the high taste (*gao pingwei*) and refined or elegant (*youya*) status of its inhabitants. Yet, as Duncan and Duncan (2003: 31) ask, '[w]hat does it mean to view something aesthetically?' Normally, to take an aesthetic attitude towards something is to react to it sensually, not analytically – not by looking beneath its surface to study or criticize the underlying social

Figure 6.2 Genteel landscapes in Vanke Garden City with workers pruning the garden in the background. (Source: author's photograph, 2005.)

relations and other conditions of its production or reproduction. Whatever is aesthetic – picturesque landscape, for instance – is seen as having value in its own right. Its existence is necessarily interdependent with other (often unjust) processes – economic, political or social – that remain unappreciated. There is also a class and ethnic basis to a particular aesthetic that helps to secure the hegemony of certain groups. Duncan and Duncan (2003: 31) further quote Terry Eagleton, who contends that:

> [T]he aesthetic is from the very beginning a contradictory, double-edged concept. On the one hand, it figures as a genuinely emancipatory force – as a commodity of subjects now linked by sensuous and fellow-feeling rather than by heteronomous law, each safeguarded in its unique particularity while bound at the same time into social harmony . . . On the other hand, the aesthetic signifies what Max Horkheimer has called a kind of 'internalized repression', inserting social power more deeply into the very bodies of those it subjugates, and so operating as a supremely effective mode of political hegemony.

For Tuan (1995), the pursuit and enjoyment of beauty and aesthetics are full of paradoxes and contradictions. On the one hand, the enjoyment of the aesthetic moments (the aesthete, for example, may take a childlike delight in transient and disconnected moments) is sometimes considered irresponsible and flippant as it does not attempt to examine the consequences that these aesthetic endeavours may have on human life, society and nature. On the other hand, aestheticism, backed by sufficient power, can also be a driving passion for power control and manipulation. As Tuan observes (1995: 19): 'The cosmetic effort that begins modestly as a rearrangement of one's hair or as the paving of a footpath of one's garden may end, in the megalomania of dictator-aesthete, in the desire for a total transformation of society and nature'.

To this extent, the hegemonic aesthetic value manifested in gated communities and the moral rhetoric of civilized modernity that framed these privileged landscapes served to legitimize territoriality, exclusion and urban segregation in gated enclaves. In particular, as Setten (2004) notes, the moral aesthetic of place is a concept that brings out binary descriptions – in this case, outsiders, especially the uncivilized migrant workers, and their cultures are deemed unfit in the aesthetic environment of gated communities. For the residents, the scenic morality might be thwarted by the unsightly presence of shabbily dressed migrant workers and their uncouth manners. When I asked residents why an enclosed residential estate is preferable, the typical answer was to protect the scenic environment (*youmei de huanjing*), the aesthetic landscape and view (*jingguan*) of their neighbourhood from outsiders who may defile the beauty of the residential landscape with their uncouth behaviour and unsightly presence. The middle-class residents' preoccupation with and fixation on preserving the beauty of the landscape in gated communities thus reveal the 'dark side' of aestheticism and romanticism as leading towards an inward-looking and exclusionary pursuit of personal desires and enjoyment.

Closely intertwined with the aesthetic aspect of landscape are other 'progressive' and civilized values that emphasize the safety (*zhian*), order (*cixu*) and environmental hygiene (*huanjing weisheng*) of neighbourhoods. Together these civilized values constituted the overarching moral (spatial) order that underpinned the territoriality of gated communities. In the following, I will elaborate the functions of these moral–spatial orders and explain how each shapes territoriality and social life in gated communities. Although the different moral orders are analytically separate, in practice they are often overlapping concerns that motivate and shape territorial practices in the gated communities.

Neighbourhood safety and migrant criminality

In September 2004, local residents in Shanghai were gripped by media reports about the disappearance of a 13-year-old school girl in the Zhabei district who was later found to have been abducted by a migrant worker from Chongqing, a city in southwestern China. (Zhaibei district in Shanghai is known to have a large 'floating population' and many migrant workers.) According to the police, a 23-year-old migrant worker was so enamoured by the good-looking young teenage girl that he abducted and sexually assaulted her while on her way home from school. What was even more alarming and outrageous was that the abductor had allegedly transported the girl forcibly back to his rural village hometown in Chongqing and forced her into marriage. The crime was finally uncovered about a week later when the Shanghai police, following a lead, located the girl's whereabouts and arrested the man. In the following weeks, the local media were rife with reports analysing the threats of migrant criminality and warned parents to teach their children to be wary of strangers.

In the Minhang district, it was further reported that crimes committed by migrant workers have been increasing steadily ever since the reform policy was adopted. A director of Minhang District Public Security Bureau claimed that 80 per cent of all crimes in the district were committed by migrants (*Shanghai Daily*, 19 November 2004). Negative representations of migrant workers are sometimes reinforced by academic research that inadvertently casts migrant workers as both deprived and depraved. For instance, a recent Chinese Academy of Social Science (CASS) study reports that:

Long separation from their wives has made the suppression of sexual needs a widespread problem among migrant workers, who have been found to be connected with a large number of recent rape cases in China. Although about 28 percent of the migrant workers brought their wives with them, they still rarely had sex because their small home was usually shared with other couples due to financial difficulties. The lack of a private room greatly reduced migrant couples' opportunities to be intimate. Most of the migrant workers said they often felt nervous and depressed. They suffered from sex illusions from time to time due to the repression of their physical needs. About 31 percent of the workers said they felt a strong sexual desire when they saw women, and about 70 percent of the men said they often looked at pornographic books and videos. As for the question of how they chose to deal with these strong feelings of sexual need, about 40 percent of them said they had no choice but to repress such urges. Another 30 percent said they would think of ways to satisfy these desires, but refused to tell how they would do so. Although these long periods of unsatisfactory sex life may have caused some migrant workers to turn to sexual violence, their understanding of the dangers posed by contagious social diseases seems to have improved in the past few years.

(*Shanghai Star*, 11 November 2004)

The above are just a sample of some recent reports on migrant workers in Shanghai. Since the mid-1980s, discourse on the criminality of migrant workers has proliferated nationally. Official reports, mass media, popular reportage literature and social science research on the 'floating population' have attempted to document and understand, and sometimes exaggerated, crime and criminality among migrants. As Zhang (2001: 139) notes, newspaper reports and magazines are often interested in 'spicy, exaggerated stories' about crime, drugs and prostitution associated with the floating population in order to attract readers. Although some of these reports and stories are not without some basis, many of them are highly exaggerated and distorted as they circulate among urban residents.

Like a stream without a source, these images and anecdotes circulate in the city, eventually running together to become elaborate myths that shape the popular urban imagination about migrants and their communities. Through repetition, circulation, and expansion, these fantasies, desires and facts merge to construct the 'reality' of the migrant communities.

(Zhang, 2001: 140)

Dominant representations of migrant workers tend to portray them as potentially dangerous people such as sexual predators or people prone to violent, antisocial behaviour and other vices because they are considered to be unconstrained by local mores and customs that bind them back in their hometowns. Local public opinion on migrant workers also frequently vacillates from more ambivalent attitudes of grudging acceptance to more extreme forms of moral repugnance and fear. Interestingly, it is not only the absence of social constraints that is considered to predispose migrant workers towards criminal conduct. Many respondents also noted how the low social status and by extension the 'inferior quality' (*di suzhi*) of migrant workers in the city also makes them less concerned with the propriety of their actions, as they do not face the same social disapprobation as higher-status people such as the more 'respectable' middle- and upper-class urban residents. Thus, as Elias (1939/1982: 238) observed: 'In dealing with those lower down the social scale, they do not need to restrain themselves, they can "let themselves go"'. For migrant workers, who are perceived as lacking in civilized values, their purported criminal inclinations and propensity to 'let go' of civilized behaviour and values thus become in keeping with, and even reinforce, their low social status. During my stay in Vanke Garden City, when an apartment was broken into, accusations were immediately levelled at the migrant workers in nearby neighbourhoods.

Despite the enclosed housing management, petty thefts were still very common. More than half of my respondents who lived in Vanke had experienced some sort of theft, ranging from stolen bicycles to shoes, flower pots, and clothes that were left to dry on the balcony. Residents often blamed lax security for allowing wandering migrant workers to enter the neighbourhood to commit thefts (ironically, many of the security guards are migrant workers). The fear of migrant criminality is further exacerbated by news reports of break-ins and even murders committed in up-market gated communities by migrant workers. (Several high-profile cases were reported recently including the brutal murder of a famous TV personality in his gated home.) Consequently, the threat of migrant criminality led residents of gated communities to be even more vigilant and paranoid about the threat of intrusion by migrant workers and outsiders. To secure the safety of the neighbourhood, a number of security measures aimed at fortifying the territories of gated communities were enforced. These included constructing even higher gates and walls (above two metres), installing surveillance equipments as well as deploying security guards at the neighbourhood entrances to 'screen out' non-residents, especially suspicious-looking migrant workers. Within gated compounds, security guards regularly patrol the neighbourhood to look out for trespassers or signs of security breaches (see Figure 6.3). For the security guards, territorial control of access into gated communities is required to protect private property and the safety of residents from the threat of marauding migrant workers. Concern for the safety of the neighbourhood (and being answerable for any security breaches) thus shapes and defines the territorial practices of guards. Exerting territorial control in Shanghai's gated communities is thus underpinned by normative concerns for securing the civilized order and safety of private neighbourhoods (see also Herbert, 1996).

As the preceding discussion has highlighted, territoriality and segregation in gated communities reflect the underlying public perception and fear of migrant criminality. If keeping out migrants and crime is of utmost concern in gated communities, maintaining order (*cixu*) and a regulated (*guifan*) environment are further crucial factors reinforcing the territorial imperatives of gated communities.

Maintaining order and civility

Enforcing physical/social order (*cixu*) is considered an important requisite for maintaining a civilized living environment in gated communities. This includes controlling the orderly flow of human and motorized traffic in and out of the neighbourhood, ensuring orderly conduct of residents and visitors and making sure that an orderly and harmonious life prevails in the neighbourhood (see Figure

Figure 6.3   The omnipresence of security guards in military uniforms patrolling the estate
in Vanke Garden City. (Source: author's photograph, 2005.)

6.4). Furthermore, it is also imperative that the physical landscape and layout in
gated communities are kept neat and tidy at all times with every minute detail
in the neighbourhood following a systematic and rational order that is planned
according to the developer's blueprint and housing regulations. For example,
the streets in gated communities are all laid out in orderly grids (with specified
dimensions) and the houses are all evenly spaced out and subdivided systematically into different zones and areas.

Within the estate, street lamps, benches and even rubbish bins all follow a
uniform design to create an overall impression of orderliness and homogeneity.

Figure 6.4 Maintaining the 'civilized order' in the neighbourhood. (Source: author's photograph, 2005.)

Signs in gated communities remind residents and visitors to adhere to rules in the estate, and housing covenants further specify various regulations that residents have to abide by in order to maintain an orderly and harmonious living environment. Any signs of disorder or clutter such as even stray litter on the street or a misplaced bicycle left on the pavement are promptly rectified. As a member of the management in Vanke Garden City emphasized to me, everything in the estate must be kept in a neat and orderly fashion (*jinjin you tiao*), following strictly the housing plans and regulation (*guifan*), leaving nothing chaotic or disorderly (*luan*) in sight. This apparent visual homogeneity and order of gated communities is, however, not to be taken for granted.

To ensure that the physical and social order of the neighbourhood is well maintained, a prime objective in gated communities is to keep out unruly 'troublemakers' from trespassing into the estate and 'messing up' the internal order and peace. Invariably, threats to the civilized order in gated communities are seen to come from migrant workers, who are often perceived to be disorderly in conduct, lacking in basic civil etiquette and ignorant of the concept of order and civility. Related to the civilized value of an orderly environment is 'discipline' (*jilu*). The discourse of civilization in contemporary China, as Brownell (1995: 25) points out, also goes hand in hand with the promulgation of 'techniques of discipline'. Foremost, self-discipline has been seen as an important concept since the founding of the People's Republic of China (PRC) and is being promoted by the state to shape and spur the productivity of the industrial workforce (see, for example, Rofel, 1999). The lack of discipline and, by extension, lack of civilized and orderly behaviour are often considered characteristics that afflict the poor moral fibre and inferior cultural disposition of migrant workers.

In Vanke Garden City, disciplining and regulating workers' conduct (many of whom are migrant workers employed at below minimum wages) are considered crucial for maintaining a civilized and well-ordered neighbourhood. For example, the uniforms of all workers in Vanke estate are carefully colour-coded and differentiated according to their tasks and occupational rank. At the top of the hierarchy are the estate management officers and managers, who are dressed in grey business suits; the security guards all wear the same navy blue coat (during winter) and green camouflage shirt and trousers (in summer); the technicians are assigned green overalls; and the cleaners and gardeners (lowest rank in the hierarchy) are dressed in standard red and beige uniforms. According to the regulations in Vanke, workers are not allowed to wander freely in the neighbourhood, and are restricted to certain areas in the neighbourhood such as their resting quarters (typically a crammed storeroom), the work areas assigned to them and the communal staff canteen. When moving from point to point, all workers (except senior management staff) are required to walk in single file and refrain from talking or laughing. Each worker is also assigned and identified by an employee identification number tag (*gonghao*) that makes it easy to keep track of them. A memeber of the management staff explained to me that these rules and management techniques are put in place to instil discipline in the otherwise unruly migrant workers and also to create the impression of a well-managed environment befitting the professional image of the property company. Such 'disciplinary techniques' are thus aimed at forging a docile and productive labouring class to service the highly lucrative real estate market in China (see also Rofel,1999).

On the whole, the physical and social order observed in gated communities is matched by an orderly and disciplined work force that constitutes the backbone of gated communities. More fundamentally, to maintain order and civility in gated communities, territorial control of space needs to be enforced in order to keep out outsiders who might disrupt the neighbourhoods with their unruly ways. To the extent that territoriality in gated communities is conditioned and shaped by strong moral concerns for safety and order, closely related to this is the desire to protect hygiene and the wholesome living environment in private neighbourhoods.

Hygiene and the 'purification' of space

Environmental hygiene (*weisheng huanjing*) is often considered another hallmark of a civilized and modern living environment. Here the concepts of dirt and purity are often invoked to justify territorial segregation and exclusion. Within gated communities, maintaining a sanitized and clean (*ganjing*) living environment free from pollution and diseases is of utmost importance, especially after the outbreak of the severe acute respiratory syndrome (SARS) epidemic in 2003. This includes the daily cleaning services provided by a legion of cleaners and sanitation workers to make sure that the living environments are kept clean and salubrious. Motorized vehicles including cars and motorcycles are restricted from entering certain zones in gated communities to prevent pollution from exhaust fumes. Rubbish bins in gated communities are emptied promptly every few hours and the streets and gardens are kept litter free. It was reported that some gated communities even have their own water purification system to supply residents with hygienic and potable water. In order to maintain the hygiene and cleanliness standard in gated communities, it is deemed necessary to prevent unsanitary elements from entering and polluting the neighbourhood. As Ruth Rogaski (2004) notes in her study on the meanings of health and disease in China at the turn of the twentieth century, the concept of hygiene or *weisheng* is not a neutral term and its significance lies beyond the mere concern for cleanliness. According to Rogaski (2004: 105):

> Translations of Western sciences about hygiene were produced in Shanghai and circulated in treaty-port cities like Tianjin. *Weisheng* was intertwined with desire, a desire for modernity – often marked as foreign – that existed just out of reach for most local Chinese. Ultimately *weisheng* as 'hygienic modernity' had a tremendous power to shape political and social realities in China, particularly when new terms of habit and hygiene standards being were enforced by occupying armies.

The modern life of Shanghai at the turn of the twentieth century in particular was marked by its desirable state of hygiene. For the urban elites and sophisticated middle class in treaty ports such as Shanghai and Tianjin, hygienic modernity was easily obtainable through the purchase of imported health and sanitary products ranging from German antibacterial medicated liquid ('keeping the skin supple and bacteria free') to Lysol household disinfectant and American Standard toilets. However, for the Chinese masses, hygienic modernity lay far away, obtainable only through a medical revolution or a moral revolution that could bring the absolute standards of the West to China (Rogaski, 2004: 226).

In contemporary Shanghai, middle-class residents in gated communities pride themselves on having refined hygienic sensibilities that separate them from the impoverished masses of 'dirty' (*zhang*) migrant workers and urban poor in old neighbourhoods. In contrast to the latter, gated communities are equipped with modern sanitation facilities. The landscape and surroundings are kept immaculately clean with everything in gated communities abiding by modern hygiene standards. Yet the desire for hygienic modernity might be thwarted by the intractable presence of the dirty migrant workers, or even by the invisible germs of disease inherent within their bodies. Public discourses in Shanghai often frame the migrant workers as being ignorant of even the most basic hygiene knowledge and practices. In addition, migrant workers are also said to be fond of unhygienic habits such as spitting, defecating/urinating in public spaces and polluting or defiling the environment (see Solinger, 1999a; Zhang, 2001). Elias (1939/1982) in particular noted how taboos and restrictions of various kinds surrounded the ejection of saliva in many societies, both 'primitive' and 'civilized'. In the latter, the prohibited tendencies stem from not just feelings of shame and repugnance, but also a 'more clearly transparent and law-like picture of specific diseases and their "pathogens"' (Elias, 1939/1982: 133; Illich, 2000). However, this rational understanding of the danger of sputum as a carrier of illness was attained only at a very late stage of the change in civilized behaviour in the nineteenth century. Even then, the reference to what is indelicate and disgusting in such behaviour still appeared separately, alongside the reference to its ill effects on health. As such, the social repugnance at the 'coarse' habits of spitting (as well as defecating in public) stems not only from concern about its miasmal effects but also what is considered the moral deficiency (lacking in civility) of migrant workers, even though health and moral concerns are clearly inseparable.

Another case in point is during the SARS outbreak in China in 2003, when many gated communities in the city enforced strict territorial controls including closing all additional side gates and entrances and 'screening' visitors entering the neighbourhood. During the outbreak, migrant workers were also blamed for transmitting the virus (SARS was believed to have originated in Guangdong province in southern China and later spread to other parts of China, including Shanghai and Beijing). More alarmingly, some of the urban residents also expressed fear that migrant workers might be potential carriers of communicable diseases such as tuberculosis or even HIV (migrant workers from the Henan, Shanxi, Yunnan and Sichuan provinces are especially the target of such discrimination due to recent media reports of the high rate of HIV infection among the rural population as a result of the illegal sale of contaminated blood in these provinces).[9] Overall, migrant workers are considered to be lacking in civilized values and failing to conform to the civilized standards in the city.

Just as the disciplining of migrant labour force in Shanghai's gated communities is centred on producing and controlling the docile and productive bodies of migrant workers, the problematization and denigration of migrants in the broader social sphere as uncivilized, backward and pollutive is further entrenched in an emergent neoliberal biopolitics that valorizes the 'self-enterprising' and 'progressive' individuals deemed to possess the requisite skills to take on the new market-oriented economy. As Ong and Zhang (2008: 14) observe, post-Mao biopolitics in China requires a new kind of ethical training in order for self-promoting subjects to manage their lives through the pursuit of private interest, but within political limits set by the authoritarian state. Foremost for the Chinese state, 'political control is exercised through the profiling of different social groups perceived to be more or less aligned with new norms of competitiveness and profitability' with the 'elite proponents stress[ing] the need for the labouring masses to improve personal attributes such as civility and self discipline in order to sustain China's role as a global player' (Ong and Zhang, 2008: 14). As Greenhalgh and Winckler (2005) further point out in their study on the governmentalization of population in China, after the founding of the PRC in 1949 managing the population became a central object in the exercise of statecraft. In particular, many of China's leaders have regarded tackling the size and 'backwardness' of China's population as an urgent task, with government policy focused initially on the location of the population (keeping rural people out of cities), but gradually coming to focus on its 'quantity' (slowing growth and limiting size) and 'quality' (enhancing not only health and education but also social morality and political commitment).[10]

In Shanghai's gated communities, the profiling and spatial sorting out of migrants and urban poor further reinforce an *embodied* neoliberal politics that imposes a hierarchical ordering on not only urban spaces but also urban inhabitants who are deemed (on account of their physical appearance and attributes) appropriate and 'dignified' enough to be granted access into gated enclaves. Zhang (2008: 30), for instance, relating her experience of accessing Kunming's middle-stratum gated neighbourhoods notes that: 'A well dressed person with an urban professional appearance is likely to pass without being questioned by the guards'. As Sibley (1995) further elaborates, the profiling and categorization of particular groups and individuals as non-conforming or dangerous results in a purification of space, which then increases the visibility of those 'who do not belong', thereby increasing the likelihood of their exclusion. The term 'purification' is used to suggest a distaste for or hostility towards mixing of unlike categories, an urge to keep things apart. In contemporary urban cultural life, purification rituals are a pervasive feature in everyday life such as in residential spaces 'where group antagonisms are manifested in the erection of territorial boundaries which accentuate difference or otherness' (Sibley, 1988: 414). In Shanghai's gated communities, maintaining and defending the purity of space and civilized values are often the defining features of 'respectable' middle-class neighbourhoods that are pure, pristine and wholesome. The concern for securing the pristine and civilized moral order of gated neighbourhoods ultimately bears serious consequences for those who are deemed to be threatening or abject, as territorial rules are enforced to preserve a 'purified community' – one that is free from the unexpected and chaotic messiness of the outside world, and free from experiences that can be emotionally threatening, dislocating and painful (Tajbakhsh, 2001: 170–171; see also Sennett, 1970).

Overall, the social construction of migrant labourers as threats to the moral–spatial order of gated communities is manifested in the moral discourse on civilized modernity which revolves around notions of safety, order and hygiene. Territoriality of gated communities is motivated and shaped by the desires to keep out migrant labourers/outsiders, who are seen as potentially violating and disrupting of the civility and moral order within gated communities. Not coincidentally, these civilized values are also the major criteria that municipal officials employ to determine whether a housing estate is awarded the coveted title of 'Civilized Residential Quarter' (*wenming xiaoqu*). More fundamentally, however, the perceived moral deficiency of migrant labourers also serves at the same time to reinforce the purported moral superiority and valorized identity of gated communities and their inhabitants.

In essence, the construction of outsiders/migrant labourers as social and moral 'others' is integral to the formation of the dominant image and identity of middle-class residents, who strive to constitute the perceived differences of migrant labourers as intrinsically foreign, inferior, abnormal, primitive, dangerous or anarchical (Connolly, 2002: 65–66). Entrenched in the formation of middle-class identity and spaces in Shanghai's gated communities is thus a paradox of difference – the constellation of the constructed otherness in the figure of the uncivilized and wayward migrant worker is both essential to the truth of the powerful identity and a threat to it. Yet, as Julia Kristeva (1991: 191) suggested, when we flee from or struggle against the 'foreigner', we are in fact fighting our unconscious – that 'improper' facet of our impossible 'own and proper'. Drawing on the psychoanalytical works of Sigmund Freud, Kristeva (1991) examines how the narcissistic self projects out of itself what it experiences as dangerous or unpleasant and transforms it into an alien and demonic double. In this instance, what is seen as irredeemably different or threatening (the migrant workers in Shanghai) appears as a defence put up by the distraught middle class to protect its own integrity by 'sheltering it from the image of a malevolent double into which it expels the share of destruction it cannot contain' (Kristeva, 1991: 184).

To put it more forcefully, the distinctness and integrity of an individual or group's identity would not have existed if they did not already co-exist as strangeness or differences associated with an abject 'other' in the first place. In other words, identity formation requires differences in order *to be*, and it converts differences into *otherness* in order to secure its own self-certainty (Connolly, 2002: 64). In this sense, the construction of middle-class (place) identity is always interconnected and constituted through a series of differences and a tendency to further describe these perceived differences in a way that gives privilege or priority to them. Thus, for the urban middle class in Shanghai's gated community, built into the dynamics of identity formation is a polemical temptation to translate encountered differences in migrant workers through which these foreign/threatening elements are seen as moral failings or abnormalities of the other (Connolly, 2002: xiv).

It is important to note that the analysis in this chapter does not imply that social groups residing in gated communities are 'cultural dupes' or automatons who respond unthinkingly or act upon an unconsciously internalized value system. Neither am I suggesting that all residents in gated communities possess similar attributes that predispose them to operate with the same class/territorial logic. Rather, it must be stressed here that territoriality and the underpinning 'civilized values' are associated with particular conditions arising from the specific local context, in this case the perceived external threat to the middle-class communities as a result of changing social demographics in Shanghai/China. In other words, these values and the resultant actions are not inherent attributes of a particular community or society but contingently defined and realized through people's perceptions, and shared definitions of particular situations. By mobilizing the discourse of civilized modernity and further inscribing this moral–cultural logic onto urban spaces, residents of gated communities thus attempted to 'soften' and 'naturalize' the exclusionary territorial landscape by reconstituting it as the pristine civilized spaces befitting Shanghai's cultivated middle class. Yet just how effective are gated communities in keeping away outsiders and migrant workers? The next section will now examine the paradoxical roles of outsiders in the physical and social reproduction of gated communities.

The paradox of gated living and exclusion

As the book has demonstrated so far, the territorialization of social relations in gated communities is undergirded by a moral order that frames spaces according to an aestheticized world-view and civilized values that emphasize the safety, order and hygiene aspects of gated neighbourhoods. The maintenance of gated communities involves not only concerted efforts to promote these civilized values but also vigilant attempts to keep out undesirable social elements that are considered to be physically and morally polluting and threatening to the community. However, this moral–spatial logic of gated communities is fundamentally at odds with the spatiality of urban social life in contemporary Shanghai.

In Shanghai's gated communities, territorial strategies to keep out migrant workers/outsiders are ultimately futile as even territorially bounded places such as gated enclaves are inextricably bound up in the external social–ecological processes that enable these places to function and exist in the first place. In particular, residents in gated communities rely extensively on cheap migrant labour to maintain and upkeep their pristine living environment – from the daily-wage cleaners whose task it is to ensure that the estates are litter-free and hygienic to the legion of construction workers, repairmen, plumbers and other service personnel employed within the gated enclave. In many gated communities, migrant workers are also employed as security guards as they are more likely than the locals to endure the long working hours and low pay. Indeed, it has become a well-established fact that rural migrant workers in Shanghai often take on the low-paid, heavy and dirty work disdained by their urban counterparts (see, for example, Ma and Xiang, 1998; Solinger, 1999a; Fan, 2002; Roberts, 2002).

In many of Shanghai's gated communities, migrant workers could be found working in the low-end service economy. In Vanke Garden City, for example, the hairdresser and 'shampoo girl' in the neighbourhood salons came from Anhui and Wenzhou provinces; the cleaners and maintenance workers in the estate hailed from Anhui, Jiangsu and Sichuan provinces; even the security guards (many of them former People's Liberation Army soldiers) originated from different regions in China. These workers stay in rundown rental apartments in nearby workers' quarters and commute daily to the estate by foot or on bicycles. In addition, many of the domestic maids and delivery workers also enter and leave the gated community quite freely on a daily basis (see Figure 6.5). In particular, these workers from outside also pose an intractable problem for the enforcement of territoriality in gated communities. A member of the estate management staff in Vanke Garden City pointed out that, although security guards make a point of verifying the identities and purposes of workers entering the estate, it is difficult to keep track of them once they are admitted. Neither do the estate management companies want to inconvenience (or raise the ire of) the residents by requiring them to register with the management office every worker/outsider who visits their homes.

It is hardly surprising to note that migrant workers in Shanghai feel that they are being treated as different from the more 'cultured' inhabitants of gated

Figure 6.5   Domestic maids and nannies from rural areas are a common sight in Shanghai's gated communities. (Source: author's photograph, 2005.)

communities. As a housekeeper (an Anhui native) who works in my neighbour's apartment revealed:

> We are always treated as being different here, especially by the local Shanghainese.[11] Even though we may work for them for years and know them very well, we are still considered as different, maybe of a lower class. Migrant workers like us who only know how to perform menial tasks are considered inferior to those middle- and upper-class folks who can afford to stay in these upscale commodity housing enclaves.

Another worker, a deliveryman from a nearby grocery store, complained that:

> Even though we may render valuable services to the residents here, helping them deliver their heavy groceries right up to their doorsteps even during the cold winter season, we are treated quite shabbily. Sometimes, the people here are over-suspicious. When they see you on a bicycle in their private neighbourhood, they think you are up to no good.

All of this points to a paradoxical situation in which those whose labour maintains the civilized order and the good life in gated communities are themselves considered uncivilized elements in the gated estates and neighbourhoods.

Migrant labours are clearly indispensable for the everyday functioning and convenience of residents in gated communities; yet at the same time, they also constitute (in the eyes of the residents and estate management companies) potential threats to the civilized enclaves. To put it more bluntly, these workers are considered the 'negative externalities' associated with gated living (Duncan and Duncan, 2003: 216). Whereas residents constantly worry that the safety and exclusive nature of their homes may be compromised by many migrant workers coming in and out of their neighbourhood, it is also clear that these workers are indispensable and vital in the everyday lives of the residents. As one resident in Vanke estate wryly admitted: 'Unless we can really say that we don't need these workers, there is no guarantee that this neighbourhood will be entirely free of outsiders and strangers. It's just an inconvenience or risk that we have to live with.'

Paradoxically then, the conditions that are necessary for the daily functioning of places such as a gated community are also the very conditions that are seen to threaten it. As such, outsiders/migrant workers may be considered as being both 'in place' and 'out of place' and gated communities are simultaneously 'open' and 'closed' spaces – open to the labour of migrant workers but closed to their bodies, which are often considered to be potentially dangerous and socially pollutive. As Roberts (2002) points out, paradoxically, rural migrants in the urban China are often considered 'willing workers' but 'invisible residents' of the city. For D. Mitchell (2000: 140), every kind of landscape further 'depends on the other: our ability to consume is predicated on "their" low wages and the miserable conditions that exist elsewhere'. The production of landscape, in this case Shanghai's gated communities, is thus inseparable from the 'social totality' that constitutes it as 'the chain of connection between and across landscapes is nearly infinite' (D. Mitchell, 2000: 141). Significantly, the aestheticized (re)production of the pristine landscape and civilized order is closely dependent on the labour of 'others'. In practically every gated community in Shanghai, migrant workers constitute the mainstay of the household service labour economy. To put it more forcefully, it is the labour of outsiders/migrant workers that helps to constitute and reproduce the civilized landscapes and the good life in gated communities. To this extent, the desire to secure an 'unspoiled' and 'purified' home space within gated communities that is free from the threatening presence of outsiders/migrant workers must always be a futile task from the beginning.

The *immanent* presence and threat of outside labour in Shanghai's gated communities is thus clearly an inescapable fact of life that the middle-class residents begrudgingly have to accept. In this sense, gated communities may be considered as paradoxical landscapes fraught with internal contradictions and tensions that disrupt and unsettle the boundaries between 'inside' and 'outside', 'us' and 'them', 'urban(e)' and 'rural', 'civilized' and 'uncivilized'. Given this, the spatial logic of exclusion in gated communities needs to be understood through the very formation of such 'constitutive outsiders' in the contested moral geographies of Shanghai's gated communities (see also Duncan and Duncan, 2003). By problematizing the binary logic of social/class identities and further destabilizing the false dichotomy between 'us' and 'them' this chapter has shown how the processes constituting social relations and place identities are in reality complex and intertwined. Rather than simply being excluded from gated communities, this chapter contends that outsiders/migrant labourers in reality form an important constitutive part in the status claims and identity formation of middle-class residents as well as the physical and social (re)production of Shanghai's fortified urban landscapes.

Summary

This chapter has demonstrated how the moral ordering of urban spaces is a key component in shaping community life and the territorial politics of gated communities. More specifically, the chapter has argued that territoriality in Shanghai's gated communities is bound up in a moral distinction between 'urban(e)' and the 'rural' that is brought together in the middle-class moral discourse on civilized modernity. Values such as the aesthetic of landscape and the safety, order and hygiene of the neighbourhood underpin and shape the community imaginary and territorial organization, which further serve to legitimize exclusion and urban segregation. By inscribing and mapping the moral–cultural logic onto urban spaces, residents of gated communities thus attempt to 'soften' and 'naturalize' exclusionary landscape by reconstituting it as the pristine civilized spaces befitting Shanghai's 'cultivated' middle class. To echo Harvey's (1997: 3) critique, gated communities in Shanghai thus 'build an image of community and rhetoric of place-based civic pride and consciousness for those who do not need it while abandoning those that do to their "under-class" fate'.

Yet, as this chapter has argued, despite concerted attempts to enclose gated communities in order to keep out uncivilized elements, the moral–spatial order of gated enclaves is fundamentally at odds with the complex spatiality of contemporary urban life in Shanghai, which is inextricably bounded to a 'social totality' in which the underclass plays a crucial role in the territorial (re)production of the good life in gated communities To this extent Shanghai's gated communities present a paradoxical situation that is fraught with internal contradictions and tensions. The next chapter extends the moral scrutiny of gated communities further by examining how the territorial (re)production of segregated middle-class landscapes of privilege are implicated in specific geographical moral concerns and the quest for 'real' and 'good' places (Sack, 2003).

7   Beyond the gates

A geographical–moral critique

> All walls are to some extent boundaries, but all boundaries are not walls. Perhaps one way of defining a better society would be to speak of it as a wall-less society, a society in which the divisions among people were not equated with the walls between them.
>
> (Marcuse, 1997b: 112)

Introduction

Throughout this book so far, I have examined the contested place-making strategies in Shanghai's gated communities and demonstrated how these privileged middle-class landscapes, far from being neutral and innocent, are implicated in a territorial politics of exclusion. In this penultimate chapter, I aim to bring together all these themes and issues that have been raised earlier in the book to address a fundamental concern of this study: how people's endeavours to shape places according to certain normative ideas and images feed into the territorial politics of exclusion that potentially undermine the normative ideals of openness and diversity in modern urban life. In the process, what kinds of geographical–moral issues are being implicated with the development of gated communities? More specifically, how do housing landscapes in Shanghai's gated communities conform to the desired visions and aspirations of its residents to include and exclude different social groups; and, corollary to that, how do social–spatial differentiations such as those observed in Shanghai's fortified middle-class enclaves disrupt, challenge and unsettle the normative ideals of city life (emphasizing openness and diversity). By engaging with some of these normative issues, this chapter aims to tease out some of the moral complexities and ambiguities of middle-class place-making in Shanghai.

At the outset, it is important to state that it is not the intention here to 'moralize' or pontificate about a particular ethical or moral position. Rather, the purpose of this chapter is twofold: first, to provide a systematic analysis of some of the normative implications of gated communities for urban life by drawing critically on Sack's (2003) geographical moral theoretical framework; and, second, to highlight the moral significance of place (and place-making) in critical debates on urban segregation and social exclusion. To focus largely on Sack's geographical moral principles in this chapter is, of course, not to discount the value and importance of other writings on urban ethics and morality (see, for example, Harvey, 1996, 2000; Badcock, 1998; Friedmann, 2000; D. Smith, 2000; Sandercock, 2003; Amin, 2006). The point here is to seek out an explicitly geographical approach to the normative questions on good cities that gives due consideration to issues on place and urban ethics.

To substantiate the arguments and discussion, this chapter is organized in the following order: after the introduction, the next section briefly examines some general normative critiques of place and place-making. The third section will examine the 'loom-like' qualities of place that constitute the 'platiality' of gated communities. Following that, the fourth section will examine some of the instrumental arguments on gated communities and highlight some of the objections and limitations of such an instrumental position. The final section then looks at some intrinsic judgements of place and how Sack's twin criteria or what he calls the 'geographic categorical imperatives' (after Immanuel Kant) of increasing awareness and of complexity and diversity can be applied to the empirical case of Shanghai's gated communities.

Normative critiques of gated communities

The recent 'normative turn' and the '(re)discovery' of moral/ethical issues in the social sciences have drawn the attention of many scholars[1] (D. Smith, 2000; see also Entrikin, 1999; Agnew, 2002: 164–178). In the field of economics, for instance, Amartya Sen (1987) laments how the study of modern economics has been impoverished by its separation from ethical discussion and argued that a closer contact between welfare economics and modern ethical studies can substantively enrich and benefit both disciplines (see, more recently, Friedman, 2006). In urban and regional planning, normative considerations have also entered the normally 'practical' and 'applied' field, with planners increasingly being interested in the role of environmental ethics and social justice in land use planning (see, for example, Fainstein, 2001).

Although discussions on ethics and morality can range far and wide, for the purpose of this book, I will focus only on issues that are directly related to the discussion on urban space and urban life. In the preceding discussion, I have dealt with issues of the 'public' and 'private', and social–spatial exclusion. This section will draw together all these themes to tease out the complexities and ambiguities of geographical–moral conceptions of place. Before proceeding further, it is useful to briefly review some relevant works and ideas.

Political theorists such as Iris Marion Young (1990) have proposed a normative model of urban life as an alternative to both the conventional notion of community and liberal individualism. What is interesting about Young's work is that she does not denounce the formation of urban enclaves as necessarily 'bad' or objectionable. In fact, the exercise of individual freedom leads naturally to group differentiation with a social and spatial expression but such sociospatial differentiation does not necessarily lead to exclusion. To put it in another way, gated communities 'represent a desire for accentuated positive freedoms', that is, the ability 'to do' something such as the freedom of personal residential choice (Atkinson and Blandy, 2005: 180). However gated communities, on the other hand, also compromise and curtail the 'negative freedoms' (Berlin, 1958) of others such as the freedom of non-gated residents to roam freely in a neighbourhood without being stopped by guards or having their movement or passageways restricted by gates and walls; or the freedom from increased crime displaced by the presence of a gated community in adjacent neighbourhoods.

Notwithstanding that, for Young (1990), the urban ideal expresses social differences as a side-by-side particularity neither reducible to identity nor completely other. In this ideal model, groups do not stand in relations of inclusion and exclusion, but overlap and intermingle without becoming homogeneous. In the good city one crosses from one distinct neighbourhood to another without knowing precisely where one ended and the other began. In the normative ideal of city life, borders are open and undecidable (Young, 1990: 238). Geographers such as Massey (1991) have argued along similar lines. For Massey, place (by extension a locality, community, neighbourhood, enclave, etc.) need not be seen as defensive, reactionary and inward looking. Instead a 'progressive sense of place' can be achieved – one that, as Massey argues, recognizes the open and porous boundaries of places as well as the myriad interlinkages and interdependencies among places. In other words, one can think of places as areas with boundaries but these boundaries are continuously being (re)drawn, (re)constructed and instantiated as 'articulated moments in [dynamic] networks of social relations and understandings' operating at multiple and diverse scales.

The contested notion of place boundaries is also a theme taken up in critical urban theories. Tajbakhsh (2001), for example, argues that a new spatial imaginary is required to think away from the fixity and hegemonic (fore)closure of space and spatiality. In particular, empirical studies employing social network perspectives offer support for the idea of a loosening of the boundedness of the local places and communities, the most important of which is the far-reaching reconceptualization of the boundary and the border in terms of its undecidability, ambivalence and hegemony. The critique of the conceptual assumptions underlying the dualism of inside/outside, self/other and so on provides many new ways to overcome the traditional ideas of non-permeable spaces. To that extent, Robert Park's image of the early twentieth-century city as 'a mosaic of little worlds which touch but do not interpenetrate', rooted as it was in assumptions from sociological objectivism, appears less and less relevant to a world characterized by identities whose primary ground is overdetermined, hybrid and overlapping (Tajbakhsh, 2001: 9). Similarly for Michael Peter Smith (2001), the criss-crossing of transnational circuits of communication and cross-cutting local, translocal and transnational social practices from 'above' and 'below' that come together in particular places at particular times throws open the contested politics of place-making that fundamentally challenges the fixed boundary and non-permeability of places. The anthropologists Gupta and Ferguson (1997) further point out that representations of localities as cohesive community formation often fail to recognize and deal with a variety of 'boundary-penetrating' social action and processes that now characterize the transnational world we live in.

Whereas the authors quoted above all emphasize a general openness and permeability of places, surprisingly few scholars have seriously considered the important linkages between place and ethics. In that respect, Robert Sack (2003) takes a more specific aim at what he terms the geographical foundation of morally 'good' and 'real' places. In his book *A Geographical Guide to the Real and the Good*, Sack (2003) takes on what he and earlier on Tuan (1998) characterize as the fundamental 'geographical problematic':

> We humans are incapable of accepting reality as it is, and so create places to transform reality according to the ideas and images of what we think reality ought to be.

That is, in specific acts of 'place-making' – from the remodelling of one's home to the large-scale transformation of 'nature' into farmlands, cities, new suburbs and gated communities – human beings are inescapably 'place-makers' and users who fashion places according to our ideas and images of what reality ought to be. Specifically, Sack highlights two particular qualities that can be used to guide us in our creation and use of places that promote morally progressive places: instrumental and intrinsic geographical judgements. In instrumental judgements, places are evaluated *relative* to the goals of projects, that is, how effectively geography is, used to support particular projects. On the other hand, intrinsic judgements provide a non-relativistic means of evaluating and judging the moral qualities of places (more on this later).

Here Sack offers two interrelated dimension of morally good and real places as places that not only enhance our awareness of the world but also expand its variety and complexity.[2] In this conception, what is being emphasized is a balance between the transparency and opacity of place, recognizing that place boundaries provide both an 'inside' and an 'outside' and so can push our attention in either direction. On the one hand, seeing through to the real means not being overly constrained by the boundaries of the place, or its practices. A relatively transparent and porous boundary can encourage this expanded awareness. On the other hand, projects that are worth undertaking, and which provide the world with complexity and variety, need to have a boundedness that allows our minds to be drawn inward to attend to these undertakings. We must focus on what we are doing, and this means that the boundaries of place must be opaque enough to temporarily block out most of the world. Still, this inward-looking aspect of being in place is only a means to undertake projects that must in the end be open to public scrutiny and contribute to both a more complex and varied reality as well as an expanded view of reality (Sack, 2003: 28).

Taken as a whole, how do gated communities in Shanghai measure up to these geographical–moral judgements? First, it can be argued that gated communities in Shanghai fall short of Young (1990) and Massey's (1991) idea of progressive places because gated communities are, by definition, explicitly territorial; and residents and managements of gated communities in Shanghai are often overzealous about guarding and maintaining boundaries and keeping out non-residents. Indeed, it is difficult to imagine how boundaries and borders of gated communities can be 'open' and 'porous', as any unauthorized boundary crossing is considered a security breach that will be detected by electronic surveillance systems and promptly attended to by vigilant security guards.

As Young (2000: 212) observes:

> Walled and gated citadels are the extreme opposed to such potential sharing of environments . . . They exist precisely to prevent openness towards neighbours. Many gated communities enclose gardens, shops, and services for the use only of those who live within the walls. Some walled enclaves encourage community among their residents; thus they are not entirely private spaces. But their purpose is to insulate residents from the surrounding city, its people, and its problems.

In other words, far from Young and Massey's model of 'progressive places', gated communities are defensive and territorial places with explicit rules of engagement (inclusion and exclusion criteria) that are strictly enforced. Yet what specifically about place qualities or the 'platiality' of gated communities allows us to make particular geographical–moral judgements? And how do place and its multiple dimensions and realms figure in our everyday life as well as in the moral domain of place-making? The following will examine the loom-like qualities of place.

The 'place' of gated communities

The importance of place has long been recognised in geographical scholarship (Tuan, 1977; Agnew, 1987; Agnew and Duncan, 1989; Entrikin, 1991; Duncan and Ley, 1993; Adams *et al.*, 2001; Paasi, 2002). Often considered as one of the 'most multilayered and multipurpose key words in our language' (Harvey, 1996: 208), place at its most fundamental level may be referred to as 'a portion of geographical space' that is 'often thought of as bounded settings in which social relations and identity are constituted' (Johnston *et al.* 2000: 582). Writing about place and region, Paasi (2002) asks geographers to 'reflect contextually on how social relations, institutional structures, ideologies, symbols and subjectivity/identity come together in discourses and practices' through which concepts such as place and region are constructed (Paasi, 2002: 808). Agnew (1987) further argues that place as a concept combines three major elements: locale (the setting in which social relations are constituted); location (the geographical area encompassing the setting for social interaction); and sense of place or the attachment between people and places (see also Pringle, 2003; Shelley, 2003). In the latter, place can also be conceived as the inscription of a collective history and of personal histories in space (Pascual-de-Sans, 2004). For the philosopher Edward Casey (2001), places are integral to the development of the 'geographical self' whereby place is regarded as constitutive of one's sense of self and vice versa. In effect, there is no place without self and no self without place (Casey, 2001: 684).

In particular, it has been argued that place matters as it is an indispensable tool capable of bringing about social consequences and effects. Place requires human agents as we are the ones who delimit an area of physical space with rules about what should or should not take place. On the other hand, place also enables and empowers us by helping to organize reality. In this respect, places cannot exist without human agency and input but, equally, we cannot exist without places. Thus, place may be said to have effects and exhibit causal properties (Sack, 2003: 233). Yet what is it about the structure and dynamics of place that helps us realize its power and efficacy?

According to Sack (1997, 2003), the best way to model how place functions as a tool is to think of it along the lines of a 'place loom'. As something like a loom, place helps us to weave together a wide range of components of reality. Specifically, the major components of place come from three domains, the empirical, the moral and the aesthetic, with each of these domains consisting of three realms. The empirical domain includes the realms of meaning, social relations and nature, which correspond to truth, justice and the natural in the moral domain (see Figure 7.1). Within each domain, place as a loom further encompasses three interrelated structural components or 'causal loops' that engage and weave together the different elements in the empirical and moral realms. For example, the casual loop of 'in/out' place rules acts as a mechanism that weaves together social relations (empirical) and justice (moral). Similarly, the spatial interaction loop connects nature with the natural realm and the surface/depth loop connects the meaning with the truth realm. Place as a tool thus helps weave together the different elements of place in the empirical and moral realms.

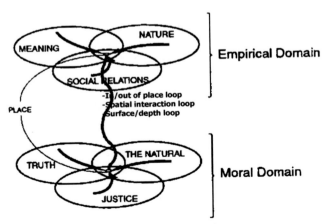

Figure 7.1   'Place loom' with corresponding realms in the empirical and moral domains. (Source: Sack, 2003: 42.)

In these terms, gated communities in Shanghai can be used to further illustrate the loom-like quality of place. Take, for example, the in/out of place rules; Shanghai's gated communities (as well as segregated places elsewhere) all possess explicit rules that govern social relations regarding who should or should not be admitted within its boundaries. These rules are often shaped by the historical and cultural context that helps to structure territorial practices and the make-up of places.

In Shanghai's gated communities, for example, 'outsiders'/rural migrant workers, who are often perceived by urban(e) residents to be 'uncivilized' and 'dangerous', are kept out. These culturally embedded notions of in/out place rules are in turn linked to a second component that is the spatial interaction loop in the nature realm. Flows and rules affect one another to the extent that changing the rules will invariably affect spatial flows. In this case, in/out place rules of gated communities help to determine the spatial interaction and flow of human bodies and traffic into the gated compounds.

These in/out place rules and spatial flows/interactions are in turn linked to the third component – the surface/depth loop in the meaning realm. By 'cleansing' the internal landscape in gated communities to create a homogeneous and purified environment (see Chapter 6), the combination of culturally embedded place rules and flows weaves together a landscape, an appearance or a surface meaning that suggests a pristine and civilized landscape behind the gates. In the case of Shanghai's gated communities, the meaning of this weave can be called into question and problematized. For example, gated communities may appear as a benevolent landscape, a retreat and private haven for middle-class families, but may in fact be a landscape of oppression and residential segregation. Overall, the empirical domain of social relations, meaning and nature in turn corresponds to the respective virtues of justice,[3] truth and the natural in the moral domain.

In the moral domain, qualities of justice (as fairness) may emerge when we consider gated communities as a site of employment with low-paying jobs and exploitative working conditions. Issues of social justice are also relevant when we consider gated communities as sites of social exclusion and class segregation. In particular, social justice may be contested when we ask how the privileged lifestyles of gated community residents can be justified given the extreme income polarization, urban inequality and the deplorable housing conditions of urban poor and migrant workers in the city. In other instances, justice may also be invoked when residents of gated communities take a housing developer to court to seek redress for any wrongdoings such as a breach of contract.

Besides concerns for justice, the moral quality of truth may also be brought under scrutiny in gated communities. For example, when residents buy into gated communities in Shanghai, it may be said that the privacy of their domicile allows them to engage with their authentic or true selves, unimpeded by the interference of the state and neighbours (see Chapter 5). Arguably, in these private enclaves, residents can be 'true to self' and enjoy greater autonomy without having to worry about outside interference. Another strand of truth may pertain to the 'authenticity' of the social and built environment within gated communities. For example, are gated communities authentic or 'fake' landscapes that are made up to appeal to the exotic tastes of home buyers? It may also be argued that gated communities are places where order and diversity are highly controlled and manipulated, hence obscuring reality and 'truth' outside.

Yet, at other times, the natural realm may prevail as the dominant virtue when we consider maintaining the health and cleanliness of the living environment in gated communities as the top priority (see Chapter 6). Another important facet of the 'natural' in gated communities lies in its role as a place for biological functions such as natural reproductive activities – child-rearing and the restoring of one's biological and psychological health (or what Sack terms 'internal nature'). Evidently, the place of gated communities matters as it is responsible for weaving together different mixes of empirical and moral elements such as social relations/justice, meaning/truth and nature/the natural. The character of a place is thus contingent on the dynamic mix of empirical and moral elements, which is always in contention and changing. Using Sack's analogy of a loom, this section has illustrated the place structure and dynamics of gated communities by highlighting how mechanisms of in/out of place rules, spatial interaction and surface/depth loops engage and weave together the empirical and moral elements in space. However, how these elements are woven together depends in large part on the moral positions undertaken by human agents. The next section will examine the instrumental position of gated communities.

Instrumental judgements of gated communities

Instrumental geographical judgements are based on how effectively geography is used to support particular projects. The role of place (its structure and dynamics) is especially important as it underpins human agency and produces effects. A key criterion in instrumental judgement is that, if geographical activity (namely, place-making) is used to effectively attain the goals of a project, then it is judged to be good.

As the preceding chapters have argued, gated communities as a particular type of place manifest a distinct form of human territoriality. Gated communities strictly enforce in/out place rules that control and regulate the spatial interaction in gated enclaves. The internal landscape of gated communities and everything that is contained within them (streets, parks, gardens, shops, playgrounds, club houses, schools, etc.) are all determined by the developer's blueprint, which maximizes potential investment returns. Even the meaning of the landscape or its surface and appearance are controlled by developers to project a marketable image of prestige and the good life (see Chapter 4). Overall, gated communities are, or at least are thought to be, an effective geographical instrument that promotes and secures the exclusive and privileged lifestyles of middle-class residents in gated communities (though such territorial control is never geographically uniform and complete, as demonstrated in Chapter 6). Nevertheless, the territorial control of space in gated communities is an effective geographical tool, as it helps to keep out undesirable elements (outsiders, crime, incivility, etc.) and ensure the 'purity' of the neighbourhood. In other words, it is good instrumentally at maintaining a segregated residential landscape. The problem with instrumental judgements is that they are always relative to the goals of the projects. As will be apparent in the following discussion, justifications for gated communities often rely on instrumental judgements that are entrenched in relativistic goals and particularistic interests. Fundamentally, the instrumental position argues that morality is a product of, and a rationalization for, particular positions and self-interests. In other words, instrumental judgement sees the moral as a product of the empirical.

The moral domain

Within gated communities, special emphasis is given to the natural realm in the moral domain. As stated earlier, the form that nature takes in gated communities is multifaceted and entails various activities such as providing a secured home space for biological activities such as child-rearing, care-giving and nurturance. In Shanghai's gated communities, all these natural reproductive activities are predicated on the provision of a wholesome living environment that is purified and free from contamination from the outside word. Thus, the realm of the natural takes over when we consider gated communities primarily as a home for biological functions – a haven of peace and a wholesome environment for providing and restoring the 'internal nature' and health of its inhabitants (see Chapter 4). Associated with the image of gated communities as the natural are other elements of justice and truth such as the 'need' for residents of gated communities to protect their private investment from the encroachment of non-residents (allegedly, the 'free-rider' problem is a form of injustice or 'unfairness' for gated community residents, who pay a premium for the upkeep and maintenance of facilities within their estate). Similarly, the realm of truth may be a dominant thread for residents who seek to secure an autonomous and authentic life behind the gates away from public interference.

All these moral considerations of the natural, justice and truth undoubtedly stem from particularistic concerns and goals. What is good or bad ultimately depends on whether a particular place supports or reinforces specific goals and motivations. Thus, for many advocates of gated communities, the privatization of housing, streets and parks as well as its exclusionary nature are seen to be highly effective and justified on the grounds of promoting efficient urban policies. A case in point here is Foldvary's (1994) 'market realist' justification of private communities as a highly effective form of urban development founded on the principle of economic efficiency and libertarian assumptions that are able to resolve the intractable 'free-rider' problems in the consumption of public goods. Using a wide range of empirical cases ranging from Walt Disney World to other proprietary communities such as the Reston planned community in Fairfax county, northern Virginia, and contractual communities such as the Village of Arden in Delaware, Foldvary argues that private communities are able to unite governance with market competition in the provision of public goods. Fundamentally, he contends that gated communities are a more efficient mode of urban provision because they allow collectively consumed goods to be supplied optimally by the market. A parallel may be drawn here with Webster's (2002) contention that gated communities may function as efficient 'collective consumption clubs' in which legal property rights over neighbourhood public goods are duly assigned by property market institutions. According to Webster (2002: 410):

> Spaces designed and managed for universal consumption but consumed principally by locals are often dysfunctional; as are those designed for local use but consumed more widely. Inefficiencies arise when the aspirations of public realm managers do not match the aspirations of consumers. The universally accessible public realm is ideal but it is not a reality for the most part. Most public spaces are used by the subsets of the populations and innovative forms of micro-urban governance need to be allowed to emerge to create a better match between the level of use of a public realm and the level of governance. The property rights assignments – the inclusion and exclusion – created by gates (markets), green belts (government) and *gemeinschaft* (community) make for efficient clubs from the point of view of members.

In all of the above claims, what is seen as good or desirable is invariably the product of the empirical – the specific conditions and circumstances that people find themselves in.

To reiterate, gated communities may be considered instrumentally good places because they are more effective spatial tools for promoting efficient market allocation of public goods (in this case, housing) and, more fundamentally, for keeping apart people from different social backgrounds and income groups through maintaining a segregated urban environment. However, such instrumental conceptions of places are often inward looking and they tend to bend the ideas of truth, justice and the natural to suit the needs of the particular project and self-interest. In this case, the loom-like qualities of gated communities in Shanghai help twist virtues of truth, justice and the natural to conform to the self-interest and privileged position of middle-class residents. In fact, 'so convincing are these twists that it may come to seem that there is no escape: self interest makes all moral judgments circular and relative' (Sack, 2003: 87).

Furthermore, instrumental judgements claim that morality is a product of context and place. In other words, the virtues of truth, justice and the natural are all driven or constructed by elements of meaning, nature and social relation, as instrumentalists see the mix of moral and its qualities as resulting from the mix of the empirical As Sack (2003: 87) warns, the instrumental position cannot avoid leading to moral relativism and/or moral absolutism, since relativism in itself cannot be a defence against tyrannical views (all views and positions have to be considered equally valid for a relativist). In fact, a relativist position may even aid and abet absolutist views. In this respect, instrumental judgements of gated communities may thus help to advance the interests of middle-class home-owners but ignore totally other concerns that lie outside the purview of such particularistic interests and positions. Worse still, instrumental judgements do not even provide an objective assessment of places other than those that already support and reinforce the existing status quo of places and other entrenched private interests. To guard against such debilitating forms of relativism, we need to turn away from instrumental logic to engage with intrinsic judgements of places in the next section.

Morally 'good' and 'real' places

Whereas instrumental judgement of place focuses on the relative goals of our projects, intrinsic geographical judgement opens itself up to the possibility of identifying qualities of the good that are largely independent of any particular project and relativistic goal. According to Sack, the intrinsic theory argues that there are two interrelated geographical judgements, each drawing on a unique facet of the good. The first recognizes that the good lies in a heightened and expanded awareness of reality and acknowledges that a major source of evil is a lack of awareness.[4] In this respect, being aware is considered a better option than not being aware, and being more aware is even better. The second criterion is based on the goodness of a plenitudinous reality; that is, a more varied and complex reality is better than a homogeneous and uniform one. According to Sack (2003: 164), '[t]he variety and complexity criterion encourages differences in viewpoints, but the seeing through requirement discourages relativism among them'. Variety and complexity of place are important not only because they provide a compelling world to see, but because they help to promote multiple points of view that are essential for us to see reality. These approaches or views moreover must be open and public and given as altruistic gifts.

According to the theory, a place can be considered good if it enhances the capacity of seeing through, not simply for those within, but for everyone else. It means that its boundaries must be permeable or transparent enough to allow the outside world in, to allow those within to see beyond, and to do so with as little distortion as possible. Both criteria are mutually reinforcing and must be applied jointly. Together, the two encourage us to create places that increase the real and our awareness of the real and to draw together elements of morally good and real places. Applying these criteria jointly orients the particular virtues within a place towards altruistic qualities and makes the various uses of truth, justice and the natural complementary. In sum, it may be said that good places are places that help make selflessness and altruistic gift-giving more likely (Sack, 2003: 181). The theory, of course, does not deny the existence of other facets of good (and conversely bad or evil) places. For example, preserving human dignity and freedom could be seen as important criteria for judging potentially good places. Likewise, places that are free from pain and human suffering may also be considered as morally good places. Nevertheless, these are often insufficient (though necessary) criteria for judging morally good places. Fundamentally, the theory contends that a primary source of evil is the lack of awareness and diversity. In other words, morally bad places and evil deeds occur because people are not fully aware of and do not understand their own actions and their consequences. They are also unable to see beyond the limited sphere of their own experience and positionality because of a lack of competing and diverse viewpoints.

In these terms, how then do gated communities in Shanghai measure up to intrinsic geographical judgements? From the point of view of increasing variety and complexity, Shanghai's gated communities certainly have some merit. On account of increasing variety, gated communities undoubtedly offer a new variety of housing styles and private property formerly unavailable in pre-reform China. As pointed out in Chapter 4, the varied housing designs and physical forms of gated housing developments clearly differ from the dreary and monotonous socialist housing landscape of yesteryear. However, the intrinsic theory requires the joint application of *both* qualities of intrinsic judgements. On the score of increasing awareness and seeing through to the real, gated communities invariably fall short of this second criterion.

In fact, gated communities by virtue of their territorial place structure intentionally obscure and 'hide' the grim reality of the outside world. In these commodified places packaged for middle-class consumption, social homogeneity and purity are artificially maintained through the spatial sorting of people based on their income and class, with social diversity being kept to a minimum 'comfortable' level. Arguably, such a highly regulated environment cannot be further from the truth of the 'real' world outside. As Chapter 6 further demonstrated, the denigration and discrimination of outsiders in Shanghai's gated communities through the distorted representations of outsiders/migrant workers as threats also reduce awareness of reality and truth. As Sack (2003: 164) notes:

> A cultural enclave that produces superstition and narrow-mindedness that disparages strangers and isolates its members from the rest of the world may be contributing to diversity, but at the expense of narrowing vision and disconnecting parts. A slum or an opium den can be 'different' and 'exotic' to those on the outside, but it imprisons those within.

In other words, the variety and complexity that these places offered were more than offset by the obstacles they presented for those inside and outside to see through to the real. In this case, not being able to see through to the real outweighs whatever variety and complexity that gated communities may have added. (For Sack, other places that violate the principle of 'seeing through' to such a degree that the lack of this principle overrides other considerations include places such as the Soviet Union behind the Iron Curtain, Nazi concentration camps and slave plantations in America's antebellum South).

Underlying the territoriality of gated communities is also a major geopsychological dynamic that comprises the compartmentalizing qualities of place. As noted earlier in Chapter 5, spatial compartmentalization can lead to an increased sense of autonomy that allows people to withdraw out of view from everyone else in order to differentiate themselves, as well as to develop a fuller and deeper sense of self. Such 'thin places', as opposed to 'thick places' with a rich web of stipulated meanings and stultifying rules, can be liberating (Sack, 1997: 10). But in so far as spatial compartmentalization can promote a critical distance towards others and the world, it can also be used to move us in the direction of instrumental judgements that tend to disconnect and narrow our vision, as the freedom that comes with the compartmentalizing qualities of place can also be unsettling, alienating and lonely. Compartmentalization can have the effect of narrowing our vision and casting us on a moral drift and self-deception (Sack, 2003: 201).

Whether or not spatial compartmentalization moves us towards intrinsic judgements that encourage us to have an open mind depends on where along the continuum the place is already located and on the exercise of our own wills. Indeed, degrees of compartmentalization and escapism are necessary and healthy, as residents of gated communities need to escape in order to relax, focus attention and undertake projects that daily life demands from them. Indeed, these forms of escapism are not necessarily bad. Just as Disney World, shopping malls, tourist sites and vacation spots are designed to provide escape and fantasy, gated communities offer residents respite from the demands of everyday life and the outside world. Yet whether these are ultimately considered as 'bad' places that do not allow us to see reality clearly depends on how deceptive and pervasive these places are. To this extent, intrinsic judgements help us decide how to weigh these and all other tendencies of compartmentalizing the world – both as compartmentalization obscures reality and yet focuses our attention upon it – and help us to know if the balance is tipped in the right direction.

On the whole, the scale of balance for Shanghai's gated communities is, arguably, tipped towards the obscuring of reality. As demonstrated throughout this book, one of the key attractions of gated living in Shanghai is precisely the ability of residents to shut out the chaotic, dangerous and uncivilized elements of urban living and retreat into secure and pristine living environments. Indeed, it is difficult to imagine how a highly defensive and guarded environment such as a gated community can facilitate greater awareness. As Young (2000) aptly observes, segregated environments such as gated communities can in fact lead to a lack of awareness that makes privilege 'doubly invisible' to the privileged themselves:

> [B]y conveniently keeping the situation of the relatively disadvantaged out of sight, [segregation] thereby renders the situation of the privileged average. Making privilege invisible to the privileged has the effect of inoculating against what sense of injustice they might have. Those who lead relatively privileged lives in a segregated society see no injustice in their situation. Indeed, they often become indignant at the suggestion that they benefit from injustice, because they experience their lives as so average, normal and full enough of troubles.
>
> (Young, 2000: 208)

Implicit in the judgement of morally good and real places is also the process of democratic place-making. To be sure, increasing awareness and diversity of places will necessarily have to engage with democratic principles that protect the free will and the rights of the people. Indeed, it will be pointless to talk about increasing awareness and diversity of places if people's individual liberty (their rights, autonomy, interests, etc.) is not fairly represented or guaranteed in the first place. Democracy is thus considered essential for expanding our awareness and encouraging diverse viewpoints to flourish. According to Sack's (2003) theory, two conceptualization of democracies – instrumental and intrinsic democracies – may be distinguished here.

In instrumental democracy, promoting and guaranteeing the rights and interests of people are considered to be of utmost importance. In the instrumentalist view, the democratic structure of place becomes an arena where interests are voiced, conflicts arise and agreements are reached through alliances, negotiations and compromises. An example of instrumental democracy is liberal democratic theory, which allows each of us to define and pursue our own interests (with the state being generally neutral about these interests). Under such instrumental democracy, what is guaranteed is the process stemming from stipulated rights that precede any definition of the good (Sack, 2003: 240).

In these terms, gated communities are arguably capable of promoting a specific form of instrumental democracy. For example, residents in Shanghai's gated communities are relatively free to decide where and how they want to live, subject to their own financial abilities and constraints. Their rights to private property are, in principle, guaranteed under the recently revised Chinese constitution (although violation of such rights remains a problem). In addition, home-owners' associations with officials elected by residents also promote a (limited) form of grassroots democracy (Read, 2003). In many commodity housing enclaves, 'rights protection' (*weiquan*) committees are formed by private property owners to protect the private interests of residents. Yet, as Ong and Zhang (2008: 12) carefully point out, in China 'economic liberalism flourishes without political liberalism and market individuation thrives without political individualism'.

However, the principle of instrumental democracy is inherently flawed and problematic. As Sack (2003: 240) readily points out, how can we know that these rights are justified without some inkling of what is good? Without a conception of the good, our supposed duty to adhere to particular rights rests on a shaky foundation. More critically, instrumental views of democracy may actually end up advancing the rights of particular dominant groups and their self-interests, regardless of whether such interests are socially desirable in the first place. Furthermore, by emphasizing rights and self-interest, instrumental democracy may make it more difficult for people to think of their obligations and duties to the wider community. Another risk of emphasizing rights in instrumental democracy is that, when we think only of receiving rights and not giving or making contributions, we may come to think of ourselves primarily as passive dependants.

Under intrinsic judgement, however, democracy is more than just about protecting the rights and interests of the people. For intrinsic judgement, democracy becomes a socioeconomic mechanism for promoting altruism and moving towards the collective good as well as a more expansive view of morality. In other words, intrinsic democracy becomes a means of arriving at a less partial position that requires those participating to voluntarily relinquish degrees of self-interest. Democratic place-making thus involves creating public places as a gift that encourages giving and sharing with others the attempt to see clearly and create variety and complexity. As Sack (2003) points out, one conceptualization of such intrinsic democracy may be found in Habermas's ideal 'speech community' in which a democratically based system of open communication encourages people to put themselves in the position of others in order to promote a view that is more detached and less self-interested. Similarly, Dewey also saw democracy as a conversation that seeks to enlighten and educate, with these associations leading to a shared sense of humanity and the common good (Sack, 2003: 242–243).

By the parameters of intrinsic democracy, gated communities are found to be lacking as there is an absence of a clear sense of a wider civic/social good (in terms of promoting altruistic goals), except in a very narrowly conceived sense of protecting individual rights and self-interests (see Chapter 5 on possessive individualism). More critically, the territorial imperative of gated communities and its exclusionary nature can hardly claim to make it a public space for open communication, let alone as an altruistic gift.

On the contrary, it can be argued that gated communities in Shanghai promote an instrumental form of 'marketplace democracy' in which citizens as consumers are free to purchase and select the lifestyles they can afford as well as to participate in decision-making regarding the management of their private estates. Indeed, it comes as no surprise that the authoritarian Chinese Communist party-state may well support, or at least condone, the assertion of such consumer interests since consumerism is now widely held to be an important engine for China's national growth and prosperity. The role of home ownership in spurring urban consumption and national economic growth is particularly salient in this respect. Deborah Davis (2006), for example, in her paper 'Urban Chinese homeowners as citizen-consumers', argues that private home ownership has empowered citizens as consumers, and in the Consumer Protection Law the party-state has provided national legislation that extends civil rights to citizens as consumers and thereby enlarges the space for consumers to be decision-makers. In essence, Davis (2006: 299) notes that the Chinese government has so thoroughly valorized free markets and consumers as essential agents in the national project of modernization that it can no longer refute the validity of consumer autonomy or maintain a firewall between the rights of Chinese consumers and the civic rights of citizens.

Yet, at the same time, it is equally clear that the Chinese state is not prepared to embrace democratic reform and has no qualms about clamping down on government critiques and political opposition. Even in the limited sphere of private home ownership, where nascent grassroots democracy is supposedly taking root, Read (2003: 48) observes that getting official approval for self-organized home-owners' associations can be difficult, in large part because of the city government's multiple reasons for looking askance at such groups. Even when home-owners' associations are approved, the government's attitudes towards these semi-autonomous groups are, at best, ambivalent. A director of the Shanghai Housing Bureau whom I interviewed has this to say about home-owners' associations and the extent of their autonomous status in Shanghai:

All home-owners' associations in Shanghai have to abide by our rules and regulations. There is no question about this . . . First and foremost, they have to register officially with us, although such registration status when approved does not guarantee that they have absolute autonomy. But they are allowed certain freedom to elect their representatives, organize social activities etc. Basically, what we are saying is that we don't necessarily disapprove of what they are doing but that does not mean that we totally approve of what they are doing. It's a thin line so if they are unsure about anything, it's advisable that they defer to us.

In some cases, groups that have been denied government recognition have fallen into inactivity for fear of offending the authorities. Overall, it may be observed that home-owners' associations and the active assertion of consumer rights in China are condoned and even encouraged as along as they do not directly challenge the state. However, the centrality of consumption in contemporary urban experience, as Christopherson argues (1994: 410–411), has impoverished the broader purposes served by urban life:

The practice of citizenship, originating in urban experience, is gradually being transformed to emulate consumer behaviour. Also emulating the consumer's world and its increasing emphasis on market segmentation is the fragmentation of political interests into ever more narrowly defined 'communities'.

The public arena thus becomes dominated by market negotiation and bargaining by diverse consumer groups each vying for their own private interests. In a marketplace democracy, gated communities may be said to define a particular mode of urban citizenship in which the rights of such citizenship are purchased through private property ownership that revolves around the visual consumption of the landscape. Places such as gated communities are democratic only in so far as they are able to promote certain instrumental goals – advancing the consumer rights and interests of the private residents – but these places invariably fall short of engaging with any broader concern for the civic good beyond the narrow bounds of individual interests and utility.

Although Sack has provided a useful model to examine the geographical–moral significance of place, the theory is not without its limitations and problems. D. Smith (2004: 431), for example, notes that Sack's 'commitment to an independent good that we do not make up implies that it is to be discovered rather than created or constructed is a hard position to defend'. Indeed, his framework appears to give short shrift to the role of human agency and emotions by assuming people to be *dispassionate* moral beings who work unremittingly towards the pursuit of an independent good. In this respect, how then can we account for and incorporate the range of human emotions (such as fear, desires, aspirations) and the actual lived experiences of gated community residents in the theory? Indeed, we may, on good grounds, criticize Sack's model for promoting an abstract and detached moral 'view from nowhere' (Nagel, 1986) that downplays the 'affective' dimension of urban social life. As Nussbaum (2001) argues, emotions can be highly discriminating responses to what is of value and importance and 'no adequate ethical theory is possible without an adequate theory of emotions'. In examining the ethical foundations of people and places, moral sentiments and emotions such as envy, resentment, fear, contempt, feelings about justice and fairness are undeniable facets of everyday life that can tell us a great deal about the significance of class differences and their spatial formation (see Sayer, 2005).

Furthermore, Sack's theory also presupposes that awareness as well as diversity and complexity is always good (in fact, for Sack, greater awareness and a more complex reality are always better). However, for many residents of gated communities, ignorance may arguably be bliss! For them, choosing not to be aware of the 'chaotic world out there' (or in fact reducing such awareness) is in many ways a self-coping mechanism to deal with the perceived messy, disorderly and threatening world outside that is seen to be beyond their control. To engage more critically with Sack's theory, we must also examine more closely the notion of awareness by considering situations in which people may actually *benefit* from being constrained in their options or from being ignorant at a particular point in time. For example, Jon Elster (2000) has proposed that people may actually choose to pre-commit or constrain their choices in order to protect themselves against self-destructive passions or inconsistencies in their preferences over time. Thus, in some circumstances, it may actually help to have fewer options or less diversity of choice. In fact, as suggested earlier, residents of gated communities may consciously choose to curtail their awareness as a self-coping mechanism. In this context, are these people then less aware? On the contrary, it may be argued that gated communities are places where residents exercise a deep form of self- and social awareness – that is, they are acutely aware and conscious of the world outside but choose to foreclose these worlds by curtailing their awareness through spatial designs and enclosure strategies. Yet it is counterintuitive to think that such forms of awareness can actually be inherently good for the society as a whole.

Whereas Sack has not been explicit in his theory about individual human agency and accountability, Duncan and Duncan (2003) have drawn attention to the 'complex complicity' of people as well as the places that we inhabit and consume. Applying a non-individualistic theory of human agency, Duncan and Duncan argue that, as consumers of places, we are accountable for the effects and consequences of our consumption practices, not only as pure individuals. More critically, we must also be conscious of the fact that, as geographical agents and selves, we are invariably intertwined in heterogeneous social and spatial networks that implicate each of us in a complex web of moral relations and obligations with people and places beyond the individual or local level. As Kutz (2000:1) notes, even though we may not participate directly in morally defective acts:

> our lives are increasingly complicated by regrettable things brought about through our associations with other people [and places] or with the social, economic and political institutions in which we live our lives and make our living. Try as we might to live well, we find ourselves connected to harms

and wrongs, albeit by relations that fall outside the paradigm of individual, intentional wrongdoing.

As place-consumers and place-makers, we may not be fully accountable for the consequences resulting from our consumption activities and spatial practices *qua* individuals, but we are nevertheless held as being complicit in the (re)production of certain undesirable conditions or oppressive places.

As demonstrated in Chapter 6, the production and consumption of the privileged landscape and pristine living environment of Shanghai's new middle class are closely dependent on the labour of poorly paid and exploited workers who help build these gated communities, prune the gardens and clean the streets (see also Duncan and Duncan, 2003; Mahler, 2003). Although it may be absurd to hold each individual resident of gated communities morally accountable for the miserable conditions of the workers, the collective responsibilities of these residents as place-consumers and place-makers do to some extent make them culpable of some moral blame and disapprobation. Even though individual residents cannot be held solely responsible for the problems of social exclusion and urban segregation existing in the city, their collective responsibilities as residents of places who contribute to or perpetuate such exclusionary and segregation practices (whether wittingly or unwittingly) are not in any sense diminished. Necessarily then, the moral interconnections of people and places need to go beyond the consideration of individual people and local places.

While Sack asserts that good places can be determined by their abilities to increase awareness and diversity, we also need to recognize that places (or their 'platiality') are not self-contained entities but are inextricably bound up with other people and places in a complex web of interrelations. A place may very well be capable of supporting diversity and awareness internally but, if the existence or flourishing of such places is predicated upon or even complicit in the (re)production of exploitative and miserable conditions elsewhere, then they can hardly be considered as morally good places, even though they may satisfy Sack's intrinsic criteria. As Kutz (2000: 1) contends: as individuals complicit in collective acts of wrongdoings, though 'we may stand outside the shadow of evil, we still do not find the full light of the good'. In the context of gated communities, there is hence the need to examine not only whether places facilitate Sack's instrumental and intrinsic judgements, but also how they are connected beyond the individual persons or local places. Clearly, in (Shanghai's) gated communities, the social totality and the complex complicity that help reproduce these segregated spaces cannot be easily dismissed, as Chapter 6 has amply demonstrated.

Conclusion

Using Sack's theory of instrumental and intrinsic geographic judgements, this chapter has provided a systematic analysis of the geographical moral implications of gated communities. As this chapter has demonstrated, gated communities can be considered effective places according to Sack's instrumental judgement, as they perform well relative to the goals set out by housing developers and middle-class urban residents. Indeed, such instrumental judgements have often been marshalled by supporters of gated communities, who argue that privately run exclusive neighbourhoods are more efficient modes of urban development because they allow collectively consumed public goods to be supplied by the market. But turning to intrinsic judgement criteria produces a very different assessment of gated communities. Within gated communities, the realities of homelessness, poverty, crime, etc. are intentionally hidden away from the residents' gaze. Of course, this is not to suggest that residents of gated communities are totally naïve about the outside world beyond their walled compounds. Rather, the point here is that gated communities as a particular type of place potentially reduce and hinder such awareness. Even though some gated communities do offer some form of variety in terms of housing and residential mix, these are at best only a highly ordered and manipulated form of 'ready-made' diversity that people buy into.

8   Conclusion

This book sets out to examine the emerging politics of middle-class place-making and how privileged social groups residing in Shanghai's gated communities use housing consumption as a form of social distinction by attempting to carve out and defend what are deemed to be their 'rightful' private spaces. Moving beyond standard commentaries on gated communities, this book explores the complex social/cultural meanings embedded in Shanghai's changing residential landscape. Primarily, the book is concerned not only with the symbolism of gated communities but also with the micro-level symbols and meanings associated with walls within the city, guarded entrances and the negotiation of middle-class identities and experiences related to housing choices. The book further challenges the commonly held assumption that gated communities are simply the 'containers' of social class and argues that Shanghai's gated enclaves may be more fruitfully viewed as critical sites of production and consumption where nascent middle-class interests, aesthetic sensibilities and identities are being territorially defined, (re)presented and contested.

As the preceding chapters have argued, territoriality, as a form of class cultural practice and a set of spatial strategies for demarcating and controlling space – thereby securing social power and prestige – plays a key role in Shanghai's middle-class spatial formation. To the extent that human territoriality is considered as the 'primary geographical expression of social power' (Sack, 1986), this book further demonstrates how the territorial production and consumption of gated communities are entrenched in a politics of 'the good life' – defined largely in neoliberal terms of a highly segregated residential landscape maintained through the territorialization of social relations and private property rights and, ultimately, securing and defending the 'civilized' lifestyle enclaves from the disenfranchised masses of migrant workers and urban poor in the city. Such place-making endeavours to shape urban spaces according to certain desired ideals and images, as this book concludes, potentially undermine the normative ideals of openness and diversity in modern urban life.

In this concluding chapter, instead of systematically reviewing the content of the book, I will examine the broader significance and some implications of this study for understanding the cultural politics of urban space and middle-class spatial practices. More pertinently, what can contemporary landscapes of power, privilege and private property manifested in Shanghai's gated communities tell us about the changing nature of urban space and society as well as the new geographies of exclusion in China's post-socialist urban regime? Furthermore, what can the proliferation of private gated communities in Shanghai tell us about the nature and trajectory of post-socialist urban transformation[1] in contemporary China? Although I have endeavoured to provide a grounded ethnographic account of the everyday life and contested (moral) geographies of gated communities, this book is, strictly speaking, not just about Shanghai's gated communities per se. In fact, many of the arguments and observations found here are also broadly relevant to other geographical/urban contexts and are constitutive of much larger processes on middle-class spatial formation, class-cultural politics and territoriality as well as normative debates on good city forms. In the following sections, I will consider some of these themes more closely and also highlight some of the main contributions and insights of this study.

Gated communities and the contested global urban future

A key argument advanced in this book is that gated communities cannot be adequately understood as the product of a taken-for-granted urban cultural form or the *inevitable* spread of an 'American-style' urbanism throughout the world. Although both of these views do find some resonances in this study, it is important to offer a more nuanced and critical account that pays attention to the local complexities and contested geographies of the city as well as the politics of place-making in Shanghai's gated communities. As indicated earlier in the study, contemporary discussions on gated communities are often marked to a large extent by polemical debates that often fail to take into account the local subtleties and complexities of meanings attached to these housing projects as well as the varied ways that gated communities have taken shape in different geohistorical as well as contemporary urban contexts.

Contrary to the view of gated communities as a universally dominating urban form originating from the United States (in particular Southern California), this study has examined how such an urban phenomenon has been locally received, contextualized and 'reworked' in Shanghai with significant and interesting divergences and convergences from conventional Anglo-American (or 'Western') analyses. Whereas gated communities in Anglo-American literature have typically been cast in a negative light (often depicted as the bulldozing of public spaces by nefarious 'private' interests), this book offers a more nuanced and diverging interpretation by arguing that Shanghai's gated communities are also sites where greater household autonomy and personal freedom may be negotiated and experienced away from the state-hegemonic public sphere that is heavily controlled by the Chinese Communist Party (CCP) government. At first sight, this may not seem like a remarkable development, especially in the Anglo-American context, but, as John Friedmann (2005: 84) carefully points out, although such expanding spaces of personal autonomy in China 'may not seem much to a Western reader, accustomed to these liberties', they are nevertheless precious and even revolutionary for those in China, who until recently have had little access to such personal liberties and autonomy. After all, for many Chinese citizens, the idea of a 'small government, big society' is a recent political invention.[2] However, as I have cautioned throughout my analysis in this book, it would be simplistic to assume that housing privatization and neoliberal urban restructuring will lead inevitably to the decline of state power in China and greater grassroots democracy.

In fact, as pointed out by many scholars, the new 'regime of living' in reform urban China is built upon the complex interplay between free-market logic and state rationale: intersecting interests of state bureaucrats and private entrepreneurs (Ong and Zhang, 2008). It is worth reiterating that economic liberalism in China has largely existed without any viable form of political liberalism on the ground. That is, citizens are free to consume and partake in economic activities as long as these activities are held within the confines prescribed by the government. However, the more interesting question is: to what extent will the products of economic liberalism spill over into the political sphere to challenge the state, especially when the consumer interests and property rights of the citizens are seen to be threatened? One needs to look no further than the recent public street protest by middle-class home-owners in Shanghai's Minhang district over the municipal government's proposed plan to extend the Maglev train line into the suburb.[3] Yet such spontaneous protests by home-owners could hardly be celebrated as a harbinger of grassroots democracy in urban China. As Jeffery Wasserstrom (2008) points out, middle-class home-owners' protests in Shanghai resemble more a form of NIMBY-ism (Not In My Back Yard) as the protesters' motivations are based, at least in the first instance, on protecting their own private self-interests and upholding their property values rather than an abiding concern with more inclusive notions of democracy or civil rights in general (even though the distinctions between self-interested motivations and broader universal concerns can actually be a fine one).

Whether a meaningful grassroots democracy[4] will eventually take root in urban China's foreseeable future is rightly debatable, but what is certain for now is that urban housing reform and the proliferation of private gated communities have dramatically altered the social and spatial fabric of cities across China. In practically every major Chinese city from Shanghai, Beijing to Kunming, the recurring urban motif is invariably a pronounced pattern of residential segregation and socio-spatial polarization with the urban landscape being fragmented into multiple nodes of up-market gated estates, 'exotic' suburban new towns, gleaming shopping malls and other luxury themed developments, all interlinked by highways and high-speed transportation networks. In Kunming, for example, a second tier 'catch-up' city often considered to be lagging behind national and global development, a new master plan to restructure the city into a pro-growth, commercialized consumer society has not only destroyed many old neighbourhoods (Zhang, 2006) but also created up-market gated communities that have progressively overtaken scenic but ecologically fragile lake areas around the Dianchi and Cuihu districts. Even in far-flung places such as Jinghong, the capital city of the Xishuangbanna autonomous prefecture in Yunnan province, the trickle-down effects of the private property boom in Kunming and other neighbouring cities have also led to the massive construction of Western-style gated residential enclaves with villas, garages, patios, gardens and lawns that are completely out of sync with the local customs and housing styles of the ethnic communities. According to the prevailing market logic, urbanites who are unable to afford the skyrocketing property prices in Kunming can live their 'Chinese dream' of owning a 'plot of land under the feet and a piece of sky overhead' (F. L. Wu, 1996: 230) for a fraction of the cost in Jinghong, where the prices of houses and villas are at least 30 per cent to 50 per cent cheaper.

Increasingly, all major social and consumption spheres are being judiciously sorted out spatially and segmented according to their market potentials and the varying income levels and purchasing powers of consumers, not to mention their 'lifestyle choices'. Well-off communities in Shanghai can virtually live their entire urban existence without ever having to step out of their privileged nodes with their customized infrastructural links. In up-market gated estates, 'smart' homes equipped with high-tech security gadgets and high-speed Internet cable connections are now standard fare. Some of the 'international' gated communities in Pudong (housing both wealthy local and expatriate families) even boast of being equipped with their own water purification facilities to provide pure drinking water for their valued inhabitants. To top it off, some elite gated communities also come fully equipped with double-steel-door reinforced bunkers in the house basements and 'panic rooms' that will keep the residents safe from gunfire, earthquakes and even poison-gas attacks (Fowler, 2007).

In their daily commute, residents in up-market gated communities travel to work in their own private vehicles (most likely, an imported Audi or BMW or, for the more 'modest' ones, a locally produced Volkswagen Passat). Even for those who have no ready access to a personal car, air-conditioned premium bus services provided by the estate management offices (strictly for ferrying residents only) will pick them up from their doorsteps and drop them off at designated places such as the airport, shopping malls and office complexes in the city area and back for a fee. Children in many of these up-market estates are chauffeured to international schools or satellite campuses of 'brand name' foreign educational institutions (bearing names such as Eton and Wellesley) and rarely mix with children from other socio-economic classes outside. Ironically, whereas many of these gated enclaves are forbiddingly closed to non-residents, they are extremely open and interconnected to a host of other valorized network spaces. As Graham and Marvin (2001: 222) remark:

> The production of such secessionary networked spaces enrolls security, urban design, financial, infrastructural and state practices in combination, to try and separate the social and economic lives of the rich from those of the poor. As secessionary enclaves become more grandiose and massive – encompassing housing, work spaces, resort and theme park activities . . . such complexes represent, in effect, a 'rebundling' of cities.

Beyond Shanghai and China, such practices of unbundling and rebundling of urban infrastructures and the resultant splintered urban landscapes are also rapidly emerging in scores of Asian cities and throughout much of the urban world. Dick and Rimmer (2003) in their survey on Southeast Asia, for example, show how private-sector-dominated planning regimes coupled with 'American-style globalization' have promoted the development of heavily secured and prestigious suburbs for expatriates and local elites such as the Forbes Park gated community in the Philippines' Makati City and the exclusive suburbs of Phayathani and Bangkapi in Bangkok, Thailand. Similarly, Leisch (2002) and Waibel (2006) have examined the formation of exclusive middle-class gated estates in Indonesia (Lippo Karawaci in Jakarta) and Vietnam (Ciputra Hanoi International City and Ho Chi Minh's Saigon South New Area development) respectively. In Malaysia, gated landed property estates are becoming increasingly popular in many urban areas such as Kuala Lumpur, Penang and Johor Bahru, both as a response to the desire by middle-class residents for a high-quality living environment and out of concern for the escalating crime rates in many big cities. In addition, these new gated estates are also being marketed by local governments as premium real estates to attract foreigners to invest and reside in the country.

In the Indonesian offshore island of Bintan, entire gated new towns and enclosed bungalow estates such as the 1,300-hectare Lagoi Bay development have also been sprouting up in the northern end of the island to attract wealthy foreign home-buyers (especially from neighbouring Singapore) with secluded resort-style living at a fraction of the cost in 'developed' cities. What all these private real estate developments have in common is their hyperbolic vision of a capitalist utopia that offers the urban elites a superior global lifestyle enclave glazed with seductive images of exclusivity, conspicuous consumption and social prestige. As M. Davis and Monk (2007) warn ominously, such a phantasmagoric 'dreamworld of neoliberalism' instantiated by custom-made 'evil paradises' for high-net-worth individuals not only enflame desires for infinite consumption and promises of total social exclusion and physical security but also are clearly incompatible with the ecological and moral survival of humanity.

Notwithstanding Davis and Monk's apocalyptic portrayal of a bleak urban future, it must be cautioned that, even though many of these gated luxury-themed developments emerging around the world may exhibit superficially similar characteristics and spatial patterns, the underlying political–economic context and urban social dynamics that shape these gated enclaves and their resultant impacts may vary significantly (see Salcedo and Torres, 2004; Manzi and Smith-Bower, 2005). For example, in Singapore, where public housing dominates a large part of the residential landscape (with over 80 per cent of the country's residents living in public flats), gated communities in the form of enclosed private condominiums exist as 'club goods' that form an integral part of the state's overall national/urban developmental plan, complementing the extensive public housing programme rather than being its direct antithesis (Pow, 2009b). On the whole, gated communities in Singapore may be understood as the product of what Vasselinov *et al.* (2007) term 'gating coalition',[5] whereby the combination of the public and private interests and actions by the local government, real estate developers, media and consumers provide the prevailing structural conditions that shape the development of gated condominium estates in Singapore. The Singapore case also reflects the dominant role of a pro-growth local government in enlisting property developers (through public–private partnership), media and local state institutions in the pursuit and management of local economic and urban growth. Indeed, the Singapore government sets the stage for the development of private gated communities and even undertakes the development of gated condominium estates through the Executive Condominium projects (a hybrid form of public–private gated estate that was spearheaded by the government to cater to the aspiring middle class who could not afford full private property market prices).[6]

In Southern California, Le Goix (2006) similarly argues that the sprawl of gated communities is to be understood not as a 'secession' from the public authority but as a form of public–private partnership – a local game offering benefits for property owners, who are granted autonomy in local governance as well as the responsibility of financing and maintenance of community infrastructure, while providing the local governments with wealthy tax-payers at barely any cost. For that reason, self-financing gated communities are especially popular in unincorporated areas, with the 1978 enactment of Proposition 13, a law limiting property tax, culminating in what some critics have termed the tax-payer revolt.[7]

Evidently, with such a great diversity of local context and urban dynamics, it is important to go beyond the universalizing and often polemical discourses on gated communities to examine in greater detail how such contentious urban forms are embedded and shaped by the prevailing political economy and sociocultural context of the city. In this respect, it will be useful to undertake further comparative work to examine the dynamics of gated enclaves developing elsewhere in other Asian and Southeast Asian cities. Beyond the unique particularities of individual case studies, cross-cultural comparative research that explores regional and national variations in residential gating may point the way towards developing an integrated critical theory on urban enclosure and fragmentation.

As Setha Low (2007) carefully points out, comparative urban analysis can help to locate culturally meaningful and theoretically significant distinctions among regional case studies that can help to shed further light on the differential trajectories as well as the social, political and economic processes that ground the social production and cultural construction of enclosed urban forms in diverse contexts. Instead of treating the dynamics of neighbourhood enclosure and urban fragmentation as the same everywhere, Low (2007) employs several useful analytical dimensions that compare urban governance, citizenship, role of state, domestic architecture, etc., in different regions to construct a layered model of urban fragmentation. More importantly, however, comparative urban scholarship should not merely add to our existing knowledge about gated communities in different urban areas but also present us with alternative and critical visions of an urban future that challenge and contest the hegemonic models of urban neighbourhood enclosure and highly privatized/territorial urban spaces driven by the ideology of privatism and neoliberal market logic.

Middle-class territoriality and geographies of exclusion

In so far as social science research on territoriality is often fixated on the macro-level analysis of the territorial state, an important insight yielded by this study is to shed light on how territoriality operates in the 'micro-scale' context of urban neighbourhoods and in less formalized everyday settings (which nevertheless have important consequences). As the book has demonstrated, the residential landscape, in this case Shanghai's gated communities, serves as an important repository of group symbols, social practices and the vehicle through which the identity and cultural practices of a class or status group are maintained and spatially reproduced. Privileged groups such as the new middle class in Shanghai, who possess the power and resources to build and shape urban spaces, further seek to protect themselves behind fortified enclaves in search for 'the good life' that revolves around the private consumption of a 'wholesome' and 'civilized' residential landscape. As Blomley (2004a: xvii) critically points out, our 'enjoyment' of property frequently depends upon dispossession of others, whether now or in the past.

The book further argues that the territoriality of gated communities not only is maintained through the enforcement of 'hard' territorial tactics (such as the construction of physical barriers and fortifications) but also operates at a more subtle and ideological level through the mobilization of a repertoire of symbols, values and rhetoric of the good life. As the book has illustrated, territoriality imbued with these values and symbols operates through a mixture of coercive strategies as well as hegemonic consent to engineer the social acceptance of particular spatial classification as natural and taken for granted. One of the important ways this is being accomplished in Shanghai's gated communities is by drawing on the moral rhetoric of civilized modernity that rests fundamentally on the social construction of migrant workers as threats to the pristine moral order of the home as well as the modern facade of the city.

The concept of moral order employed here parallels the Durkheimian notion of a social collective (see also Wacquant, 2004), including specific social and cultural ideals of the good life and its physical manifestations as imagined and constructed by the Chinese middle class. As such, middle-class territoriality in Shanghai's gated communities is motivated and shaped as much by the residents' aspirations to cultivate class distinction and an appropriate habitus as by their desires to keep out migrant workers, who are seen to potentially defile the moral order (aesthetics, safety, order and hygiene) in their gated neighbourhoods. To this extent, this book has provided a new analytical angle by showing how the moral considerations of urban places overlap and intersect with class boundaries and cultural politics. Although Bourdieu (1984) had been widely noted for his penetrative analysis of how class distinctions are being articulated through processes of cultural differentiation, his work has also been criticized as greatly underestimating the importance of moral boundaries while exaggerating the importance of cultural and socioeconomic boundaries (Lamont, 1992: 5). In fact, for Bourdieu, moral discourses are subsumed within class hierarchies and do not seem to have any autonomy at all. According to him, people who value morality do so to make up for their lack of 'real' capital that is valued by the market:

the rising petite bourgeoisie endlessly remakes the history of the origins of capitalism. In social exchanges, where other people can give real guarantees, money, culture or connections, it can only offer moral guarantees; (relatively) poor in economic, cultural and social capital, it can only 'justify its pretensions', and get the chance to realize them, by paying in sacrifices, privations, renunciations, goodwill, recognition, in short, virtue.

(Bourdieu, 1984: 333)

As this book has demonstrated, moral virtues are deployed even by those with relative wealth and, where such moral boundary-drawing coincides with sociocultural boundaries of class distinctions, it tends to be marked by the territorial place-making strategies that further reinforce the social–spatial class boundaries. As is evident in the case of Shanghai's gated communities, safeguarding the moral community by securing the civilized enclave with well-kept houses and gardens, litter-free streets and an aesthetically pleasing and pristine living environment has as much to do with the staging and performance of middle-class status distinctions as it has with demonstrating the moral superiority of its inhabitants over others. More fundamentally, such moral aesthetic order parallels the logic of neoliberal hegemony such that class and social exclusion are refigured and become depoliticized while the defence of luxury and privileges are simply recast as differing standards of civility, lifestyle values and the living environment.

A broader point can also be made here on the role and function of civility in urban life. Whereas (urban) civility has often been held up as a positive moral virtue that helps to ease social tensions and facilitate social interactions in a democratic and pluralistic society, the repressive aspects of the 'civilizing projects' undertaken by urban elites often end up becoming instruments of social control that stifle urban heterogeneity and social differences, targeting especially the lower classes and immigrant populations (Boyd, 2006: 873; see also Valentine, 1998). If indeed, as Boyd (ibid.) suggests, 'civility is most conspicuous in its absence' (such as when urban dwellers are being confronted by the 'uncivilized' behaviours of rural migrants), this study further demonstrates how urban civility may in fact become a highly contentious notion with the urban population increasingly being segmented and polarized along the lines of a neoliberal biopolitics that problematizes the 'inferior quality' of China's rural migrant stock as unskilled and uncivilized floating population/bodies that are rendered morally and socially out of place in the gleaming new cities of reform China.

Another significant contribution of this study is to shed light on the emerging class dynamics in reform China by examining how the cultural reproduction of middle-class lifestyle is implicated in the geography of difference. In particular, the study has highlighted the role cultures of privilege play in producing and reproducing hierarchies of economic distinction. However, this is not to suggest that middle-class cultures are reducible as simply the product of economic structures. Rather, culture and economics are seen as mutually constitutive elements, with neither reducible to the other. Equally important, when analysing class-cultural politics of consumption, is to pay critical attention to the spatial dynamics that help (re)produce class spaces and identity. As Leichty (2003: 255) points out, class is an inescapably locational idea: it necessarily implies a geography in which difference (however imagined and/or enforced) is mapped onto social space. Class as cultural practice and performance is about locating oneself and one's class 'others' in social space. In this sense, gated communities are thus prime locales for understanding the spatial dynamics of class practice and their spatial claims. As this book has consistently argued, gated communities are not just inert spatial containers of class interests and spatial practices but critical sites for the performance of middle-class identities (Chapter 4) and enactment of private property rights (Chapter 5). Not only that, gated communities are also important *pedagogical* spaces where residents in Shanghai cultivate and acquire their class disposition/sensibility while learning to be respectable members of the middle class. As Chapter 6 has further demonstrated, by inscribing and mapping the moral–cultural logic onto urban spaces, residents of gated communities thus attempt to 'soften' and 'naturalize' the exclusionary landscape by reconstituting it as the pristine and civilized living space befitting Shanghai's 'cultivated' middle-class residents.

By critically interrogating the territorial politics of gated communities in Shanghai, this book has also gone beyond the simple dichotomy of exclusion versus inclusion to challenge the binary construction of class territorial membership in urban communities. A key idea highlighted in this study is how the 'self/others', 'insider'/'outsider' dichotomy typically presented in studies on gated communities (and, more broadly, research on urban segregation) is not as rigid and water-tight as commonly presumed. As Chapter 6 has shown, outsiders/migrant labourers in reality form an important constitutive part in the physical and social reproduction of Shanghai's gated communities. In fact, it may be argued that migrant workers are both 'in place' and 'out of place' simultaneously in gated communities.

Through problematizing the binary logic of social/class identities and further destabilizing the false dichotomy between 'us' and 'them', this book hopes to show how the processes constituting social relations and place identities are in reality complex and intertwined. Rather than simply being excluded from gated communities, this study contends that outsiders/migrant labourers are in essence an important constitutive element of Shanghai's fortified enclaves. Ultimately, this book aims to contribute towards formulating a progressive politics of identity by recognizing that the 'outsider' or 'foreigner' is always within us (Kristeva, 1991). As Connolly (2002: xiv) reiterates, to confess to a particular identity (whether class, gender, racial or other) is also to belong to difference. To this end, coming to terms affirmatively with the complexity of the interconnections between self/others and insider/outsider is a good starting point to help support and reflect on an ethos of identity and difference suitable for a democratic culture of deep pluralism to emerge.

Urban ethics and the 'geographical problematic'

If indeed people are incapable of accepting reality as it is, and hence have to transform places according to their idealized images and notions, such place-making endeavours, or what has been termed the 'geographical problematic', are also invariably bound up with certain ethical and moral concerns. When we construct new places or alter or destroy old ones, we also create new conditions that may potentially hinder (or improve) the moral qualities of existing places. As Tuan (1989: vii) notes, in practically every human geographical activity 'moral issues arise at every point if only because, to make any change at all, force must be used and this raises questions of right and wrong, good and bad'.

Building on some of these ideas, this book further brings together issues of territoriality, class boundaries and moral–spatial claims, to address the overarching question concerning the constitution of 'good' places that are consonant with the modern ideals of city life (openness, diversity, democracy, social justice). Using Sack's theory on instrumental and intrinsic geographic judgements, this book emphasizes the relevance and importance of adopting a geographical–moral perspective and systematically critiques the spatial ethics and the moral texture of everyday spaces and social life behind the gates. In this sense, gated communities may be considered as key sites for critical reflection on the moral content of neoliberalism. Although gated communities can be considered effective places according to Sack's instrumental judgement since they perform well relative to the goals set out by housing developers and middle-class urban residents, they fall short of intrinsic criteria as their territorial structure intentionally obscures and 'hides' the reality of the outside world. As commodified landscapes packaged for middle-class consumption, social homogeneity and purity are artificially maintained in gated communities. As a contested site of and for place-making, gated communities in Shanghai thus instantiate the urban politics and societal tensions over the right to public/private spaces as well as broader normative concerns on urban democracy, citizenship and social justice.

Yet, as David Smith (2000: 202) points out, any normative inquiry needs to develop a geographically sensitive ethics of place alongside a careful consideration of local place history, culture, politics, etc. Fundamentally, any normative geographical conception of place needs to grapple with the local complexities and ambiguities of place-making. Nevertheless, if Walzer (1994: xi) is right that 'there are makings of a thin and universalist morality [or 'good places'] inside every thick and particularistic morality,' then what needs to be theorized is how exactly the 'thick' and 'thin', 'global' and 'local', 'universal' and 'particular' are intertwined in Shanghai's urban landscapes of privilege and exclusion. By teasing out some of these context-sensitive moral ideas and complexities inherent in place-making, this book hopes to reiterate the importance of considering the interlinkages between place, ethics and morality. If the contentions surrounding gated communities and the privatization of urban spaces are ultimately debates on the kinds of urban spaces and cities that we would like to see being built and inhabited, it would be pertinent to pay critical attention to these geographical moral practices that underpin urban place-making.

Appendix
Notes on research methodologies and fieldwork

If the book *China Bound* (Thurston *et al.*, 1997) – a practical guide on 'surviving' the academic research environment in China – is anything to go by, conducting fieldwork, as even the most seasoned of field researchers will attest, entails many months of extensive preparation, conscientious planning and careful negotiation with the complex Chinese bureaucracy while leaving room for serendipitous encounters. Being prepared, as the book's authors counsel, can often mean 'the difference between a headache and a productive day'. Albeit written specifically with the American academic audiences in mind, the book nevertheless provides some useful general lessons for all. Not least, for the nature of my research project, conducting ethnographic fieldwork is also profoundly mediated by the complex relationship between the ethnographer and research subjects, which is further conditioned by specific local and larger sociopolitical circumstances. In the following, I will provide some clarifications as well as reflections on the field methodologies employed.

In this study, I have attempted to cover a spectrum of both middle-class gated communities that target the majority of the commodity housing market – the relatively well-to-do and affluent though not the richest urbanites – as well as the more luxurious high-end gated communities or 'golden ghettoes' (Giroir, 2002) that cater to a small fraction of nouveau riche or 'bourgeois' consumers (estimated to be about 1 per cent or less of the entire population; A. Chen, 2002: 410). Generally speaking, the line between middle-class and luxurious high-end gated communities is not clearly defined and is drawn arbitrarily on the basis of the fluctuation of housing prices, different property locations and real estate market conditions as well as subjective perception. By the last criterion, for example, a poor migrant worker may consider an average commercial housing enclave that is financially out of reach for him/her to be a luxurious high-class dwelling whereas a well-heeled home-buyer may be more discerning in distinguishing between high- and mid-priced properties. In general, luxury residential enclaves in Shanghai with a unit rate of more than 10,000–15,000 yuan per square metre are concentrated in certain prime locations in or near the downtown Puxi area – mainly in the Huangpu, Jing'an and Luwan districts as well as the Pudong Lujiazui area.

To compound the issue further, a commercial residential estate located in Shanghai's suburbs may contain all the luxurious and 'modern' accoutrements befitting high-end housing projects (e.g. private swimming pool, club house) but may cost less than a comparable development found in the city centre on account of different land prices. Notwithstanding these ambiguities, gated communities in Shanghai all display similar territorial characteristics and tendencies through the primary mechanism of spatially sorting residents according to their income, class and lifestyle. On the whole, estimates put the number of urban residents in Shanghai who are realistically able to afford private commodity housing enclaves at between 5 and 10 per cent of the entire urban population (D. Davis, 2000: 9). Not coincidentally, this figure corresponds to some of the estimates of the size of the middle-class urban population in China (see Chapter 3).

In order to understand why middle-class urban residents are moving into private gated communities in Shanghai, it is useful to adopt a hermeneutic approach and try to understand individuals and their household's unique resources, motivations, desires and aspirations as well as their past housing experiences in shaping their housing consumption. In such interpretive social research, researchers are primarily interested in making sense of the actions and intentions of people as 'knowledgeable agents'; more accurately, researchers are attempting to make sense of how people *themselves* make sense of events and opportunities confronting them in their everyday life. For geographers, Ley (1988: 121) further notes that an interpretive approach considers:

> [P]laces, regions or landscapes as the result of the active construction of social groups, a human achievement with all the flux, dynamism, discontinuity and local nuances. Places are not the inevitable outcome of seemingly irreversible and impersonal forces. Rather people make over places in their own image as they confront the opportunities and limits of a local environment . . . every place is an object for a subject, an intersection of human objectives, physical possibilities and contextual contingencies, developing together through time.

To this end, the study employs a combination of qualitative research tools, namely a 'community ethnography' approach and 'participant observation' whereby the researcher becomes a resident of the community under study in an attempt to gain a more precise understanding of the values and practices of its everyday life. Specifically, participant observation is often described as an inductive research methodology that progressively makes sense of social circumstances as data accumulate, and involves an intellectual process of going back and forth between concept formation and data collection. To ensure the reliability and accuracy of the inductive fieldwork strategy as well as the conclusions drawn from my analysis, I find it useful to discuss some of my observations with 'knowledgeable natives' such as local researchers and 'insiders' of the housing industry, and have them countercheck some of my hypotheses and findings.

Vis-à-vis the 'natives', my positionality as an overseas Chinese (*huaqiao*) researcher from Singapore is also noteworthy here. Being conversant in Mandarin (*putonghua*) and with a very rudimentary understanding of the Shanghainese dialect, I am considered by the local respondents as ethnically Chinese, sharing (though not completely) many similar cultural traits and practices. Yet at the same time, being a non-citizen of the PRC state and having grown up and lived outside China, I am also seen and treated as an 'outsider'. Whereas my liminal status as both 'insider' and 'outsider' to Chinese society has provided me with a unique vantage point to observe urban social life in Shanghai, my identity as a Chinese Singaporean also brings along with it some advantages as well as pitfalls when conducting research. Many respondents, upon learning that I am from Singapore, will automatically assume that I am there to invest in real estate properties. Such a 'mistaken' identity works both *for* and *against* my research agenda. On the positive side, I am often warmly received by property agents and home-owners, who will allow me to tour the interiors of many gated community estates. Among the latter group, after overcoming their initial suspicion, many 'house-proud' local respondents are quite enthusiastic to show me around their neighbourhood, given the novelty of a foreigner taking a keen interest in their new living environment.

On the other hand, people are also less forthcoming in sharing with me some of the less desirable aspects of Shanghai's urban life, for fear of turning away a potential home-buyer (for the real estate agents) and, for the locals, the worry of presenting themselves and their home 'turf' in a less than positive light and hence 'losing face' in front of a fellow ethnic Chinese from overseas. This self-presentation and management of impression is, however, often a two-way process, as I learnt in an episode when I was turned away at the door (more on this later). Quite evidently, when conducting research the positionality of the researcher in relation to the local respondents can significantly influence access to the field as well as types of information (see Cochrane, 1998; McDowell, 1998; Herod, 1999).

In addition to ethnographic fieldwork, I also conducted semi-structured in-depth interviews, discourse analysis of housing advertisements and brochures, and library research. Quantitative real estate data and various 'lifestyle' survey results published by property research companies and housing developers were also solicited to provide a background macro-understanding of housing reform policies and their differential impacts on urban residents. Specifically, participant observation entails observing and interacting on a daily basis with residents as well as workers in the gated community (including employees of the property management office, cleaners, security guards, employees at various shops and restaurants) as they go about performing their daily tasks. During my stay at Vanke Garden City, I also participated in the daily activities of the residents, shopping for groceries at the nearby market and the local convenience stall (*bianlidian*), dining occasionally at the local eateries and restaurants, visiting the local barber and laundry shops, etc. In addition, I also attended social gatherings (Lunar New Year celebrations, Mooncake Festival gatherings, Vanke Community Family Day, etc.) and spoke to the local officials of the residential committees (*juweihui*). Unfortunately, I did not have a chance to participate in any home-owners' meetings during my stay in Vanke Garden City as I was told that the old committee had 'retired' and new committee was yet to be formed. In any case, I was told that only full-fledged home owners (and not renters like myself) are allowed to participate in any home-owners' meetings and voting.

Through participating in other neighbourhood social activities and interacting with the residents and workers on a daily basis, I was able to gain insight into the dynamics of the everyday life in gated communities. In addition, I also rely on quantitative data drawn from household survey conducted by Vanke Corporation (published in 2004) that provides insights into the reasons and motivations why people chose to move into Vanke Garden City. More formally, I have also conducted semi-structured interviews with 120 residents staying in Vanke Garden City to find out about their reasons and motivations for moving into a gated community such as this as well as their opinions on the desirability of living in an enclosed housing development. The sampling strategy relies on purposeful sampling to include as many local residents from different parts of the gated neighbourhood as possible. These households vary in the length of their housing tenure in Vanke Garden City, with about 60 per cent having stayed there for five years or more, 30 per cent between two and three years and the remainder for less than a year (10 per cent).

Typically, residential households in Vanke Garden City, like in many other middle-class gated communities in Shanghai, are nuclear families comprising young to middle-aged couples with usually one child and retired parents. These residents are also mostly in professional (*zhuanye*)/managerial (*guanli ceng*) positions or hold 'white-collar' (*bailing*) occupations and may be work in both the public sector and also private and international joint ventures. In addition, there are also residents who are private entrepreneurs (*siying qiyejia*) and business people (*shengyiren*) who own capital ranging from small retail shops or restaurants to mid-size factories. In some cases, it is quite common for residents to own more than one apartment or house in addition to the one they are currently staying in. In fact, several of the residents I spoke to have two or more commodity housing units which they bought for investment purposes. From my interviews and observation, it is also not uncommon for the combined household income of residents in private gated communities to be several times more than the national average. A household survey, for example, indicated that the income structure of Vanke Garden City residents is heavily skewed towards the upper end, with 32 per cent of residents having a monthly household income of between 5,000 and 10,000 yuan and 42 per cent with a monthly income of more than 10,000 yuan (or an annual income of 120,000 yuan). To put this in perspective, for the latter group, their annual income is at least 3.5 times the average annual income of ordinary workers (about 10,998 yuan) in the city (see F. L. Wu, 2005: 246).

As the primary focus of my study is to examine the changing lifestyle and cultural reproduction of middle-class residents in Shanghai's gated communities, I am less concerned with the experiences of expatriate families (see, however, F. L. Wu and Webber's 2004 study on 'foreign gated communities' in Beijing). The interviews with residents were all conducted within the gated community, usually in the gardens, community centres or club houses or outside shops and restaurants as well as in other commonly shared facilities and spaces in the gated communities. Generally an appropriate time for conducting such interviews is during the evenings when families take a stroll in the gardens after dinner. In the day time, only old people and young children are at home. As suggested earlier, I initially encountered some problems soliciting for interviews as people were generally suspicious of an 'outsider' asking them personal questions about their lifestyle and habits. In addition, workers in the gated communities were also reluctant to talk to me for fear of reprisals from their employers (the property management company). To circumvent these problems, I first introduced myself as a new tenant (stating my house number, 'number 5, unit 302') who had just moved into the neighbourhood and wanted to find out more about the surroundings. Sensing that the respondents had warmed up, I then made clear my position as a researcher studying gated communities in Shanghai and would like to seek their opinions on some issues, even though, at the end of the day, many of them still insisted that I was a 'covert' real estate investor/speculator from Singapore. As I later rationalized, their impressions might be due in part to media reports about the recent forays of many Singapore real estate companies (for example, Capitaland and Keppel Land) into mainland Chinese cities and also the high-profile China–Singapore Suzhou Industrial Park.

The interviews were conducted mainly in Mandarin with different family members including the head of household (usually the father or husband in a Chinese nucleus family) and the mother/wife regarding their decisions to move into the gated community. During my preliminary fieldwork, I observed that there were several elderly residents and young children living in gated communities, possibly in extended families. I also interviewed these senior family members and children to find out about their experiences living in a gated community. In addition, I surveyed nearby commercial areas (shopping centres, markets and restaurants) and also interviewed residents staying adjacent to the gated communities in order to understand the general context surrounding the everyday life of gated community residents. For example, it would be useful to note the shopping habits of residents living in gated communities in order to establish whether they do interact substantially with the external social environment. I also interviewed developers, architects and real estate agents and collected marketing brochures, sales data and advertising documents for content analysis.

To gain access into the field, I relied on personal contacts of friends who knew of residents staying at a particular gated neighbourhood. Invariably, such visits would 'snowball' to other contacts living within the same neighbourhood or in gated communities elsewhere. More frequently, the strategy I adopted was to call on the sales/rental office of the selected gated community to express my interest in viewing the houses. Appointments were then scheduled, usually beginning with a 10- to 15-minute 'sit-down' session with the housing agent to discuss housing preferences, followed by a tour of the neighbourhood and sometimes viewing of 'showroom' apartments or the actual houses for sale or rental. Normally, the whole appointment lasted no more than one or two hours. In such visits, the housing agents will usually 'size up' the clients and accord different treatments depending on their perceptions of the client's level of income and 'sincerity'. As noted earlier, managing impressions and 'keeping up appearances' is important. In one of my visits to an up-market gated community at the Pudong Lujiazui Area, I was turned away at the door because I was dressed 'inappropriately' in jeans and sneakers and carrying a backpack (my usual fieldwork attire during Shanghai's hot summer months). The housing agent, through the security guard at the door, told me that the houses were sold out. I later made a phone appointment two days later and turned up in more formal 'office wear' (business shirt and trousers with leather shoes) and was warmly received. When I remarked about the incident two days ago to an agent (albeit a different one), she apologized profusely but went on to explain that they just wanted to be sure that the clients were bona fide and 'sincere' about purchasing the houses as they did not want to 'waste time' on people who were just curious and/or couldn't afford to stay in the property (see Chapter 6 on embodied neoliberal politics).

Besides some difficulties gaining access into gated communities, I have also encountered some problems interviewing government officials, many of whom are suspicious or dismissive of foreign researchers. A director of the Shanghai Housing Bureau once told me bluntly during an interview that 'outsiders will not be able to understand the complex situation in China'. In addition, official endorsement of commodity housing estates and gating in China also makes 'negative' information on the issue hard to find because Chinese media and researchers tend to avoid contradicting the government (Miao, 2003: 49). As with any fieldwork in a foreign country, institutional support provided by the host country is crucial and can sometimes 'make or break' a research project (Thurston *et al.*, 1994). Though often considered one of China's most cosmopolitan and 'open-minded' cities, negotiating through Shanghai's state bureaucracy can still pose a difficult challenge for (foreign) academic researchers.

During my preliminary fieldwork in 2003, I first established useful contacts with various key research institutes in Shanghai, including researchers from the Shanghai Academy of Social Sciences (SASS) and the Shanghai Urban Development Planning Bureau as well as academics from the Department of Geography at the East China Normal University. When I later returned to Shanghai for formal fieldwork in 2004, I was fortunate to be affiliated to the SASS as a visiting scholar, which enabled me to access research materials and data in their libraries but more importantly to establish contacts with researchers in SASS who have institutional connections with government officials as well as property developers in Shanghai. An important function of the SASS is to issue 'letters of recommendation' (*jieshao xing*), which prove to be crucial in opening doors for interviews with developers and government officials. Through the Foreign Affairs Office (*waishi banshichu* or simply *waiban*) at the SASS, I was able to resolve pressing logistical and administrative issues such as securing a year-long multiple entry visa as well as the more mundane task of registering for my temporary residence permit with the local Public Security Bureau.

Notes

1 Introduction

1 Vanke Corporation is one of the most reputable and prestigious commodity housing developers in mainland China. Helmed by a former People's Liberation Army soldier by the name of Wang Shi (often described as 'China's Donald Trump' for his flamboyant management style), the company first started out in Shenzhen, Guangdong Province, in the early 1980s and was involved in a number of business ventures before making its big break in real estate business following housing reform policies in the late 1980s and early 1990s. Capitalizing on the poorly regulated real estate industry in China, Vanke began its real estate venture in Shanghai and developed its prototype model housing community, Vanke Garden City, in 1994. As one of the first commodity housing estates in China, Vanke Garden City was immensely popular amongst 'white-collar' (*bailing*) middle-class home buyers. The prototype housing community has since been replicated in several developments elsewhere in China. Currently, Vanke Corporation, which has a turnover of more than US$930 million, has housing projects in 20 major cities in China including Beijing, Shanghai, Shenzhen, Wuhan, Nanjing, Chengdu, Dalian and Shenyang. According to a report in *Time Magazine*, with its scale and intensity of operation in China, Vanke Corporation is touted to become the world's largest housing provider in the next decade (*Time Magazine* 27 June 2005; see also Vanke Company Report, 2000; Lu, 2004; Vanke, 2004).

2 One US dollar is approximately equivalent to 8.0762 yuan during the period this research was conducted.

3 See http://house.online.sh.cn (accessed 16 March 2006).

4 During transition from a planned economic system to a market-oriented one, the government sees maintaining social stability as its topmost political concern, and gating as a quick solution to crime control and maintaining social stability. Governments at all levels in China have included gating residential estates as part of their housing programmes.

5 The usual protocol of ensuring the anonymity of interview sources is observed in this study.

6 A more famous example here was the attempt by Liang Sicheng (son of the late Qing dynasty reformer Liang Qichao) to save the old Beijing city walls in the 1950s. Together with an urban planner called Chen Zhangxiang, Liang submitted a proposal to the Chinese government entitled the 'Proposal on Location of City Centre of The Central People's Government', which elaborated, amongst other planning issues, their ideas on preserving historic city structures including the ancient city walls. However, on account of the socialist radicalism of the 1950s, Liang and Chen's ideas were attacked as a 'bourgeois conspiracy' that was aimed at maintaining the backward feudal past of the 'old society' and hindering the modern development of socialism. Soon

afterwards, in the 1950s and 1960s, many of Beijing's old city walls were demolished (see P. Rowe and Kuan, 2002).

7　By using the term 'gated community', I am not suggesting that China's gated developments are an offshoot of American-style (gated) urbanism; neither am I suggesting that gated urban forms are entirely novel in the Chinese context. Rather, I deploy the term first in a descriptive manner to examine the nature and morphology of enclosed commodity housing enclaves in contemporary Shanghai; and second in a heuristic sense to draw comparisons with theoretical debates on gated communities found in Anglo-American urban literatures and beyond.

8　Gated communities are often associated with a number of terms such as 'master-planned communities', 'proprietary developments', 'enclosed guarded condominiums', 'defensive housing complexes', 'residential club communities', 'Community Association Institutes' (CAS), 'Common-Interest Housing' (CIH) and 'neighbourhood-level private governance'.

9　The distinction between *categories of practice* and *categories of analysis* is highlighted by Brubaker (1996) in his work on nationalism. Mindful of the need to avoid socially and intellectually reifying the notion of the nation, Brubaker argues for the need to study nationalism (the ways it comes to structure public perception, to inform thought and experience, to organize discourse and political action) without invoking nations as substantial entities. 'Instead of focusing on nations as real groups, we should focus on nationhood and nationness, on "nation" as practical category, institutionalized form, and contingent event. "Nation" is a category of practice, not (in the first instance) a category of analysis' (Brubaker, 1996: 7). In the same way, this study is concerned with practical uses of class and how the process of middle-class place-making actively shapes and structures social and spatial relations within gated communities and urban spaces.

10　The view of culture adopted in this study is aligned with Swidler's (1986) conception of culture as a metaphorical 'tool-kit' consisting of symbols, codes, stories, rituals, rhetoric, etc., which people use in varying configurations to solve different kinds of problems. Fundamentally, Swidler's 'culture as tool-kit' metaphor diverges from Weber's and Parson's functionalist notions of culture as an inventory of unified societal values and traditions that are internalized by members of a society and in turn direct their actions. The cultural tool-kit drawn from both the material world (architectural styles, spatial strategies, landscape cues) and symbolic environments (cognitive and emotional meanings; values, beliefs, ideologies, etc.) thus enables social actors to creatively use cultural tools in various combinations to solve different kinds of problems. In this sense, culture's causal significance lies not in strictly defining ends of actions but in providing a selection of cultural components that are used by people to construct strategies of action. By aligning the conception of culture with Swidler's tool-kit metaphor, this study focuses on how residents actively draw upon a wide cultural repertoire of 'the good life' in constructing landscapes of privilege and exclusion.

11　The main focus of this study is on commercially developed private housing enclaves built in Shanghai after the housing reform. As such, the study does not include traditional housing complexes that were later retrofitted with gates and fences for security reasons. These often contain poor-quality housing built prior to the reform and can hardly be considered as lifestyle enclaves.

12　Qualitative research and interpretations on inner-city neighbourhoods and social life can be traced back to several notable ethnographic works done by urban sociologists associated with the University of Chicago and elsewhere (see, for example, Wirth's 1928 study on Chicago's Jewish ghetto, Whyte's 1955 study on Boston's Italian district and Gans's 1962 study on urban villagers). During the 1970s and 1980s, increasing intellectual exchanges and dialogues between geography and other cognate disciplines such as sociology and anthropology enabled urban social geographers to engage more deeply with interpretive research, which spawned several ethnographic studies with a geographical focus (see Ley, 1974; Cybriwsky, 1978; Western, 1981; Duncan and Duncan, 1984; Jacobs, 1996).

13 Situated centrally in the southwestern part of the city, Minhang District consists of nine towns, three subdistricts and one municipal industrial zone. The district is largely a residential area covering approximately 370 square kilometres, though it is also home to a number of production facilities and key public infrastructures such as the Minhang Economic and Technological Development Zone and Hongqiao International Airport (the main air transportation hub in Shanghai before Pudong International Airport started operation in 1999). At the end of 2007, the district had over 1.8 million permanent residents. This is often considered as one of the most habitable areas outside of central Shanghai, and housing development has quickly become one of the main sources of local government revenue since the 1990s with the rapid development of commodity housing estates in the district. In 2001 and 2002 respectively, the district was awarded the national title of a 'garden urban district' and the United Nations–Habitat's Dubai International Award for Best Practices to Improve the Living Environment. In 2007, the district's per capita urban housing area was 22.33 square metres and the per capita urban disposable income stood at 20,154 yuan, both figures are much higher than Shanghai's overall average. See http://www.shanghaidaily.com/minhang/index.asp (28 July 2008). More recently, middle-class residents in the district made the news headlines for staging a rare public protest in Shanghai demanding that the municipal government scrap plans to build an extension line for the high-speed magnetic levitation train into their neighbourhood (more on this in Chapter 8).

2 Making middle-class spaces

1 Historically, the construction of physical boundaries (walls, fences, barricades) has long been practised in many societies and cultures. The early Roman cities were heavily fortified with walls which symbolized both aggression and defence. Medieval walled cities, as Lewis Mumford (1961) observed, served more than just a utilitarian/military function, also reflecting the distribution of power. These 'walls of custom' performed an important psychological function by binding different classes and 'keeping them in their places'. For instance, a typical pattern in the medieval city was the citadel or fortress on the hill (inhabited by the lords who dominated the city) surrounded at its base by residents of the city (merchants, workers, artisans) who were in turn separated by city walls from agricultural serfs and labourers located outside the city (Marcuse, 1997b: 106). Low (2003: 13) further notes that a system of walls, spatial segregation and class division is deeply ingrained in Europe as well as in the United States as a means for wealthy people to protect themselves from the local population. Perhaps the oldest and longest wall of all is the Great Wall of China, built after 228 BC. Measuring 1,500 miles long and between 18 and 30 feet high, the wall was built for defence against invasions from the northern tribes (see Wheatley, 1971; Heng, 1999; Xu, 2000).

2 As Stuart Elden (2007) critically points out, 'territory' and 'terror' share common etymological roots. Quoting the work of William Connolly, Elden illustrates how 'territory' is formed from both the Latin word *terra* (land or terrain) but also from the notion of *territorium*, a place from which people are warned or frightened away (*terrere*). Elden further argues that 'creating a bounded space is, already, a violent act of exclusion; maintaining it as such requires constant vigilance and the mobilization of threat; and challenging it necessarily entails a transgression' (2007: 822).

3 As Blomley (2004a,b) argues, it is critical for scholars, not least geographers, to *take property more seriously* as it is deeply social and political, not only structuring immediate relations between people but also shaping the broader political geogra-

phies of the city. In particular, 'property implies diverse and often contradictory social beliefs and representations (masculine citizenship, race, visions of the economy, claims to community, and so on)' and spatial conflicts and struggles over urban development frequently turn on contests over the meaning, moralities, and politics of property (Blomley, 2004a: xvii). It is thus important to challenge the dominant and essentialized views of (private) property claims as 'property is more definitionally, politically and empirically heterogeneous than the dominant ownership model presupposes' (Blomley, 2004a: xv–xvi).

4 The word for privacy in Chinese (*yinsi*) literally means something hidden, something that is protected from anyone knowing, and carries a pejorative connotation.

5 Although, during that time, Western notions of individualism did influence and encourage the belief that *si*, denoting self-interest, could be a means towards the achievement of the common good, the rhetoric of *gong* (public) had a powerful appeal. This *gong* rhetoric was often derived from indigenous political traditions, such as the notion of *datong* (the great harmony) attributed to Confucius in which the famous phrase 'All under Heaven is for the common good' (*tianxia wei gong*) views the public (*gong*) as infinitely superior to the private realm (*si*). These ideas were later taken up and debated by Chinese scholars and reformers such as Kang Youwei and Liang Qichao, the latter attempting to promote private virtue (*side*) not as merely a residual or purely instrumental value but as complementary to public virtue (*gongde*). However, the view was pushed aside under Sun Yat-sen's political programme, which laid out the Nationalist doctrine and belief that public institutions, service and interest were morally superior to private institutions, although not to the exclusion of respect for private property and for the family as an autonomous institution.

6 It is not my intention to reduce the discussion of privacy to its economic underpinnings. However, it has been suggested by some authors that the level of privacy one enjoys is typically associated with social status and material well-being. For example, in Pellow's (1993) study on family intimacy and the private life of city dwellers in Shanghai, she argues that it was following the economic reform and the general improvement in material/housing conditions that the average Chinese family could enjoy greater privacy and private spaces in their new apartments. Yan (2003), quoting the works of Prost, Braudel and Rybczynski, further notes that, in France, workers and peasants often lived in extremely crowded housing conditions until the turn of the twentieth century; and, in the United States, it was during the first half of the twentieth century that American families in a suburban dwelling began to enjoy a family room and a master bedroom with its own bathroom (Yan, 2003: 138).

3 Urban reform, the new middle class and the emergence of gated communities in Shanghai

1 The idea of developing Pudong is not entirely new. The original plans to develop Pudong could be traced back to Sun Yat-sen, widely recognized as the 'founding father' of modern China. After the 1911 Nationalist revolution, Sun had declared as one of his national reconstruction projects the development of the 'Great Port of Pudong'. However, the 1946 'Master Plan for Shanghai' (including the Pudong area) prepared by the Shanghai City Planning Board was soon discarded after the downfall of the nationalist Kuomintang Party in 1949 and was resurrected by Shanghai's city planners only after the adoption of open door policy in the late 1980s and 1990s.

2 As pointed out by Zhou and Ma (2000), although there are similarities between Chinese and North American suburbanization processes, there are also major differences. In particular, unlike the polycentric spatial structure of suburban growth in North American cities, suburbanization in China is still at an early stage with suburbs dominated by central cities. Also, the role of the state in China has been more pronounced in driving and shaping the suburbanization process.

3 'Neoliberalism' here refers to the ascendancy of economic doctrines that argue for the privatization of public services and the privileging of private property rights and private accumulation as well as promoting the competitive ethos of self-interest and self-advancement. To be sure, neoliberal thinking can often be traced to post-war writings of Friederich Hayek and Milton Friedman that are subsequently appropriated by scholars and activists to describe the organizational, political and ideological reorganization of capitalism through 'free-market' doctrines at the national or supranational levels. More recently, scholars have began to examine the 'urbanization of neoliberalism' at the city level to examine the interface between neoliberalism and urban restructuring (see, for example, N. Smith, 1996, 2002; Swyngedouw *et al.*, 2002; Leitner *et al.*, 2006). Cities, in this context, have become increasingly important geographical targets and institutional laboratories for a variety of neoliberal policy experiments including local entrepreneurialism, place-marketing, privatization of municipal public sector, restructuring of urban housing (razing of public housing and commodification of housing as private good), property-led mega-project development programmes and new strategies of social control and socio-spatial polarization. In this sense, urban spaces are mobilized as an arena both for market-oriented economic growth and for elite consumption.

4 After the 1949 Revolution, land in China was effectively nationalized and private land ownership ceased to exist by the 1950s. Public land was freely available to the people and government enterprises. The market-orientated economic reform in the 1980s not only brought an end to the monopoly public economy, but ended the institution of free land use. An amendment to the 1982 Chinese constitution was proposed and approved by the National People's Congress in 1988, which decreed that the right of land use can be transferred in accordance with the law. Essentially, land-use right transfer grants the land-use right, by bid, auction or agreement, to land-use applicants for a fixed period (usually 40 to 70 years) after a lump-sum payment has been made. Critics have charged that urban land reform is rigged by 'predatory rent-seeking' practices and corruption (see, for example, Y. P. Wang and Murie, 2000).

5 Shanghai's commercial banks extended loans worth 102.3 billion yuan (US$12.33 billion) to the real estate industry in 2004, an increase of 20.4 billion yuan from 2003. The outstanding value of individual housing loans hit 72.8 billion yuan in Shanghai in 2004, up by 10.6 billion yuan from 2003. According to the People's Bank of China, loans to the real estate sector, including mortgages and development loans, made up 76 per cent of all money loaned by local commercial banks in Shanghai in 2004 (*Xinhua News*, 16 May 2005).

6 The idea of improving the protection of private property was first brought up at the 16th National Congress of the Communist Party of China in November 2002. On 14 March 2004, a major amendment on private property protection was put to the vote and was passed by the Second Session of the 10th National People's Congress in Beijing. Specifically, Article 13 of the revised constitution states that the lawful private property of citizens is inviolable. The state protects according to law the right of citizens to own and inherit private property. See http://english.gov.cn/2005–08/05/content_20813.htm (22 May 2008). Subsequently, in 2007, China's landmark Property Law containing 247 articles providing equal protection to both state and private properties was put into effect. However, those from the conservative camp have expressed concerns that, although the new property law would undoubtedly increase protection for home-owners and prevent land seizures, it would also erode China's socialist principles.

7 According to a *China Daily* report (29 July 2005), China's affluent class, which accounts for less than 20 per cent of the total population, owns more than 80 per cent of the country's bank deposits. However, they contribute less than 10 per cent to the nation's personal income tax revenue.

8 The government has recently implemented a series of measures aimed at curbing

skyrocketing prices of commodity houses and real estate speculation, including raising the central bank's one-year lending rate from 5.31 per cent to 5.58 per cent and
the one-year deposit rate from 1.98 per cent to 2.25 per cent; tightening control on
property development loans; and levying business tax on the full profits from house
sales that are transacted within two years of purchase.

9 In a skewed income structure as in contemporary China, the middle-class concept
does not always map neatly with the 'median income' group, as income distribution in
China is heavily concentrated at the lower end. As several analysts have pointed out,
China's income distribution structure can be described as pyramid-shaped, with an
overwhelming majority of the population located at the bottom rungs of low-income
earners (the working-class strata) and the top 20 per cent of households earning more
than 50 per cent of total income. Given the skewed income distribution structure and
the relatively small number of high-income earners, it is thus not surprising that the
middle class has often been conflated and used interchangeably to also mean the rich
and upper class.

10 For this reason, Goodman (2008) cautions against transposing Western (more specifically northern European) developmental experiences onto contemporary China. As
he carefully points out, in the first half of the nineteenth century in northern Europe,
the new bourgeoisie were a new middle class created by the process of industrialization. As this process deepened, the modern state became more complex, producing
managerial and professional classes, which in turn formed a new middle class that
neither owned capital nor controlled the state, but derived income and status from
service and management. The demand for a widening of the franchise and the emergence of liberal democracy during the nineteenth century in Europe are often seen as
the necessary results of the emergence of the bourgeoisie (Goodman, 2008: 23–24).
Clearly, the Chinese new middle class has emerged under very different political–
economic circumstances and conditions, which made Goodman sceptical of the view
often proposed by some Western observers of equating the rise of industrialization
and economic development in China with the emergence of peace-ensuring liberal
democracy. Arguably, the pattern of economic development in China fits more closely
with that of Germany, Japan and Russia during the late nineteenth century than with
that of Britain or the United States in that, for the former group of countries, the state
played a central role in industrialization, as opposed to the laissez-faire capitalism of
the earlier European experience, which is based on the protection of the sovereign
individual outside the state.

11 Although the term 'middle class' is frequently invoked in both academic and popular parlance, it remains an elusive concept that is difficult to define and pin down.
Marxist 'materialist' theory, for example, focuses almost exclusively on interclass
politics between the capitalists and working class, giving short shrift to the role of the
middle class and its internal social dynamics. Weber, on the hand, although failing to
adequately characterize interclass conflict, nevertheless provided important insights
that are able to shed light on middle-class social life (Leichty, 2003: 16). Although this
study is not concerned with a theoretical exposition on the concept of the class, it is
instructive to make clear the concept of 'new middle class' and new rich in Shanghai/
China.

12 As Zhang (2008: 25–26) pointed out, *jieji* is a highly politicized term that is closely
associated with the brutal social repression and violent class struggles during Mao's
rule in China whereas *jiecheng* is a more contemporary and vernacular term referring to socioeconomic differentiation and status distinction. More than just a term
signifying economic distinction, *jiecheng* is also a cultural reference that is deeply
intertwined with one's ability to generate income and to consume a new lifestyle
that articulates the newly acquired social position of the new urban middle class in
Chinese society.

13 According to estimates, the typical expenses for China's middle class, taking a typical

young family as the base, are as follows: 1,500–5,000 yuan (US$181.20–$603.90) for food and beverages per month, 600–1,500 yuan (US$72.50–$181.20) for medical insurance, 300–5,000 yuan (US$36.20–$603.90) for education, 500–1,000 yuan (US$60.40–$120.80) for communication and transportation, 1,000–5,000 yuan (US$120.80–$603.90) for clothes and beauty treatments, and 600–3,500 yuan (US$72.50–$422.70) for sports and entertainment activities. In short, a typical young family needs to earn at least 10,000 yuan (US$1,207.70) per month if they want to lead a standard middle-class life. For a mid-level middle-class family, the couple needs to earn 20,000 yuan (US$2,415.50) per month, whereas 40,000 yuan (US$4,830.90) indicates an upper middle-class family (see G. R. Chen and Yi, 2004).

14 Although commodity housing proliferated in Shanghai only during the mid-1990s, the precursor to commodity housing is the residential housing that was first built in 1979 for people with overseas remittances. These residential buildings for people with overseas remittances could only be sold to the returned overseas Chinese and their relatives. Foreign exchange was used for settling accounts. In 1992, these buildings were converted into 'high-standard commodity residence' buildings for domestic sale.

15 For example, Y. P. Wang and Murie (2000) point out that, within the same work-unit housing compound, the driver of the director of a work-unit could well live in the same dwelling as his superiors although they would have occupied different sizes of flats and enjoyed different levels of housing benefits and entitlements. Essentially, during the socialist era, spatial segregation by class or income was nearly non-existent.

16 Many of these up-market neighbourhoods in contemporary central Shanghai mirror the old distinction of the 'uptown' areas in the city or what is locally known as the *Shangzhijiao*. In the uptown neighbourhoods, places such as the Huangpu and Luwan districts containing the French and international settlements were often considered prosperous places where foreigners and people with high status resided during the Concession era. In these upper-end areas of Shanghai today, one can still find many old villas and foreign-designed dwellings although many new prestigious real estate developments such as the mixed-used development in Xintiandi have been constructed there since the 1990s. By contrast, the lower-end areas such as Zhabei, Putuo and Yangpu districts in downtown Shanghai (*Xiazhijiao*) are often considered by the locals to be inferior and poor neighbourhoods. In between these two 'upper' and 'lower' end areas are 'middling' neighbourhoods such as Nanshi (Gamble, 2003: 113). While it is often impossible to draw a precise demarcation of the upper- and lower-end areas, these urban spatial distinctions have come to shape Shanghai residents' mental maps of rich and poor areas in the city for decades. However, such urban neighbourhood distinctions are not always static and have evolved over time. For example, Pudong in the olden days was considered one of the worst areas in the city, arguably even inferior to the poor neighbourhoods at the lower end, not least because it was physically separated from the main city by the Huang river. There is an old local saying that Shanghainese would rather own a bed in Puxi (west of the Huangpu river) than own a house in Pudong (east of the river) (*ningyao puxi yizhang chuang, buyao pudong yijianfang*). Clearly, this perception has changed dramatically now, as houses especially along the banks of Pudong are some of the most expensive properties in Shanghai.

4 Marketing the Chinese dream home

1 Non-representational thinking in geography is closely associated with the works of Nigel Thrift, alongside other geographers (see Dewsbury *et al.*, 2002; Lorimer, 2005; Cosgrove, 2008). Some of the tenets of non-representational theorizing include the denial of the efficacy of symbolic representational models of the world, whose main focus is on the 'internal', and a shift to focus on the 'external' where 'basic terms and objects are forged in a manifold of actions and interactions' (Thrift, 1996: 7). In this

sense, practice constitutes our sense of the real. However, Thrift is also careful to point out that non-representational thinking does not deny the value of cognitive processes or the reality of cultural representation. 'It is, rather, to situate these imagined understandings as only a part of a broader process of knowledging' (ibid.: 8).

2 As Knapp and Lo (2005) as well as other scholars on Chinese domestic architecture have pointed out, the Chinese character for 'house' (*jia*) is also the same as that for 'home' and 'family'. The Chinese character for *jia* (pictographically depicting a pig under a roof or in a house) signifies the family as historically an economic unit of production (pig-rearing) as well as consumption (pig-eating) (Jervis, 2005: 223). Although contemporary urban families are no longer bounded by the agrarian tradition, the Chinese family or *jia* continues to serve as an important foundation that shapes and organizes personal and social life. In reform China more specifically, the ascendance of the private family based on horizontal conjugal ties (rather than vertical patriarchal or corporate family structures) has also transformed the house/home as a private haven for the nuclear family, catering to the changing needs for private conjugal spaces and the privacy of individual family members (see Yan, 2003; see also Chapter 5 for more on the shifting meanings of home and privacy in Shanghai's gated communities).

3 Since 1950, the Chinese Communist Party (CCP) has been selecting *lao muo* or 'labour heroes', hailing proletarian workers such as street sweepers, toilet cleaners, bus conductors, plumbers and miners as model workers to be emulated by the citizens. In recent years, the selection of model workers has departed from convention by also including millionaire businessmen and wealthy celebrities as potential labour heroes. In 2005, the NBA sports star and Shanghai native Yao Ming was selected as a national model worker despite much contention within the rank and file of the CCP, who felt that his millionaire and celebrity status has put him out of touch with ordinary workers in China (*Xinhua News*, 20 April 2005).

4 Rem Koolhas was commissioned to design the controversial new China Central Television (CCTV) headquarters in Beijing and Paul Andreas is involved in a number of high-profile projects such as the National Theatre in Beijing and Shanghai's Pudong International Airport.

5 The terms 'villa' and 'mansion' are often used indiscriminately in Shanghai's real estate advertisements and even low-rise apartments may sometimes be misrepresented as villas or mansions.

6 Western-style villas were by no means the only form of elite housing in Shanghai in the past. Other prestigious housing types during pre-liberation days include new-style *shikumen* (stonewall) apartments or *xinshi linong* and garden alleyway houses. The Western-style villas were generally considered the most luxurious housing type of the time.

7 Like gated communities elsewhere, Vanke Garden City has a set of housing covenants and by-laws that prevent residents from altering the exterior of their houses or encroaching on common property areas within the estate. These housing covenants and by-laws are, however, frequently flouted by residents in many housing estates in Shanghai.

8 Salacious reports of businessmen and political officials keeping 'second wives' and mistresses (*bao ernai*) have rapidly surfaced in post-reform China, with some of these illicit affairs being linked to high-profile cases of corruption charges involving senior-ranking political cadres and city mayors. Whereas the mistress or 'modern concubine' phenomenon in China has been well documented (for example Shih, 1998), the existence of up-market gated communities as the private liaison grounds for these extramarital affairs has also been highlighted in news reports and even on the website of the National Population and Family Planning Commission of China. In the latter, local government officials have highlighted difficulties in enforcing the state's family planning policies and keeping track of children born out of wedlock in some of these

up-market gated communities, which are often closed off to non-residents and even the local police (*Dongfang Morning Post*, 18 January 2005). See also Chapter 5 for further discussion on privacy of gated estates and the conflicts with state control.

5 Constructing a new private order

1 See http://xmwb.news365.com.cn/ (16 April 2006).
2 See http://www.privacyinternational.org (20 May 2006).
3 As Bonnie McDougall (2004: 1) reminds us, the terms 'private' and 'privacy' have overlapping meanings but are not entirely synonymous. In English, 'private' may refer to private versus public realms, i.e. private institutions, service and interests in distinction to public institutions, service and interests; whereas in the noun 'privacy' it refers more to a state of intimacy, seclusion and interiority to which access is controlled.
4 There are limited rights to privacy in the Chinese constitution. For example, Article 38 states that the personal dignity of citizens of the People's Republic of China (PRC) is inviolable and that insult, libel, false accusation or false incrimination directed against citizens by any means is prohibited. Articles 37 and 39 define, respectively, the protection of freedom of the person and the residence. Article 40 provides for the freedom and privacy of correspondence of the citizen. Despite these provisions, the Chinese government admits that it has room for improvement in applying *any* laws fairly and systematically. Law enforcement officials can issue search warrants on their own authority or else simply ignore legal requirements for independent oversight. Authorities also monitor telephone conversations, facsimile transmissions, international and domestic mail, email, text-messaging and Internet communications. In addition, the security services also routinely monitor and enter residences and offices to gain access to computers, telephones, and fax machines. All major hotels have a sizable internal security presence, and hotel guestrooms are sometimes searched for sensitive materials (*Privacy International*, 16 October 2004, http://www.privacyinternational.org; see also *Constitution of the People's Republic of China*, 2004).
5 In recent years, in a bid to improve the city's image and food safety record, the Shanghai municipal government has clamped down on open-air 'wet markets' in several parts of the city and relocated these businesses to 'modern' indoor markets. In addition, foreign supermarket chains such as the French Carrefour, the US Walmart and Thai-owned Lotus Company are sprouting up all over the city and suburbs, even though many Shanghai residents still continue to buy their daily grocery products from itinerant hawkers in open-air market places.
6 To some extent, the same may be said about the work-unit apartments that were built in Shanghai after the 1950s. These 'new apartment villages' (*gongren xincun*) have built-in kitchens and washing facilities with separate rooms and have lost the earlier communal aspect of *shikumen* living. The average size of the *xincun* flat is only 50 square metres and the lack of personal spaces and privacy is still a concern, especially when there are children and old folks in the house.
7 The Residential Committees were first established by the Chinese Communist Party when it took power in 1949, building on the old practice of state-sponsored community security or the *bao-jia* system in the earlier periods. Under the planned economy, the residential committees under the control of their 'Street Offices' (*jiedao banshichu*) hardly played any formal political role in neighbourhood administration except to help publicize government propaganda, mediate petty disputes among residents and also monitor the personal activities and behaviour of residents (see Frolic, 1980). The more important tasks of administering neighbourhood organization and providing residential services were handled by the work-units instead. However, with the decline of the influence of work-units after the economic reform, the residential committees in many urban neighbourhoods have now taken on greater responsibili-

ties, acting as the liaison between the grassroots and the municipal authorities and police. However, in many up-market gated communities that are privately managed and run, the residential committees, long considered as state-linked and paternalistic neighbourhood organizations, are often sidelined and in some respects supplanted by the 'semi-autonomous' home-owners' associations and professional property management companies.

8 The issues of self-governance of urban neighbourhoods through home-owners' associations and local community development (*shequ jianshe*) have in recent years been widely debated in China. In December 2007, the state-run China Central Television (CCTV) even broadcast a dialogue programme entitled 'Grassroots democracy in urban China'. Interestingly, it was pointed out that, whereas the Ministry of Civil Affairs was tasked with the setting up of local community development programmes to replace work-unit-dominated neighbourhood administration, it was the Ministry of Construction that was in charge of governing urban home-owners' associations under the 1994 ordinance (Order No. 33 'Methods of Managing New Urban Residential Neighbourhoods'). However, for the latter, there are many government restrictions and, as Benjamin Read (2003, 2008) points out, getting official approval for self-organized home-owners' associations can be difficult, in large part because of the city government's multiple reasons for looking askance at them. Far from wanting to boost home-owners' capacity to exercise power over their homes and housing complexes, government officials felt they should be tamped down and put in their place (Read, 2003: 55). In addition, once set up, many home-owners' associations become riddled with many internal conflicts and problems. For instance, a lot of the home-owners' associations in China are not actually controlled by the home-owners themselves but are instead dominated by the property developers and management companies. Sometimes the home-owners themselves become factionalized and get bogged down in internal conflicts, so that the associations fail to even function properly. Nevertheless, in some estates in Shanghai, home-owners' associations actually do function quite well, holding regular meetings and elections and representing the residents' interests, albeit within the parameters set by the state.

9 I am not suggesting that such personal freedom or liberties are enjoyed only by residents of gated communities per se. To be sure, the loosening up of state control is a broad set of structural changes experienced in reform China with its ramifications and effects felt across a wide spectrum of people from rural to urban areas. The point I am making here is that personal autonomy and liberty are more readily accessible in private gated communities with their enclosed management style and private status.

10 In stark contrast to the state-controlled CCTV, the national television network with 13 channels, Phoenix's InfoNews Channel offers more innovative news shows modelled after Western media such as CNN. The channel also provides live, exclusive reporting on Taiwan – a first since the government banned virtually all news from the island that it considers a renegade province. In addition, Phoenix InfoNews also provides in-depth reporting on what are deemed to be politically and socially sensitive Chinese news stories and events such as the 2004 mining disaster in which 166 miners died after a poorly regulated coal-mine exploded in western China's Shaanxi province (*Asia Times*, 9 December 2004).

11 See http://www.chinafpa.org.cn/ (26 May 2006).

12 A prominent advocate for this view is Judith Thomson (1974), who argues that, in every single case, what is known as the supposed right to privacy proves in fact to be another right already in existence. In other words, rights to privacy can in each particular case be reduced to other rights, in particular rights over the person and property. (For arguments against this reductionist view, see Rossler, 2005: 67–68; also Scanlon, 1975.)

13 This is not to suggest that alternative ways of understanding and talking about private property do not exist in China. The phenomenon of private property is arguably

much more complicated and ambiguous (J. M. Zhu, 2002; Ho and Lin, 2003) than the simple dichotomy between public and private. Deborah Davis (2004), for example, has demonstrated how family members mobilize a wide range of discourses about family justice and moral values such as filial piety when arbitrating property rights. Not withstanding that, the point of this chapter is to examine how residents in gated communities assert and protect their own immediate interests and private property.

14   The literature on governmentality can be traced to the writings of Michel Foucault (1982, 1991), who extended the notion of governance beyond state-centric processes. Historically, in the evolution of modern Western statecraft, the governing of society and the regulation of human life, often in the name of enhancing the welfare and quality of life of the population, precipitated the creation of a new biopolitics centred on the increased ordering and administration of the population by the state. This resulted in the emergence of an elaborate discursive/bureaucratic structure and organized practices (mentalities, rationalities and technologies of power) through which citizen-subjects are formed (see also Rose, 1999; Larner, 2000).

15   Yan's (2003) work is one of the few scholarly attempts to examine in detail the issue of privacy and family life in post-reform China. Although his book is based on rural ethnographic evidences, his observations and arguments on the privatization of the family and rise of individualism are broadly applicable to the urban context in China. As he notes in the preface of his book (2003: xiii), many of the structural forces that transform the rural society can also be found in cities that have undergone similar socialist policies and economic reform.

16   The rise of individualism has been a much-debated social issue in China. Social analysts have cited a number of trends such as the rise in divorce rates (21 per cent in 2004, nearly five times more than in 1979) as one indication of rising individualism in China (*China Daily*, 10 April 2005). Recently, state-endorsed patriotic songs were at the centre of a public uproar as the lyrics were seen to encourage young people to pursue their own dreams and success, departing from the traditional understanding of patriotic songs that usually promote values such as selflessness, collectivism and heroism (*China Daily*, 17 March 2005).

17   In order to generate funding for commercial housing development, the Chinese government introduced the Housing Provident Fund (HPF) Scheme in Shanghai in 1991. Fashioned in part after Singapore's Central Provident Fund (CPF) system, all employees are required to contribute a proportion of their salaries to the HPF and employers contribute a similar amount. Accounts for individual workers were set up in the Construction Bank of China. Workers are then allowed to withdraw their HPF savings when they retire, or alternatively use their HPF savings to purchase homes in the private housing market or other approved housing developments. The HPF is now implemented in most cities in China, although there are some variations in the operation of the scheme (see S. C. W. Yeung and Howes, 2006). However, many residents I spoke to revealed that the HPF is only sufficient to cover a very small portion of their housing expenditure, as wages in China (especially for those working in the public sector) are still very low and this is compounded by the fact that housing prices in big cities such as Shanghai have appreciated many times beyond the reach of many ordinary workers.

18   The theory of possessive individualism is fundamentally flawed on two accounts (Macpherson, 1985). First, it generates an impoverished view of human life, making acquisition and consumption central and obscuring deeper human purposes and capacities. It further reduces the functions of human life to the maximization of utility and the narrow pursuit of self-interest. Second, possessive individualism also holds out a false promise. Most people cannot really enjoy even an impoverished individuality, freedom and equality, which possessive individualism ostensibly offers to all, because a system based on private property and so-called free exchange inevitably generates a concentration of ownership of all the means of production except labour.

In fact, most people are compelled to sell their labour and are free and equal individuals in name only. In reality, they are subordinates to the owners of capital, who are able to use the power that ownership brings to control those without capital and to extract benefits from them (Carens, 1993: 3).

19 Wang, however, seems to have overstated her case and clearly ignores the individual human agency as well as their complex experiences and motivations when she argues that 'the post-communist personality is so thoroughly at the mercy of the stimuli thrown up by the market reforms' that it is characterized by 'hedonism without individualism' (X. Y. Wang, 2002: 8).

6 Securing the civilized enclaves

1 As L. Zhang (2001: 210) usefully points out, the notion of *suzhi* parallels Bourdieu's (1984) concept of habitus in that they both refer to a person's disposition, behaviour and way of living, which are shaped by one's upbringing and unlikely to be altered overnight. However, it is contentious who has the right to define or determine *suzhi* in Chinese society because the discourse of *suzhi* both is conditioned by and in turn shapes power relations and social domination. Zhang (2001) goes on to suggest that, paradoxically, whereas migrant communities in the city are often stigmatized as people with poor *suzhi*, successful migrant entrepreneurs such as the Wenzhou migrants are known for their legendary business acumen, shrewdness and business competence. The urbanites' complaints of the migrants' low *suzhi* partly reveal their own insecurity and jealousy, as they are being symbolically displaced by particular groups of successful migrants and thus failing to assume a prominent place in the post-Mao socioeconomic order (L. Zhang, 2001: 211).

2 Most of the suspicion or hostility directed against 'outsiders' in gated communities is invariably targeted at migrant workers, more than the local urban poor. The latter are considered less threatening and problematic as they are seen to be rooted in the local community and way of life. Besides, poor communities with local *hukou* are also assisted by municipal welfare services whereas rural migrant workers with no urban *hukou* status are left to their own devices. Given this, it is often thought that institutional exclusion from local welfare services and support coupled with the absence of strong local community ties will cause these rural migrant workers to be more prone to commit crime and disrupt social order in the city.

3 For Bourdieu (1984), moral and cultural disposition appear to be quite distinct. Whereas cultural capital is accrued by people as a form of class distinction, moral virtues such as the symbolic authority of honesty and trustworthiness are often utilized by poorer people who have no real capital to offer to the market (1984: 365).

4 As Cohen (1993) contends, the conceptual transformation of the population in China's countryside from farmers into peasants was a reversal of the sequence of events in rural Europe, where modernization was seen to turn peasants into farmers. In Europe, the end of peasantry was linked to the formation of modern nation-states, and to growing rural–urban ties in the context of industrialization, and modernization of communications and agriculture as well as the spread of formal education. In China, Western influence and pre-Communist industrialization and modernization had their greatest impact in the cities, especially the major foreign-dominated 'treaty ports'. The effect was the modern creation of the severe rural–urban contrasts, which in the Western historical imagination are seen to be characteristic of Europe's pre-modern era.

5 Here, the *China Daily* editorial makes no apparent distinction between farmers and peasants.

6 See also Emily Honig's (1992) insightful historical account on the derogatory construction of Subei people as ethnic outsiders in Shanghai. Mostly refugees from floods, famine or war in their native districts, Subei migrants in Shanghai dominated

the ranks of unskilled labourers and were often despised and stigmatized as being poor, ignorant, dirty and unsophisticated.

7 The moral dimension of state power has drawn critical attention from scholars in recent years. In these discussions, the state is often seen to be actively involved in promoting the 'proper' moral and social development of its citizenry. For example, Bunnell (2002) argues that the Malaysian government's concern over the inappropriate conduct of its Malay citizens in the rapidly modernizing capital city, Kuala Lumpur, has led to the contested governance of urban(e) 'Malayness'. Brownell's (1995) study on sports culture in China further explores the similar theme of how the state regulates and controls national sporting events and the development of a 'body culture' through invoking various moral ideas about civilization and discipline. Overall, these works stress the nationalistic goals of the state to mobilize moral discourses to work towards the creation of an internally cohesive nation-state as well as 'morally well-developed' citizenry that is productive and dedicated to the nation's overall welfare. This sense of 'internal morality' is typically nurtured through national campaigns and public education but is also developed through the process of defining a morally inferior 'other' in the national psyche (Herbert, 1996: 141).

8 In Fernand Braudel's (1995) work on the history of civilizations, he noted that the word 'civilization' (a neologism) emerged late, and unobtrusively, in eighteenth-century France. It was formed from 'civilized' and 'to civilize', which had long existed and were in general use in the sixteenth century. The word then spread through Europe (together with the word 'culture'). By 1772 and probably earlier, the word 'civilization' had reached England and replaced 'civility', despite the latter's long history. Yet in other European countries the word took on various forms, such as *Zivilization* in Germany (alongside its older counterpart *Bildung*), or was met with resistance. For example, in Holland, the word met opposition from *beschaving*, a noun based on the verb *beschaven* meaning to refine, ennoble or civilize, although the word *civilisate* did later appear. In Italy, the word too encountered similar resistance in the old word *civilita* (Braudel, 1995: 3).

9 A report in *China Daily* (6 September 2005) quoted a China health expert as stating that transient migrant workers are a 'high AIDS risk' and constitute one of the main reasons for the spread of HIV infection in the country. According to the report, poorly educated rural workers often engage in high-risk sexual practices such as engaging in the illegal sex trade. The expert warned that greater preventive measures need to be taken, 'otherwise, they [migrant workers] will carry the virus all over the country and it will cause a tragedy in China's public health system'. See also C. Smith and Hugo (2008) on the spread of HIV/AIDS and migration in China.

10 According to Greenhalgh and Winckler (2005), under Mao Zedong, China's booming population was sometimes considered as an asset to the country and sometimes as an impediment to national progress. Under Deng Xiaoping, however, the large size and 'low quality' of China's population was considered unequivocally as a serious obstacle to China's modernization efforts. In response to this, post-Mao leaders had placed limiting population growth as a central concern in the country's new programme of national reform. Under Jiang Zeming, population policy premised on maintaining low fertility also shifted towards raising population quality. By Hu Jintao's era of the early 2000s, population and reproduction policy has moved beyond addressing purely demographic concerns to be reframed as 'social policy' addressing specific social problems such as gender imbalance, old age security and rural–urban distribution. By and large, limiting population growth and improving its quality have become a central preoccupation of Chinese statecraft (Greenhalgh and Winckler, 2005: 2).

11 Many migrant workers I spoke to consider private home ownership as one of the most important criteria towards qualifying 'as a Shanghainese'. In the late 1980s, many local governments implemented some form of 'urban citizenship for sale' programme through the issuance of 'blue stamp' *hukou* (Cartier, 2001: 252–253). Eligibility is

mainly based on the economic contributions of applicants and education level. But more frequently, urban citizenship or blue stamp *hukou* were offered to those who could afford to purchase private property at full market prices. Even though this system has been discontinued in Shanghai, many of my respondents still think that the first step towards being a Shanghainese is to be able to afford a private home in the city. Migrants who have achieved economic success and been awarded local *hukou* are often called 'new Shanghainese' or *xin shanghairen*.

7 Beyond the gates

1 The 'normative turn' in no way denies earlier contributions of the social sciences on moral and ethical issues. After all, social/cultural anthropologists have long been interested in the moral codes and orders of different societies (Howell, 1997). For example, Malinowski's (1926) work *Crime and Custom in Savage Society* posed many pertinent questions on why people in different societies behaved according to social rules and norms, and whether their behaviour was constrained by the fear of punishment or it was due to some higher social 'bonding forces' at work. Other anthropologists have also been interested in examining 'gift exchange' as a form of moral economy or as a 'total social phenomenon' (Mauss, 1925) involving legal, economic, moral, religious and aesthetic dimensions (see also more recent works, for example by Yan, 1996, on gift exchange in a Chinese village). Geographers too have been interested in the connection between geography and morality but, as Sack (2003: 5) points out, the connection has been filtered largely through the study of religion and mythology. Only in recent decades have geographical literatures taken explicit positions and offered systematic arguments on morality (see, for example, Harvey, 1973, 1996, 2000; D. Smith, 1998; Tuan, 1989).

2 The theory adopts a critical realist approach that assumes that reality exists and the good is an independent part of reality. In other words, as Sack (2003: 8) notes: 'we can be realist not only about empirical reality but that we can be moral realist too'. See, however, Bauman's (1993) opposing view on morality as endemically and irredeemably non-rational and hence resistant to codification and formalization.

3 There are different prevailing notions of justice (distributive, procedural and retributive) appealing to principles such as strict egalitarianism, welfare maximization and fairness (see, for example, Rawls, 1999). In this instance, the theory is addressing the distributive notion of justice based on the principle of giving all members of society a 'fair share' of the benefits and resources available.

4 The conception of evil in Sack's model draws heavily from the works of Hannah Arendt. Most notably, Arendt (1963) had argued that evil is banal and does not have 'depth nor any demonic dimension'. Atrociously evil acts are not so much committed by inherently diabolical or downright wicked people but can be seen as the result of 'sheer thoughtlessness' and the lack of full awareness of one's own action. As Sack (2003: 180) further contends, 'evil is far less remote when we think of it arising from not choosing to be aware (as opposed to being fully aware and then choosing evil over good)' and that 'incremental decisions to avoid being open-minded can lead to the morally wrong choices'.

8 Conclusion

1 The terms 'transformation' and 'transition' and their semantic implications need to be qualified and considered carefully when they are used to describe China's contemporary social and political changes. As Ma (2002: 1545–1546) points out, the concept of 'transition' used in post-socialist development assumes a process of change towards a preconceived and fixed target that is inappropriate for China's case, in which economic reform appears to be aimed at several moving targets. Instead Ma prefers to use

the term 'transformation', which, in his opinion, avoids the implication of the inevitability of transiting towards a Western capitalist style of production and instead stresses the unpredictable processes and outcomes in China's prolonged reform programmes. Pannell (2002: 1572), however, has chosen the term 'urban transition', which he uses to refer to 'the movement of population from rural to urban locations, the shift of their work activities to things normally associated with urban locations, such as from manufacturing and various other services and the changing nature of their lifestyles in cities and towns'. Yet other authors use the two terms quite interchangeably, perhaps to describe the transitory aspects as well as more radical transformative dynamics of urban change in contemporary urban China (see also Friedmann, 2005; Logan, 2008). Clearly there is no consensus here over which term is more appropriate though it is worthwhile to be cognizant of the different usages of these terms here.

2 The idea of 'small government, big society' (*xiao zhenfu, da shuhui*) was promulgated as China's approach to enlarging the functions of society and the people while reforming the political system and streamlining state bureaucratic control. First coined by Liao Xun, a young research fellow in the Chinese Academy of Social Sciences (CASS), the idea represents a first major effort to create the foundation of a new kind of civil society in China, but one that is paradoxically implemented from above and not from below (Brødsgaard, quoted in Friedmann, 2005: 85).

3 Allegedly, the middle-class residents in Minhang were infuriated that the extension of the noisy magnetic levitation or Maglev train lines into their neighbourhood would depreciate their property values, disturb the tranquillity of their homes and perhaps even pose health hazards to the residents, especially the children and elderly. Arguably, what makes these middle-class protesters unique and different from others is that this new middle-class social stratum has more resources at its disposal (money, education, communication tools such as mobile phones, the Internet and video cameras) that were missing or less prevalent in earlier periods of PRC history. Also, when they buy expensive homes in these new housing developments it gives them a strong impetus to protect that investment. Often considered the new movers of China's market-driven economy, they could be alienated by the Chinese state if their concerns are not addressed adequately.

4 Ironically it was the rural villages that got the first head start in experimenting with grassroots democracy through open direct election of village officials. In 1978, village elections were first introduced in China and were subsequently conducted on a trial basis from 1988 onwards. The Chinese National People's Congress formally passed the 'New Organic Law of the Village Committee' in 1998, which mandated all village committee officials to be elected competitively by local villagers. Notwithstanding some initial implementation problems, village elections in provinces such as Jilin, Fujian, Yunnan and Hainan have generally been considered to have resulted in positive changes by empowering locally elected officials and promoting village citizenship. From the late 1990s, experimental direct elections were extended to townships as well for electing urban residential committee members in cities like Qingdao, Shanghai and Beijing (see B. G. He, 1996). It has often been pointed out by some critics that it is ironic that China started experimenting with democratic elections in the rural villages where people are often considered by the state to be poor and backward.

5 The concept of 'gating coalition' is derived from Logan and Molotch's (1987) classic thesis on 'urban growth machine' politics.

6 The 'Executive Condominium' (essentially a gated condominium estate) programme was introduced in 1995 by the Singapore government to cater to the 'sandwich' middle class, identified as young university graduates and professionals who can afford more than public housing but find private property out of their reach. To manage this rising tide of envy among the young and upwardly mobile electorates, the People's Action Party party-state has responded by promoting the development of such subsidized gated estates. Comparable in design and facilities to private condominiums,

Executive Condominiums (ECs) are developed and sold by private developers but at a lower price (about 30 per cent below market rate) and come with a generous government housing grant (of up to S$30,000). However the purchase of an EC is based on various eligibility criteria. EC buyers must be Singapore citizens with a family nucleus comprising at least another Singapore permanent resident or Singapore citizen. The combined income level per month should also be no more than S$10,000. Through the building of the EC, the state attempts not only to institutionalize middle-class privileges by helping them achieve their private housing aspirations but also in the process maintain state legitimacy and rule (Chua and Tan, 1999). To date 22 EC housing projects have been built in Singapore.

7   Under Proposition 13, passed by voters in California in 1978, property taxes in the state are limited to 1 per cent of a property's assessed value. Although the stated purpose of the provision was to protect home-owners, another motive, as Fulton (1999) points out, was to constrain local city governments from liberal spending practices. One drastic effect of the enactment of this proposition was that it severely restricted many local governments' ability to raise revenues through property taxes, forcing many of them to 'fiscalize' their land-use policies and to compete for lucrative real estate developments. Critics of gated communities often charged that the tax law resulted in financially strapped localities and a declining standard of public infrastructure, which provided the incentives and structural conditions for the proliferation of self-funded and self-contained gated communities, where 'community' infrastructures and amenities are paid for privately through home-owners' association dues and other fees. Despite this, the proposition remains popular among many voters and was upheld by the US Supreme court as constitutional. Similar statutes have also been enacted, for example Proposition 2½ in Massachusetts, which was passed in 1980.

Bibliography

Adams, P., Hoelscher, S. and Till, K. (eds) (2001) *Textures of Place: Exploring Humanist Geographies*, Minneapolis: University of Minnesota Press.

Adrey, R. (1997) *The Territorial Imperative: A Personal Inquiry into the Animal Origins of Property and Nations*, New York: Atheneum.

Agnew, J. (1987) *Place and Politics: The Geographical Mediation of State and Society*, Boston: Allen & Unwin.

—— (2002) *Making Political Geography*, London: Edward Arnold.

Agnew, J. and Duncan, J. (eds) (1989) *The Power of Place: Bringing Together Geographical and Sociological Imaginations*, Boston, MA: Unwin and Hyman.

Alexander, J. (2004) 'Cultural pragmatics: social performance between rituals and strategy', *Sociological Theory* 22: 527–573.

Amin, A. (2006) 'The good city', *Urban Studies* 43: 1009–1023.

Anagnost, A. (1997) *National Past-Times: Narrative, Representation, and Power in Modern China*, Durham, NC: Duke University Press.

Anderson, K. (1988) 'Cultural hegemony and the race definition process in Vancouver's Chinatown: 1880–1980', *Environment and Planning D: Society and Space* 6: 127–149.

—— (1991) *Vancouver's Chinatown: Racial Discourse in Canada, 1875–1980*, McGill–Queen's University Press.

Arendt, H. (1963) *Eichmann in Jerusalem: A Report on the Banality of Evil*, New York: Viking.

—— (1998) *The Human Condition*, Chicago: University of Chicago Press.

Aries, P. and Duby, G. (1991) *A History of Private Life*, Cambridge, MA: Belknap Press, Harvard University Press.

Asia Times. Online. Available at http://www.atimes.com (last accessed 20 April 2005).

Atkinson, R. and Blandy, S. (2005) 'International perspectives on the new enclavism and the rise of gated communities,' *Housing Studies* 20: 177–186.

Bachelard, G. (1964) *The Poetics of Space*, Boston: Beacon Press.

Badcock, B. (1998) 'Ethical quandaries and the urban domain', *Progress in Human Geography* 22: 586–594.

Baudrillard, J. (1981) *For a Critique of the Political Economy of the Sign*, trans. with introduction by Charles Levin, St. Louis: Telos Press.

Baum, R. (1996) *Burying Mao*, Princeton, NJ: Princeton University Press.

Bauman, Z. (1993) *Postmodern Ethics*, Oxford: Blackwell.

Baumgartner, M. P. (1988) *The Moral Order of a Suburb*, Oxford: Oxford University Press.

Berlin, I. (1958) *Two Concepts of Liberty*, Oxford: Clarendon Press.

Blakely, E. J. and Snyder, M. G. (1997) *Fortress America: Gated Communities in the United States*, Washington, DC: Brookings Institution Press.

Blomley, N. (2004a) *Unsettling the City: Urban Land and the Politics of Property*, London: Routledge.

—— (2004b) 'Un-real estate: proprietary space and public gardening', *Antipode* 36: 614–641.

Bondi, L. (2005) 'Working the spaces of neoliberal subjectivity: psychotherapeutic technologies, professionalisation and counselling', *Antipode* 37: 497–514.

Bourdieu, P. (1984) *Distinction: A Social Critique of the Judgement of Taste*, Cambridge, MA: Harvard University Press.

—— (1990) *In Other Words: Essays towards a Reflexive Sociology*, Stanford, CA: Stanford University Press.

Boyd, R. (2006) 'The value of civility', *Urban Studies* 43 (5–6): 863–878.

Brain, D. (1997) 'From public housing to private communities: the discipline of design and the materialization of the public/private distinction in the built environment,' in J. Weintraub and K. Kumar (eds) *Public and Private in Thought and Practice: Perspectives on a Grand Dichotomy*, Chicago: University of Chicago Press.

Braudel, F. (1995) *A History of Civilizations*, New York: Penguin Books.

Brenner, N. and Theodore, N. (eds) (2002) *Spaces of Neoliberalism: Urban Restructuring in North America and Western Europe*, Oxford: Blackwell.

Brownell, S. (1995) *Training the Body for China: Sports in the Moral Order of the People's Republic*, Chicago: University of Chicago Press.

Brubaker, R. (1996) *Nationalism Reframed: Nationhood and the National Question in the New Europe*, Cambridge: Cambridge University Press.

Bunnell, T. (2002) '*Kampung* rules: landscape and the contested government of urban(e) Malayness', *Urban Studies* 39: 1685–1701.

—— (2006) *Malaysia, Modernity and the Multimedia Super Corridor: A Critical Geography of Intelligent Landscapes*, London: RoutledgeCurzon.

Cahoone, L. (1996) *From Modernism to Postmodernism: An Anthology*, Oxford: Blackwell.

Caldeira, T. (1999) 'Fortified enclaves: the new urban segregation', in J. Holston (ed.) *Cities and Citizenship*, Durham, NC: Duke University Press.

—— (2000) *City of Walls: Crime, Segregation, and Citizenship in São Paulo*, Berkeley, CA: University of California Press.

Carens, J. (1993) *Democracy and Possessive Individualism: The Intellectual Legacy of C. B. Macpherson*, Albany, NY: State University of New York Press.

Cartier, C. (2001) *Globalizing South China*, Oxford: Blackwell.

Casey, E. (2001) 'Between geography and philosophy: what does it mean to be in the place-world?', *Annals of the Association of American Geographers* 91: 683–693.

Castells, M. (1996) *The Rise of the Network Society*, Oxford: Blackwell.

Chan, K. W. and Zhang, L. (1999) 'The Hukou system and rural–urban migration in China: processes and changes', *China Quarterly* 160: 818–855.

Chen, A. (2002) 'Capitalist development, entrepreneurial class, and democratization in China', *Political Science Quarterly* 117: 401–422.

Chen, G. R. and Yi, Y. (2004) *Zhongguo zhongchan diaocha* (*A Study on the Middle Class in China*), Beijing: TJ Press.

China Daily. Online. Available at http://www.chinadaily.com.cn/home/index.html (last accessed 26 December 2005).

China Statistical Yearbook 2002. No. 21, National Bureau of Statistic of China: China Statistic Press.

China Vanke Co. Ltd. Online. Available at http://www.vanke.com/main/ (last accessed 28 March 2006).

Christopherson, S. (1994) 'The fortress city: privatized spaces, consumer citizenship', in A. Amin (ed.) *Post-Fordism: A Reader*, Oxford: Blackwell.

Chua, B. H. and Tan, J. E. (1999) 'Singapore: where the middle-class sets the standard', in M. Pinches (ed.) *Culture and Privilege in Capitalist Asia*, London: Routledge.

Cochrane, A. (1998) 'Illusions of power: interviewing local elites', *Environment and Planning A*, 30: 2121–2132.

Cohen, M. (1993) 'Cultural and political inventions in modern China: the case of the Chinese "peasant"', in W. M. Tu (ed.) *China in Transformation*, Cambridge, MA: Harvard University Press.

Connell, J. (1999) 'Beyond Manila: walls, malls, and private spaces', *Environment and Planning A* 31: 417–439.

Connolly, W. (2002) *Identity/Difference: Democratic Negotiations of Political Paradox*, expanded edition, Minneapolis: University of Minnesota Press.

Constitution of the People's Republic of China (2004) Beijing: People's Publishing House.

Cosgrove, D. (2008) *Geography and Vision*, London: IB Tauris.

Cosgrove, D. and Daniels, S. (eds) (1988) *The Iconography of Landscape: Essays on the Symbolic Representation, Design and Use of Past Environments*, Cambridge: Cambridge University Press.

Cosgrove, D. and Jackson, P. (1987) 'New directions in cultural geography', *Area* 19: 95–101.

Coy, M. and Pohler, M. (2002) 'Gated communities in Latin American mega-cities: case studies in Brazil and Argentina', *Environment and Planning B* 29: 355–370.

Cresswell, T. (1996) *In Pace/Out of Place: Geography, Ideology and Transgression*, Minneapolis: University of Minnesota Press.

—— (2001) *Tramp in America*, London: Reaktion Books.

Crilley, D. (1994) 'Architecture as advertising: constructing the image of redevelopment', in G. Kearns and C. Philo (eds) *Selling Places: The City as Cultural Capital, Past and Present*, New York: Pergamon Press.

Cybriwsky, R. (1978) 'Social aspects of neighborhood change', *Annals of the American Geographers* 68: 17–33.

Davis, D. (ed.) (2000) *The Consumer Revolution in Urban China*, Berkeley: University of California Press.

—— (2002) 'When a house becomes his home', in P. Link, R. Madsen, and P. Pickowicz (eds) *Popular China*, Lanham, MD: Rowman & Littlefield.

—— (2003) 'From welfare benefit to capitalized asset: the re-commodification of residential space in urban China', in R. Forrest and J. Lee (eds) *Housing and Social Change: East–West Perspective*, London: Routledge.

—— (2004) 'Talking about property in the new Chinese domestic property regime', in F. Dobbin (ed.) *The Sociology of the Economy*, New York: Russell Sage Foundation.

—— (2006) 'Chinese homeowners as citizen-consumers,' in S. Garon and P. Maclachlan (eds) *The Ambivalent Consumer: Questioning Consumption in East Asia and the West*, Ithaca, NY: Cornell University Press.

Davis, M. (1990) *City of Quartz*, London: Vintage Books.

Davis, M. and Monk, D. (eds) (2007) *Evil Paradises: Dreamworlds of Neoliberalism*, New York: New Press.

Deleuze, G. and Guattari, F. (1988) *A Thousand Plateaus: Capitalism and Schizophrenia*, Minneapolis: University of Minnesota Press.

Dewsbury, J., Harrison, P., Rose, M. and Wylie, J. (2002) 'Enacting geographies', *Geoforum* 33: 437–440.

Diamant, N. (2001) 'Making love "legible" in China: politics and society during enforcement of civil marriage registration 1950–1966', *Politics and Society* 29: 447–480.

Dick, H. and Rimmer, P. (2003) *Cities, Transport and Communications: The Integration of Southeast Asia since 1850*, New York: Palgrave Macmillan.

Dongfang Morning Post. Online. Available at http://www.dfdaily.com/ (last accessed 3 March 2006).

Dovey, K. (1985) 'Home and homelessness', in I. Altman. and C. Werner (eds) *Home Environments*, New York: Plenum.

—— (1999) *Framing Places: Mediating Power in Built Form*, Architext Series, London: Routledge.

Drummond, L. (2000) 'Street scenes: practices of public and private space in urban Vietnam', *Urban Studies* 37: 2377–2391.

Duara, P. (2004) 'The discourse of civilization and decolonization', *Journal of World History*. Online. Available at http://www.historycooperative.org/journals/jwh/15.1/duara.html (last accessed 18 October 2005).

Duncan, J. (1980) 'The superorganic culture in American cultural geography', *Annals of the Association of American Geographers* 70: 181–198.

—— (1992) 'Elite landscapes as cultural (re)productions: the case of Shaughnessy Heights', in K. Anderson and F. Gale (eds) *Inventing Places: Studies in Cultural Geography*, Melbourne: Longman.

—— (1998) 'Classics in human geography revisited', *Progress in Human Geography* 22: 567–573.

Duncan, J. and Duncan, N. (1984) 'A cultural analysis of urban residential landscapes', in J. Agnew, J. Mercer and D. Sopher (eds) *The City in Cultural Context*, London: Allen and Unwin.

—— (2001) 'Sense of place as a positional good: locating Bedford in space and time', in P. Adams, S. Hoelscher and K. Till (eds) *Textures of Place: Exploring Humanist Geographies*, Minneapolis: University of Minnesota Press.

—— (2003) *Landscapes of Privilege: The Politics of the Aesthetic in an American Suburb*, London: Routledge.

Duncan, J. and Ley, D. (eds) (1993) *Place/Culture/Representation*, London: Routledge.

Durkheim, E. (1984) [1893] *The Division of Labor in Society*, New York: Free Press.

Dutton, M. (2000) *Street Life China*. Cambridge: Cambridge University Press.

Elden, S. (2007) 'Terror and territory', *Antipode* 39: 829–845.

Elias, N. (1939/1982) *The Civilizing Process*, trans. E. Jephcott, Oxford: Blackwell.

Ellin, N. (1999) *Postmodern Urbanism*, Princeton, NJ: Princeton Architectural Press.

Ellis, R. (1993) 'The American frontier and the contemporary real estate advertising magazine', *Journal of Popular Culture* 27: 119–133.

Elster, J. (2000) *Ulysses Unbound: Studies in Rationality, Precommitment, and Constraints*, Cambridge: Cambridge University Press.

Entrikin, N. (1991) *The Betweenness of Place: Towards a Geography of Modernity*, Baltimore: Johns Hopkins University Press.

—— (1999) 'Political community, identity and cosmopolitan place', *International Sociology* 14: 269–282.

Etzioni, A. (2000) *The Limits of Privacy*, New York: Basic Books.

Fainstein, S. (2001) *The City Builders: Property Development in New York and London 1980–2000*, Lawrence: Kansas University Press.

Fan, C. (2002) 'The elite, the natives, and the outsiders: migration and labor market segmentation in urban China', *Annals of the American Geographers* 92: 103–124.

Feuchtwang, S. (2002) 'Reflections on privacy in China', in B. McDougall and A. Hansson (eds) *Chinese Concepts of Privacy*, Leiden: Brill.

Flusty, S. (2000) 'Thrashing downtown: play as resistance to the spatial and representational regulation of Los Angeles', *Cities* 17: 149–158.

Foldvary, F. (1994) *Public Goods and Private Communities: The Market Provision of Social Services*, Brookfield, VT: Edward Elgar Publishing.

Foucault, M. (1982) 'The subject and power', in R. Dreyfus and P. Rabinow (eds) *Michel Foucault: Beyond Structuralism and Hermeneutic*, Brighton: Harvester.

—— (1991) 'Governmentality', in G. Burchell, C. Grodon and P. Miller (eds) *The Foucault Effect: Studies in Governmentality*, Hemel Hempstead: Harvester Wheatsheaf.

Fowler, G. (2007) 'In China, the wealthy show off wealth with lavish homes', *Wall Street Journal*. Online. Available at http://www.realestatejournal.com/buysell/regionalnews/20071022-fowler.html (last accessed 4 April 2008).

Fraser, D. (2000) 'Inventing oasis: luxury housing advertisements and reconfiguring domestic space in Shanghai', in D. Davis (ed.) *The Consumer Revolution in Urban China*, Berkeley: University of California Press.

Friedman, B. (2006) *The Moral Consequences of Economic Growth*, New York: Vintage.

Friedmann, J (2000) 'The good city: in defense of utopian thinking', *International Journal of Urban and Regional Research* 24: 460–472.

—— (2005) *China's Urban Transition*, Minneapolis: University of Minnesota Press.

—— (2007) 'Reflections on place and place-making in the cities of China', *International Journal of Urban and Regional Research* 31: 257–279.

Frolic, M. (1980) *Mao's People: Sixteen Portraits of Life in Revolutionary China*, Cambridge, MA: Harvard University Press.

Fulton, W. (1999) *Guide to California Planning*, Point Arena, CA: Solano Press Books.

Gamble, J. (2003) *Shanghai in Transition: Changing Perspectives and Social Contours of a Chinese Metropolis*, London: RoutledgeCurzon.

Gans, H. (1962) *The Urban Villagers: Group and Class in the Life of Italian-Americans*, New York: Free Press of Glencoe.

Genis, S. (2007) 'Producing elite localities: the rise of gated communities in Istanbul', *Urban Studies* 44: 771–798.

Giroir, G. (2002) 'The phenomenon of the gated communities in Beijing or the new forbidden cities', *Bulletin de l'Association de Géographes Français* 4: 423–436.

Glasze, G, Webster, C. and Frantz, K. (eds) (2006) *Private Cities: Global and Local Perspectives*, London: Routledge.

Gleeson, B. (1999) *Geographies of Disability*, London: Routledge.

Goffman, E. (1963) *Stigma: Notes on the Management of Spoiled Identity*, Englewood Cliffs, NJ: Prentice-Hall.

Gold, J. and Gold, M. (1994) ' "Home at last": building societies, home ownership and the imagery of English suburban promotion in the interwar years', in J. Gold and S. Ward (eds) *Place Promotion: The Use of Publicity and Marketing to Sell Towns and Regions*, New York: Wiley.

Goodman, D. (2008) *The New Rich in China: Future Rulers, Present Lives*, London: Routledge.

Goss, J. (1993) 'The "magic of the mall": an analysis of form, function, and meaning in the contemporary retail built environment,' *Annals of the Association of American Geographers* 83: 18–47.

Graham, S. and Marvin, S. (2001) *Splintering Urbanism: Network Infrastructures, Technological Mobilities and the Urban Condition*, London: Routledge.

Grant, R. (2005). 'The emergence of gated communities in a West African context: evidence from Greater Accra, Ghana', *Urban Geography* 26: 661–683.

Greenhalgh, S. and Winckler, E. (2005) *Governing China's Population: From Leninist to Neoliberal Biopolitics*, Stanford, CA: Stanford University Press.

Griffiths, R. (1998) 'Making sameness: place marketing and the new urban entrepreneurialism', in N. Oatley (ed.) *Cities, Economic Competition and Urban Policy*, London: Paul Chapman Publishing.

Gupta, A. and Ferguson, J. (1997) 'Beyond culture: space, identity, and the politics of difference', in A. Gupta and J. Ferguson (eds) *Culture, Power and Place*, Durham, NC: Duke University Press.

Harvey, D. (1973) *Social Justice and the City*, London: Edward Arnold.

—— (1979) 'Monument and myth', *Annals of the Association of American Geographers* 69: 362–381.

—— (1996) *Justice, Nature and the Geography of Difference*, Oxford: Blackwell.

—— (1997) 'The new urbanism and the communitarian trap', *Harvard Design Magazine*, Winter/Spring: 1–3.

—— (2000) 'Cosmopolitanism and the banality of geographical evils', *Public Culture* 12: 529–564.

—— (2005) *A Brief History of Neoliberalism*, London: Oxford University Press.

Hayden, D. (2002) *Redesigning the American Dream: Gender, Housing and Family Life*, New York: W. W. Norton & Company.

He, B. G. (1996) *The Democratization of China*, London: Routledge.

He, J. M. (ed.) (2004) *Xinziyou Zhuyi Pingxi [Analyses of Neo-Liberalism]*. Beijing: Social Sciences Documentation Publishing House.

Heng, C. K. (1999) *Cities of Aristocrats and Bureaucrats: The Development of Medieval Chinese Cityscapes*, Singapore: Singapore University Press.

Herbert, S. (1996) *Policing Space: Territoriality and the Los Angeles Police Department*, Minneapolis: University of Minnesota Press.

Herod, A. (1999) 'Reflections on interviewing foreign elites: praxis, positionality, validity, and the cult of the insider', *Geoforum* 30: 313–327.

Hogan, T. and Houston, C. (2002) 'Corporate cities, urban gateways or gated communities against the city? The case of Lippo, Jakarta', in T. Bunnell, L. Drummond, and K. C. Ho (eds) *Critical Reflections on Cities in Southeast Asia*, Singapore: Times Academic.

Honig, E. (1992) *Creating Chinese Ethnicity Subei People in Shanghai 1850–1980*, New Haven, CT: Yale University Press.

Hook, D. and Vrdoljak, M. (2002) 'Gated communities, heterotopia and a "rights" of privilege: a "heterotopology" of the South African Security Park,' *Geoforum* 33: 195–219.

Howell, S. (ed.) (1997) *The Ethnography of Moralities*, London: Routledge.

Huang, T. Y. (2004) *Walking between Slums and Skyscrapers: Illusions of Open Space in Hong Kong, Tokyo and Shanghai*, Hong Kong: Hong Kong University Press.

Huang, Y. (2003) 'A room of one's own: housing consumption and residential crowding in transitional urban China,' *Environment and Planning A* 35: 591–614.

—— (2006) 'Collectivism, political control and gating in Chinese cities', *Urban Geography* 27: 507–525.

Illich, I. (2000) 'The dirt of cities, the aura of cities, the smell of the dead and utopia of an odorless city', in M. Miles, I. Borden and T. Hall (eds) *The City Cultures Reader*, London: Routledge.

Jackson, P. (1989) *Maps of Meaning: An Introduction to Cultural Geography*, London: Unwin Hyman.

Jacobs, J. (1996) *Edge of Empire: Postcolonialism and the City*, London: Routledge.

Jenks, C. (2005) *Culture*, 2nd edn, London: Routledge.

Jenner, W. (1992) *The Tyranny of History: The Roots of China's Crisis*, London: Penguin.

Jervis, N. (2005) 'House united, house divided: myths and realities, then and now', in R. Knapp and K. Y. Lo (eds) *House Home Family: Living and Being Chinese*, Honolulu: University of Hawaii Press.

Johnston, R., Gregory, D., Pratt, G. and Watts, M. (2000) *The Dictionary of Human Geography*, Oxford: Blackwell Publishers.

Jurgens, U. and Gnad, M. (2002) 'Gated communities in South Africa – experiences from Johannesburg,' *Environment and Planning B* 29: 337–353.

King, A. (1984) *The Bungalow: The Production of a Global Culture*, Oxford: Oxford University Press.

—— (2004) *Spaces of Global Cultures: Architecture, Urbanism, Identity*, London: Routledge.

King, A. D. and Kusno, A. (2000) 'On Be(ij)ing in the world: "postmodernism", "globalization" and the making of transnational space in China,' in A. Dirlik and X. Zhang (eds) *Postmodernism and China*, Durham, NC: Duke University Press.

Knapp, R. (2000) *China's Walled Cities*, Oxford: Oxford University Press.

Knapp, R. and Lo, K. Y. (eds) (2005) *House Home Family: Living and Being Chinese*, Honolulu: University of Hawaii Press.

Kraus, D. (2000) 'Public monuments and private pleasures in the parks of Nanjing: a tango in the ruins of the Ming emperor's palace,' in D. Davis (ed.) *The Consumer Revolution in Urban China*, Berkeley: University of California Press.

Kristeva, J. (1991) *Strangers to Ourselves*, New York: Columbia University Press.

Kuhn, P. (1990) *Soulstealers: The Chinese Sorcery Scare of 1768*, Cambridge, MA: Harvard University Press.

Kutz, C. (2000) *Complicity, Ethics and Law for a Collective Age*, Cambridge: Cambridge University Press.

Lakoff, G. (2002) *Moral Politics: How Liberals and Conservatives Think*, Chicago: University of Chicago Press.

Lamont, M. (1992) *Money, Morals and Manners: The Culture of the French and American Upper-Middle Class*, Chicago: Chicago University Press.

Larner, W (2000) 'Neo-liberalism: policy, ideology, governmentality', *Studies in Political Economy* 63: 5–26.

Lasch, C. (1995) *The Revolt of the Elites and the Betrayal of Democracy*, New York: W. W. Norton & Company.

Laswell, H. (1979) *The Signature of Power*, New York: Transaction Books.

Latham, E. (1979) *The Poetry of Robert Frost: The Collected Poems, Complete and Unabridged*, London: Holt Paperbacks.

Law, L. (2002) 'Defying disappearance: cosmopolitan public spaces in Hong Kong', *Urban Studies* 39: 1625–1645.

Le Goix, R. (2006) 'Gated communities: sprawl and social segregation in Southern California', in R. Atkinson and S. Blandy (eds) *Gated Communities*, London: Routledge.

Lee, L. O. (1999) *Shanghai Modern: The Flowering of a New Urban Culture in China 1930–1945*, Cambridge, MA: Harvard University Press.

Lees, L. (2001) 'Towards a critical geography of architecture: the case of an ersatz colosseum', *Ecumene: A Journal of Cultural Geographies* 8: 51–86.

Lee, J. and Zhu, Y. P. (2006) 'Urban governance, neoliberalism and housing reform in China', *Pacific Review* 19: 36–61.

Leichty, M. (2003) *Suitably Modern: Making Middle-Class Culture in a New Consumer Society*, Princeton, NJ: Princeton University Press.

Leisch, H. (2002) 'Gated communities in Indonesia', *Cities* 19: 341–350.

Leitner, H., Peck, J. and Sheppard, E. (2006) *Contesting Neoliberalism: Urban Frontiers*, New York: Guilford Press.

Ley, D. (1974) *The Black Inner City as Frontier Outpost: Images and Behavior of a Philadelphia Neighborhood*, Monograph Series No. 7, Washington, DC: Association of American Geographers.

—— (1988) 'Interpretive social research in the inner city,' in J. Eyles (ed.) *Research in Human Geography*, Oxford: Blackwell.

Li, S. M. (2000) 'Housing consumption in urban China: a comparative study of Beijing and Guangzhou', *Environment and Planning A* 32: 1115–1134.

Lin, S. F. (2004) 'A good place need not be nowhere: the garden and utopian thought in the six dynasties', in Z. Cai (ed.) *Chinese Aesthetics: The Ordering of Literature, the Arts, and the Universe in the Six Dynasties*, Honolulu: University of Hawaii Press.

Logan, J. (ed.) (2008) *Urban China in Transition*, Oxford: Blackwell.

Logan, J. and Molotch, H. (1987) *Urban Fortunes: The Political Economy of Place*, Berkeley: University of California Press.

Lorimer, H. (2005) 'Cultural geography: the busyness of being "more-than-representational" ', *Progress in Human Geography* 29: 83–94.

Low, S. (2003) *Behind the Gates: Life, Security and the Pursuit of Happiness in Fortress America*, London: Routledge.

—— (2007) 'Towards a theory of urban fragmentation: a cross cultural analysis of fear, privatization and the state', *Cybergeo*. Online. Available at http://www.cybergeo.eu/index3207.html (last accessed 7 March 2008).

Lu, H. C. (2000) *Beyond the Neon Lights: Everyday Shanghai in the Early Twentieth Century*, Berkeley: University of California Press.

—— (2002) 'Nostalgia for the future: the resurgence of an alienated culture in China', *Public Affairs* 75: 169–187.

Lu, X. Z. (2004) *Wang Shi shizenyang lianchengde* (*Wang Shi: How to Succeed*), Beijing: Zhejiang Renming Publication.

Ma, L. J. C. (2002) 'Urban transformation in China: a review and research agenda 1949–2000', *Environment and Planning A* 34: 545–569.

Ma, L. J. C. and Xiang, B. (1998) 'Native place, migration, and the emergence of peasant enclaves in Beijing', *China Quarterly* 155: 546–581.

McCann, E. J. (1995) 'Neotraditional developments: the anatomy of a new urban form', *Urban Geography* 16: 210–233.

McDougall, B. (2001) 'Privacy in contemporary China: a survey of student opinion, June 2000', *China Information* 15: 140–152.

—— (2002) *Love-Letters and Privacy in Modern China: The Intimate Lives of Lu Xun and Xu Guangping*, Oxford: Oxford University Press.

—— (2004) 'Privacy in modern China', *History Compass* 2 AS 097: 1–8.

McDougall, B. and Hansson, A. (eds) (2002) *Chinese Concepts of Privacy*, Boston, MA: Brill.

McDowell, L. (1998) 'Elites in the city of London: some methodological considerations', *Environment and Planning A* 30: 2133–2146.

—— (1999) *Gender, Identity and Place*, Cambridge: Polity Press.

Macpherson, C.B. (1962) *Political Theory of Possessive Individualism: Hobbes to Locke*, Oxford: Clarendon Press.

—— (1985) *The Rise and Fall of Economic Justice, and Other Papers*, Oxford: Oxford University Press.

Mahler, K. (2003) 'Workers and strangers: the household service economy and the landscape of suburban fear', *Urban Affairs Review* 38: 751–786.

Malinowski, B. (1926) *Crime and Custom in Savage Society*, London: Routledge & Kegan Paul.

Mann, M. (1984) 'The autonomous power of the state: its origins, mechanisms and results', *European Journal of Sociology* 25: 185–213.

Manzi, T. and Smith-Bowers, B. (2005) 'Gated communities as club goods: segregation or social cohesion?', *Housing Studies* 20 (2): 345–359.

Marcus, C. (1997) *House as a Mirror of Self: Exploring the Deeper Meaning of Home*, Berkeley: Conari Press.

Marcuse, P. (1997a) 'The enclaves, the citadel, and the ghetto: what has changed in the post-Fordist US city', *Urban Affairs Review* 33: 228–264.

Marcuse, P. (1997b) 'Walls of fear and walls of support', in N. Ellin (ed.) *Architecture of Fear*, New York: Princeton Architectural Press.

Marshall, A. (2001) [1907] *Elements of Economics of Industry: Being the First Volume of Elements of Economics*, UK: BookSurge Publishing.

Massey, D. (1991) 'A global sense of place', *Marxism Today* June: 24–29.

Mathewson, K. (1998) 'Classics in human geography revisited', *Progress in Human Geography* 22: 567–573.

Matless, D. (2000) 'Moral geographies', in R. J. Johnston, D. Gregory, G. Pratt and M. Watts (eds) *Dictionary of Human Geography*, 4th edn, Oxford: Blackwell.

Mauss, M. (1925) *The Gift: The Form and Reason for Exchange in Archaic Societies*, trans. Ian Cunnison, with an introduction by E. E. Evans-Pritchard, New York: Norton Press.

Maxwell, K. (2004) *Gated Communities: Selling the Good Life*, Masters Thesis, School of Planning, Dalhousie University.

Miao, P. (2003) 'Deserted streets in a jammed town: the gated community in Chinese cities and its solution', *Journal of Urban Design* 8: 45–66.

Mitchell, D. (1995) 'There's no such thing as culture: towards a reconceptualization of the idea of culture in geography', *Transactions of the Institute of British Geographers* 20: 102–116.

—— (2000) *Cultural Geography: A Critical Introduction*, Oxford: Blackwell.

Mitchell, K. (1997) 'Conflicting geographies of democracy and the public sphere in Vancouver, BC', *Transactions of the Institute of British Geographers* 22: 162–179.

Mitchell, W. J. T. (1994) 'Introduction', in W. Mitchell (ed.) *Power and Landscape*, Chicago, IL: University of Chicago Press.

Monk, J. (1992) 'Gender in the landscape: expressions of power and meaning', in K. Anderson and F. Gale (eds) *Inventing Places: Studies in Cultural Geography*, Melbourne: Longman.

Moore, B. (1984) *Privacy Studies in Social and Cultural History*, Armonk, NY: M. E. Sharpe.

Mumford, L. (1961) *The City in History: Its Origins, its Transformations, and its Prospects*, New York: Harcourt, Brace & World.

Nagel, T. (1986) *The View from Nowhere*, Oxford: Oxford University Press.

Newman, O. (1972) *Defensible Space: Crime Prevention through Urban Design*, New York: Macmillan Press.

Nussbaum, M. (2001) *Upheavals of Thought: The Intelligence of Emotions*, Cambridge: Cambridge University Press.

Olds, K. (2001) *Globalization and Urban Change: Capital, Culture, and Pacific Rim Mega-Projects*, Oxford: Oxford University Press.

Ong, A. W. (1999) *Flexible Citizenship: The Cultural Logic of Transnationality*, Durham, NC: Duke University Press.

—— (2008) 'Self fashioning Shanghainese: dancing across spheres of value', in L. Zhang and A. W. Ong (eds) *Privatizing China: Socialism from Afar*, Ithaca, NY: Cornell University Press.

Ong, A. W. and Zhang, L. (2008) 'Introduction: privatizing China; powers of self, socialism from afar' in L. Zhang and A. W. Ong (eds) *Privatizing China: Socialism from Afar*, Ithaca, NY: Cornell University Press.

Paasi, A. (2002) 'Place and region: regional worlds and words', *Progress in Human Geography* 26: 802–811.

Pannell, C. (2002) 'China's continuing urban transition', *Environment and Planning A* 34: 1571–1584.

Pascual-de-Sans, A. (2004) 'Sense of place and migration histories: idiotopy and idiotiope', *Area* 36: 348–357.

Peck, J. and Tickell, A. (2002) 'Neoliberalizing space', *Antipode* 34: 380–404.

Peleman, K. (2003) 'Power and territoriality: a study of Moroccan women in Antwerp', *Tijdschrift voor Economische en Sociale Geografie* 94: 151–163.

Pellow, D. (1993) 'No place to live, no place to love: coping in Shanghai', in G. Guldin and A. Southall (eds) *Urban Anthropology in China*, New York: E. J. Brill.

People's Daily. Online. Available at http://www.people.com.cn/ (last accessed 30 March 2006).

Pile, S. and Keith, M. (1997) *Geographies of Resistance*, London: Routledge.

Pow, C. P. (2009a) 'Neoliberalism and the aestheticization of new middle-class landscapes', *Antipode* 41: 371–390.

—— (2009b) 'Public intervention, private aspiration: gated communities and the condominization of housing landscapes in Singapore', *Asia Pacific Review* 50 (2): forthcoming.

Pringle, D. G. (2003) 'Classics in human geography revisited', *Progress in Human Geography* 27: 607–609.

Putnam, R. (2001) *Bowling Alone: The Collapse and Revival of American Community*, New York: Simon & Schuster.

Rawls, J. (1999) *A Theory of Justice*, revised edition, Oxford: Oxford University Press.

Rapoport, A. (1977) *Human Aspects of Urban Form: Towards a Man–Environment Approach to Urban Form and Design*, New York: Pergamon Press.

—— (1980) 'Cross-cultural aspects of environmental design', in I. M. Altman, A. Rapoport and J. F. Wohlwill (eds) *Human Behavior and Environment: Advances in Theory and Research*, New York: Plenum Press.

Read, B. (2003) 'Democratizing the neighborhood? New private housing and homeowner self-organization in urban China', *China Journal* 49: 31–59.

—— (2008) 'Property rights and homeowner activism in new neighborhoods', in L. Zhang and A. W. Ong (eds) *Privatizing China: Socialism from Afar*, Ithaca, NY: Cornell University Press.

Roberts, K. (1997) 'China's "tidal wave" of migrant labor: what can we learn from Mexican undocumented migration to the United States?', *International Migration Review* 31: 249–293.

—— (2002) 'Rural migrants in urban China: willing workers, invisible residents', *Asia Pacific Business Review* 8: 141–158.

Rofel, L. (1999) *Other Modernities: Gendered Yearnings in China after Socialism*, Berkeley: University of California Press.

—— (2007) *Desiring China: Experiments in Neoliberalism, Sexuality and Public Culture*, Durham, NC: Duke University Press.

Rogaski, R. (2004) *Hygienic Modernity: Meanings of Health and Disease in Treaty-Port China*, Berkeley: University of California Press.

Rose, N. (1999) *Powers of Freedom: Reframing Political Thought*, Cambridge: Cambridge University Press.

Rosen, G. and Razin, E. (2008) 'Enclosed residential neighborhoods in Israel: from landscapes of heritage and frontier enclaves to new gated communities', *Environment and Planning A* 40 (12): 2895–2913.

Rosen, R. (2004) 'The victory of materialism: aspirations to join China's urban moneyed classes and the commercialization of education', *China Journal* 51: 27–51.

Rossler, B. (2005) *The Value of Privacy*, trans. R. Glasgow, New York: Polity Press.

Rowe, P. and Kuan, S. (2002) *Architectural Encounters with Essence and Form in Modern China*, Cambridge, MA: MIT Press.

Rowe, W. (1989) *Hankow: Conflict and Community in a Chinese City 1796–1895*, Stanford, CA: Stanford University Press.

Ruggeri, L. (2007) ' "Palm Springs": imagineering California in Hong Kong', in M. Davis and D. Monk (eds) *Evil Paradises: Dreamworlds of Neoliberalism*, New York: New Press.

Sack, R. (1986) *Human Territoriality: Its Theory and History*, Cambridge: Cambridge University Press.

—— (1997) *Homo Geographicus: A Framework for Action, Awareness, and Moral Concern*, Baltimore, MD: Johns Hopkins University Press.

—— (2003) *A Geographical Guide to the Real and the Good*, London: Routledge.

Salcedo, R. and Torres, A. (2004) 'Gated communities in Santiago: wall or frontier?', *International Journal of Urban and Regional Research* 28: 27–44.

Sanchez, T., Lang, R., and Dhavale, D. (2005) 'Security versus status? A first look at the census's gated community data', *Journal of Planning Education and Research* 24: 281–291.

Sandercock, L. (2002) 'Difference, fear, and habitus: a political economy of urban fears', in J. Hillier (ed.) *Habitus A Sense of Place*, Aldershot: Ashgate.

—— (2003) *Cosmopolis II: Mongrel Cities in the 21st Century*, London: Continuum.

Saunders, P. and Williams, P. (1988) 'The constitution of the home', *Housing Studies* 3: 81–93.

Sayer, A. (2005) *The Moral Significance of Class*, Cambridge: Cambridge University Press.

Scanlon, T. (1975) 'Thomson on privacy', *Philosophy and Public Affairs*, 4: 655–669.

Sen, A. (1987) *On Ethics and Economics*, Oxford: Basic Books.

Sennett, R. (1970) *The Uses of Disorder: Personal Identity and City Life*, New York: Alfred A Knopf.

—— (1992) *The Fall of the Public Man*, New York: W. W. Norton.

Setten, G. (2004) 'The habitus, the rule and the moral landscape', *Cultural Geographies* 11: 389–415.

Shanghai Daily. Online. Available at http://www.shanghaidaily.com/ (last accessed 15 May 2006).

Shanghai Economy Yearbook 2003. No.19, Shanghai: Shanghai Municipal Government Publications.

Shanghai Metropolitan Transport White Paper 2002 (Shanghaishi jiaotong baipishu baogao 2002), Shanghai: Shanghai Municipal Government Publications.

Shanghai Real Estate Guide (Shanghai Loushi), Shanghai: Jansen Media Pte.

Shanghai Real Estate Guide (Fall 2004), Shanghai: Jing Ying Color Printing Co.

Shanghai Star. Online. Available at http://app1.chinadaily.com.cn/star/index.html (last accessed 5 March 2006).

Shanghai Statistical Yearbook 2004, Shanghai: Shanghai Statistical Bureau, Beijing: China Statistical Publisher.

Shanghai Urban Planning Administration Bureau (2004) *Summary of the Comprehensive Plan of Shanghai 1999–2020 (Shanghaishi chengshi zongtigaiyao 1999–2020)*, Shanghai: Shanghai Urban Planning and Design Institute, 2004.

Shelley, F. (2003) 'Classics in human geography revisited', *Progress in Human Geography* 27: 605–607.

Shen, H. (2005) ' "The first Taiwanese wives" and "the Chinese mistresses": the international division of labour in familial and intimate relations across the Taiwan Straits', *Global Networks* 5: 419–437.

Shih, S. M. (1998) 'Gender and the new geopolitics of desire: the seduction of mainland women in Taiwan and Hong Kong media', *Signs* 23: 287–319.

Shurmer-Smith, P. (1998) 'Classics in human geography revisited', *Progress in Human Geography* 22: 567–573.

Sibley, D. (1995) *Geographies of Exclusion: Society and Difference in the West*, London: Routledge.

—— (1988) 'Purification of space', *Environment and Planning D* 6: 409–421.

Smith, C. and Hugo, G. (2008) 'Migration, urbanization, and the spread of sexually transmitted diseases: empirical and theoretical observations in China and Indonesia,' in J. Logan (ed.) (2008) *Urban China in Transition*, Oxford: Blackwell.

Smith, D. (1998) 'Geography and moral philosophy: some common ground', *Ethics, Place and Environment*, 1: 7–34.

—— (2000) *Moral Geographies: Ethics in a World of Difference*, Edinburgh: Edinburgh University Press.

—— (2004) Review of *A Geographical Guide to the Real and the Good*, *Annals of the American Geographers* 94: 428–431.

Smith, M. P. (2001) *Transnational Urbanism: Locating Globalization*, Oxford: Blackwell.

Smith, N. (1996) *The New Urban Frontier: Gentrification and the Revanchist City*, London: Routledge.

—— (2002) 'New globalism, new urbanism: gentrification as global urban strategy', in N. Brenner and N. Theodore (eds) *Spaces of Neoliberalism: Urban Restructuring in North America and Western Europe*, Oxford: Blackwell.

Sommer, M. (2000) *Sex, Law, and Society in Late Imperial China*, Stanford, CA: Stanford University Press.

Solinger, D. (1999a) *Contesting Citizenship in Urban China: Peasant Migrants, the State, and the Logic of Market*, Berkeley: University of California Press.

—— (1999b) 'Citizenship issues in China's internal migration: comparisons with Germany and Japan', *Political Science Quarterly* 113: 455–478.

Sorkin, M. (1992) *Variations on a Theme Park: The New American City and the End of Public Space*, New York: Hill and Wang.

Soto, Hernando de (1989) *The Other Path: The Invisible Revolution in the Third World*, London: IB Tauris.

—— (2000) *The Mystery of Capital: Why Capitalism Triumphs in the West and Fails Everywhere Else*, New York: Basic Books.

Stapleton, K. (2000) *Civilizing Chengdu: Chinese Urban Reform 1895–1937*, Cambridge, MA: Harvard University Press.

Sudjic, D. (2005) *The Edifice Complex: How the Rich and Powerful Shape the World*, London: Allen Lane.

Sun, L. P., Li, Q. and Shen, Y. (2004) 'The trend in the middle–near future and the latent crisis during the transformation of social structure in China' (Zhongguo shehui jiegou zhuanxing de jinzhongqi qushi yi qianzai weiji), in P. L. Li, Q. Li and L. P. Sun (eds) *Social Stratification in China's Today* (Zhongguo shehui fenceng), Beijing: Social Sciences Documentation Publishing House.

Swidler, A. (1986) 'Culture in action: symbols and strategies', *American Sociological Review* 51: 273–286.

Swyngedouw, E., Moulaert, F. and Rodriguez, A. (2002) 'Neoliberal urbanization in Europe: large-scale urban development projects and the new urban policy', in N. Brenner and N. Theodore (eds) *Spaces of Neoliberalism: Urban Restructuring in North America and Western Europe*, Oxford: Blackwell.

Tafuri, M. (1979) 'The Disenchanted Mountain', in G. Ciucci, Co F. Dal, M. Manieri-Elia, and M. Tafuri (eds) *The American City*, Cambridge, MA: MIT Press.

Tang, X. B. (2000) *Chinese Modern: The Heroic and the Quotidian*, Durham, NC: Duke University Press.

Tajbakhsh, K. (2001) *The Promise of the City: Space, Identity, and Politics in Contemporary Social Thought*, Berkeley: University of California Press.

Taylor, P. (1999) 'Places, spaces and Macy's: place–space tensions in the political geography of modernities', *Progress in Human Geography* 23: 7–26.

Thompson, E. P. (1966) [1963] *The Making of the English Working Class*, New York: Vintage Books.

—— (1978) 'Eighteenth-century English society: class struggle without class?', *Social History* 3: 133–165.

Thomson, J. (1974) 'The right to privacy', *Philosophy and Public Affairs* 4: 295–314.

Thrift, N. (1996) *Spatial Formations*, London: Sage.

Thurston, A., Turner-Gottschang, K. and Reed, L. (1994) *China Bound Revised*, Washington, DC: National Academy Press.

Till, K. (1993) 'Neotraditional towns and urban villages: the cultural production of a geography of "Otherness"', *Environment and Planning D* 11: 709–732.

—— (2001) 'New urbanism and nature: green marketing and the neotraditional community', *Urban Geography* 22: 220–248.

Time Magazine, November 11, 2002; June 27, 2005, New York: Time Inc. (www.time.com).

Tomba, L. (2004) 'Creating an urban middle class: social engineering in Beijing', *China Journal* 51: 1–26.

Tong, Z. Y. and Hays, R. A. (1996) 'The transformation of the urban housing system in China', *Urban Affairs Review* 31: 625–658.

Tuan, Y. F. (1977) *Space and Place: The Perspective of Experience*, Minneapolis: University of Minnesota Press.

—— (1982) *Segmented Worlds and Self: A Study of Group Life and Individual Consciousness*, Minneapolis: University of Minnesota Press.

—— (1986) 'Strangers and Strangeness,' *Geographical Review*, 78 (1): 10–19.

—— (1989) *Morality and Imagination: Paradoxes of Progress*, Madison: University of Wisconsin Press.

—— (1990) *Topophilia: A Study of Environmental Perception, Attitudes, and Values*, New York: Columbia University Press.

—— (1995) *Passing Strange and Wonderful: Aesthetics, Nature, and Culture*, New York: Kodansha International.

—— (1998) *Escapism*, Baltimore: Johns Hopkins University Press.

Valentine, G. (1998) 'Food and the production of the civilised street', in N. Fyfe (ed.) *Images of the Street: Planning, Identity, and Control in Public Space*, New York: Routledge.

Vanke Corporate Report 2000. Shanghai: China Vanke Co.

Vanke (2004) *Vanke Garden City (Shanghai) Tenth Anniversary Commemorative Book*, Shanghai: Shanghai Academy of Social Sciences.

Vasselinov, E., Cazessus, M. and Falk, W. (2007) 'Gated communities and spatial inequality', *Journal of Urban Affairs* 29: 109–127.

Waibel, M. (2006) 'The production of urban space in Vietnam's metropolis in the course of transition: internationalization polarization and newly emerging lifestyles in Vietnam society', *TRIALOG 89* 2: 43–48.

Wacquant, L. (2004) *Body and Soul: Notebooks of an Apprentice Boxer*, New York: Oxford University Press.

Walzer, M. (1994) *Thick and Thin: Moral Argument at Home and Abroad*, Notre Dame, IN: University of Notre Dame Press.

Wang, H. (2003) *China's New Order: Society, Politics, and Economy in Transition*, ed. and with an introduction by Theodore Huters, Cambridge, MA: Harvard University Press.

Wang, X. Y. (2002) 'The post communist personality: the spectre of China's capitalist market reforms', *China Journal* 47: 1–17.

Wang, Y. P. and Murie, A. (1999) 'The process of commercialization of urban housing in China', *Urban Studies* 33: 971–989.

—— (2000) 'Social and spatial implications of housing reform in China', *International Journal of Urban and Regional Research* 24: 397–417.

Warren, S. and Brandeis, L. (1890) 'The right to privacy', *Harvard Law Review* 4: 193–220.

Wasserstrom, J. (2008) 'NIMBY comes to China', *The Nation*. Online. Available at http://www.thenation.com/doc/20080204/wasserstrom (last accessed 20 February 2008).

Webster, C. (2002) 'Property rights and the public realm: gates, green belts and gemeinschaft', *Environment and Planning B* 29: 397–412.

Webster, C. and Glasze, G. (2006) 'Dynamic urban order and the rise of residential clubs', in G. Glasze, C. Webster and K. Frantz (eds) *Private Cities: Local and Global Perspectives*, London: Routledge.

Webster, C., Glasze, G. and Frantz, K. (2002) 'The global spread of gated communities', *Environment and Planning B* 29: 315–320.

Webster, C., Wu, F. L. and Zhao, Y. J. (2006) 'China's modern gated cities', in G. Glasze, C. Webster and K. Frantz (eds) *Private Cities: Local and Global Perspectives*, London: Routledge.

Weintraub, J. (1995) 'Varieties and vicissitudes of public space', in P. Kainitz (ed.) *Metropolis: Center and Symbol of Our Times*, New York: New York University Press.

Western, J. (1981) *Outcast Cape Town*, Minneapolis: University of Minnesota Press.

Wheatley, P. (1971) *The Pivot of the Four Quarters: A Preliminary Enquiry into the Origins and Character of the Ancient Chinese City*, Edinburgh: Edinburgh University Press.

White, G. (1993) *Riding the Tiger: The Politics of Economic Reform in Post-Mao China*, Stanford, CA: Stanford University Press.

Whyte, M. and Parish, W. (1984) *Urban Life in Contemporary China*, Chicago, IL: University of Chicago Press.

Whyte, W. F. (1955) *Street Corner Society*, Chicago, IL: University of Chicago Press.

Wilson, P. (1988) *The Domestication of the Human Species*, New Haven, CT: Yale University Press.

Wirth, L. (1928) *The Ghetto*, Chicago, IL: University of Chicago Press.

Wolch, J. and Dear, M. (1989) *The Power of Geography: How Territory Shapes Social Life*, Boston, MA: Unwin Hyman.

Wu, F. L. (1996) 'Changes in the structure of public housing provision in urban China', *Urban Studies* 33: 1601–1627.

—— (2003) 'The (post-) socialist entrepreneurial city as a state project: Shanghai's reglobalisation in question', *Urban Studies* 40: 1673–1698.

—— (2004) 'Transplanting cityscapes: the use of imagined globalization in housing commodification in Beijing', *AREA* 36: 227–234.

—— (2005) 'Rediscovering the "gate" under market transition: from work-unit compounds to commodity housing enclaves', *Housing Studies* 20: 235–254.

Wu, F. L. and Webber, K. (2004) 'The rise of "foreign gated communities" in Beijing: between economic globalization and local institutions', *Cities* 21: 203–213.

Wu, W. P. (2002) 'Temporary migrants in Shanghai: housing and settlement patterns', in J. Logan (ed.) *The New Chinese City: Globalization and Market Reform*, Oxford: Blackwell.

—— (1999) 'City profile Shanghai', *Cities* 16: 207–216.

Xinming Evening News. Online. Available at http://xmwb.news365.com.cn/ (last accessed 16 April 2006).

Xinhua News. Online. Available at http://www.xinhuanet.com/ (last accessed 2 February 2006).

Xu, Y. (2000) *The Chinese City in Space and Time: The Development of Urban Form in Suzhou*, Honolulu: University of Hawaii Press.

Yan, Y. X. (1996) *The Flow of Gifts: Reciprocity and Social Networks in a Chinese Village*, Stanford, CA: Stanford University Press.

—— (2003) *Private Life under Socialism: Love, Intimacy, and Family Change in a Chinese Village 1949–1999*, Stanford, CA: Stanford University Press.

—— (2005) 'The individual and transformation of bridewealth in rural north China', *Journal of the Royal Anthropological Institute* 11: 637–658.

Yang, M. (1997) 'Mass media and transnational subjectivity in Shanghai: notes on (re) cosmopolitanism in a Chinese metropolis', in A. W. Ong and D. Nonini (eds) *Ungrounded Empires: The Cultural Politics of Modern Chinese Transnationalism*, London: Routledge.

Yeung, S. C. W. and Howes, R. (2006) 'The role of housing provident fund in financing affordable housing in China', *Habitat International* 30: 343–356.

Yeung, Y. M. and Sung Y. W. (eds) (1996) *Shanghai: Transformation and Modernization under China's Open Policy*, Hong Kong: Chinese University Press.

Young, I. M. (1990) *Justice and the Politics of Difference*, Princeton, NJ: Princeton University Press.

—— (2000) *Inclusion and Democracy*, New York: Oxford University Press.

Zarrow, P. (2002) 'The origins of modern Chinese concepts of privacy: notes on social structure and moral discourse', in B. McDougall and A. Hanson (eds) *Chinese Concepts of Privacy*, Boston, MA: Brill.

Zhang, L. (2001) 'Contesting crime, order and migrant spaces in Beijing', in Nancy N. Chen (ed.) *China Urban: Ethnographies of Contemporary Culture*, Durham, NC: Duke University Press.

—— (2006) 'Contesting spatial modernity in late socialist China', *Current Anthropology* 47: 461–484.

—— (2008) 'Private homes, distinct lifestyles: performing a new middle-class', in L. Zhang and A. W. Ong (eds) *Privatizing China: Socialism from Afar*, Ithaca, NY: Cornell University Press.

Zhang, X. Q. (1999) 'The impact of housing privatization in China,' *Environment and Planning B* 26: 593–604.

Zheng, Y. N. (2004) *Will China Become Democratic: Elite, Class and Regime Transition*, Singapore: Eastern Universities Press.

Zhou, Y. and Logan, J. (2005) *Suburbanization of Urban China: A Conceptual Framework*. Online. Available HTTP: http://www.albany.edu/chinanet/neworleans/Zhou-Logan.doc (last accessed 23 April 2008).

Zhou, Y. X. and Ma, L. J. C. (2000) 'Economic restructuring and suburbanization in China', *Urban Geography* 21: 205–236.

Zhu, J. M. (2002) 'Urban development under ambiguous property rights: a case of China's transition economy', *International Journal of Urban and Regional Research* 26: 41–57.

Zukin, S. (1991) *Landscapes of Power: From Detroit to Disney World*, Berkeley: University of California Press.

—— (1995) *The Cultures of Cities*, Oxford: Blackwell.

Index